PRISONERS

OF THE

REICH

GERMANY'S CAPTIVES
1939–1945

David Rolf

LEO COOPER
LONDON

First published 1988 by Leo Cooper Ltd

Leo Cooper is an independent imprint of
the Heinemann Group of Publishers,
Michelin House, 81 Fulham Road,
London, SW3 6RB

LONDON   MELBOURNE   JOHANNESBURG   AUCKLAND

ISBN 0-85052-681-7

Photoset in Great Britain by
Rowland Phototypesetting Ltd, Bury St Edmunds. Suffolk
and printed in Great Britain by Mackays of Chatham plc, Chatham, Kent

To the memory of
my Mother and Father

CONTENTS

LIST OF ILLUSTRATIONS

ACKNOWLEDGEMENTS

The author and publishers would like to thank the following for permission to reproduce photographs in their possession: The Imperial War Museum – Nos 1, 3, 4, 11, 12, 19, 20, 21, 22, 23, 24; W. A. Lawrence Esq – Nos 2, 6, 7, 8, 9, 10; H. Wagner Esq – No 5; J. Christopherson Esq – Nos 13, 14, 15, 16, 18; R. G. Reading Esq – No 17.

PREFACE

TWICE DURING THE first two months of war, a GPO messenger boy delivered urgent telegrams to my maternal grandparents' home. The first informed them of the death of their younger son, killed on 17 September, 1939, when HMS *Courageous* sank with the loss of over 500 men after a German U-boat torpedoed her as she turned into the wind at dusk. One month later to the day came news that their other son had failed to return from air operations over Germany. Anxiously awaiting further news they found out that he was a prisoner of war.

My first recollections of this uncle whom I had hardly known is of a gaunt figure in airforce blue being overwhelmed by rejoicing relatives when he returned home in 1945. To me he seemed someone from another world. Some details of his life as a POW must have impressed themselves on my young mind since I gathered enough to realize, much later, that colourful accounts of German prison camps, with their breathtaking suspense and frequent escapes, seemed oddly at variance with what I had half-glimpsed years before. It was time to tell another story.

I am deeply indebted to many ex-POWs who sent me precious diaries, wrote long accounts, provided war-time photographs, filled in questionnaires or made tapes of their recollections and for the genuine and delightful hospitality of many whom I was privileged to meet in the course of researching this book. Their names, and those of relatives who allowed me to use material from ex-POWS who never returned from the war or died in the intervening years, are recorded later.

My major concern has been to recount, as accurately as possible, the experiences of men who were not, either by inclination or opportunity, escapers. The band of POWs committed to trying a 'home run' from permanent camps was, in any case, very small and highly select. I admire the courage and singlemindedness with which they pursued that aim.

For the great mass of POWs a different kind of fortitude was called for and it is their story which I have attempted to tell. Former prisoners have also been keen to let their story be known: 'I have been wanting to get the past off my chest for a long time,' wrote Private

Broomhead in a letter to me, 'and after seeing some of the films about POW life I thought it time to let people read and see the other side of the coin.' In similar vein, Sapper Kirk foresaw, while in prison camp, that films would be made after the war about POW life; 'Sadly,' he said, 'they did not tell our story.' And a plea from Rifleman Porter has been in my mind since he replied to my request for POW experiences: 'I do hope your book will help put the record straight.' I have, incidentally, used throughout this work the rank held by each man when he was captured.

While researching in the German military records, Dr L. Neugebauer of the *Bundesarchiv-Militärarchiv* at Freiburg, was instrumental in turning my attention to material that I would otherwise have missed and answered a number of my questions about German military organization. Jürgen Seibel, a long-time friend, gave up much time to help me work through the German archives and corrected German phrases and terms used in this book. Nevertheless, for such grammatical infelicities and errors of fact that remain, I am, of course, solely responsible. While in the Federal Republic, Fraser and Margaret Cameron have afforded me ever-generous hospitality as have Manfred and Ludgera Best.

I have worked also in the extensive records held in the Public Record Office at Kew and the Imperial War Museum. To their staffs I am indeed grateful. Philip Reed, Deputy to the Keeper of the Department of Documents at the Museum, has been unfailingly helpful in producing much original material from the archives there. Ministry of Defence staff also enabled me to see some items relating to POWs still held by them. Editors of provincial newspapers throughout the country kindly printed my requests for contacts with ex-POWs as have the editors of various specialist newsletters and magazines, including the Royal British Legion, RAF Association, RAF POW Association, Air-Gunners' Association, Coastal Forces Veterans' Association, Dunkirk Veterans' Association and IVB Ex-POW Association.

R. M. A. Hirst provided me with very useful information on the history of Camp King, formerly Dulag Luft, near Frankfurt. Mrs A. Willis kindly sent me a number of specialised volumes produced by ex-POWs which were published shortly after the war and Mrs R. Hartley provided various POW newspapers as did A. Fry, J. Stafford and C. Upton. Dr B. G. Owen supplied an extensive diary transcript of Private Johnston, a former POW. A number of POW letters in his possession were kindly loaned to me by J. A. Woolfenden and A. Stalewski provided items relating to Stalag Luft III and Stalag VIIIB.

Private V. C. Davis, an ex-POW himself, transcribed a number of accounts for me, giving freely of his time, while Lynne Edwards and then Pauline Smith coped splendidly with typing successive drafts of this work from my own rough manuscript. Technical help in preparing a final word-processor version was given by John Shearwood.

Mary and Launa have lived with this work over its long period of research and writing. They have supported me in times when the material seemed about to overwhelm me and when I had serious doubts about whether the subject was simply too big to be undertaken by one writer. That it has been completed at all is a tribute to their encouragement and to the knowledge that many former prisoners who gave generously of their time and recollections, wished to see this account in print. I hope they will find it has been worthwhile.

Crown-copyright material in the Public Record Office is reproduced by permission of the Controller of Her Majesty's Stationery Office. Material in the Imperial War Museum is published with the permission of the Museum's Trustrees or holder of the copyright.

The research for this work would not have been possible without a grant from the Twenty-Seven Foundation and I gladly acknowledge the Foundation's financial support.

PART ONE

INTO CAPTIVITY

'Well here I am a Prisoner of War in Germany, this was one of the last places I thought I should get to.'

Flight-Sergeant Steele in a letter home, December, 1940. [Shot down over France, 9 December, 1940; killed on the morning of 19 April, 1945 when British Typhoons accidentally strafed a marching column of British POWs at Gresse, near Mecklenburg, Germany.]

I
SURRENDER

B ARBED WIRE, SEARCHLIGHTS, sentries, guard dogs; such were the
components of Hitler's new order for Europe in the summer
of 1940. Hastily assembled, the Stalags, Oflags and Dulags* awaited
vast numbers of men trapped before Dunkirk and on the plains of
Northern France.

From the far shores of the Baltic Sea to the high Alpine pastures of
the Swiss and Italian frontiers, and from the icy waters of the Vistula in
the east to the formidable natural boundary of the Rhine on her
western flank, Germany's prisoners were destined to suffer in many
different kinds of camps.

Now, over forty years later, their names and locations can still
awaken emotional memories for many ex-POWs. In them, they left
behind much of their youth and friends who did not survive the ordeal
of captivity.

It is, however, not at all easy to understand what life as a prisoner of
the Germans must have been like. When Petty Officer Macey got
home from POW camps in Italy and Germany, he tried to explain this
to his friends but found that 'you would not and others would not
understand fully what I was trying to convey to you. It is an experience which must be lived through in order to understand it in its
fullest entirety. That is all I can say.'

Every man who was captured went through a traumatic ordeal
which was most personal and his reaction differed according to place,
time, and circumstance. The only common feeling was one of surprise
that he should be 'in the bag' at all. As Commander Scurfield wrote to
his wife while a POW before falling, tragically, victim of a British air
strike in 1945, 'We were prisoners . . . – the last thing I ever expected
to be – but by God's Providence we were alive.'

Although this was to be a crucial event in their lives, most fighting
men were hardly conscious of the moment that sent them into
captivity. In battle the pressure of events was generally so great that

* *Stalag*: abbreviation of *Stammlager* = a central prison camp for Other Ranks
  Oflag: *Offizierenlager* = central camp for officers
  Stalag Luft: *Stammlager Luftwaffe* = central camp for RAF prisoners
  Dulag: *Durchgangslager* = transit camp

the infantryman sheltering desperately from enemy fire, the navigator crouched at the escape hatch about to jump into the void below or the sailor with lungs half-full of oily water reacted without thought to the most powerful human instinct of self-survival. So it was often a large dose of luck coupled with the random nature of survival which decided who should die and who should survive to end up in a German prison camp.

Since they never expected to be captured, most men had very little knowledge of what this involved and had given virtually no thought to the matter before finding themselves at the wrong end of a German bayonet or machine pistol.

Equally little attention had been paid to this at the highest levels of British government, even though over 135,000 men of the armed forces eventually found themselves in captivity in the struggle against the Nazis.

Only the fall of Tobruk, in July, 1942, which Viscount Alanbrooke later confessed was 'a staggering blow', raised the problem for military leaders and politicians at home. They could hardly ignore the fact that 33,000 British, Canadian, Indian and South African defenders, despite many individual acts of bravery, had been forced into a humiliating surrender by an attacking force of roughly half their number.

Even after this military catastrophe no general instructions were issued as to how and why individuals should surrender and what might be expected to happen to them if they did. The reason for this was simple. Fighting men were not told much about such matters in case it weakened their resolve to carry on the struggle with every ounce of their strength against the enemy.

This lack of information could have a devastating result on men who were suddenly captured: 'I was totally unprepared to be a POW,' noted Captain Irwin, 'We had received no instructions whatsoever concerning being taken prisoner. I believe that we were badly trained for war.'

There was also a saying commonly heard on many operational bomber stations that the best aircrew were those with the least imagination. There was some truth in this because too much thought about the possibility of sudden and violent death could cause a man to act irrationally or lose control entirely at critical moments in the heat of battle.

Most men who went to war managed to push that fear into the deepest recesses of their mind and kept it there by believing that it was only other people who 'bought it' or by taking a fatalistic view that once your number was up there was nothing you could do about it anyway.

Sergeant Lowman of Bomber Command, shot down in 1944, remembered that cavalier attitude to death: 'At the time one volunteers to become aircrew you could not have any idea of the high loss rate. When you do start to work up to appreciate this of course, you still delude yourself that it will never be you. On being shot down four of my crew were killed and on reaching prison camp, meeting an old colleague who was on the Air Gunners' course with me, we accounted for nearly all the course (approx. 40) and they were all dead.'

Faced by such ferocious odds against surviving, men tried to keep death at arm's length; and, since they rarely thought seriously about being killed, the idea of being captured or suffering long-term imprisonment seemed an even more remote possibility.

For men of the British Expeditionary Force taken prisoner in the Spring of 1940, there was much bitterness at what they believed was the failure of their superiors. 'There was no lack of courage during the short, sharp campaign', thought Lance-Corporal Hancy, 'but owing to the enemy's superiority of tanks, forces and air support we were overcome and most of us were convinced that we had been rather "let down" by the Powers that were in so-called control at that time.'

When they were forced into defeat and surrender by the German *Blitzkrieg* which advanced with such apparent invincibility towards the Channel ports, many soldiers thought members of the Wehrmacht were superhuman. Private Dyson, ordered to throw down his rifle, ammunition, steel helmet and ammunition pouches, could not remember being frightened at the time because 'events had moved so quickly and I was probably more shocked at their efficiency. They were, in every respect, twenty years in advance of our army with their camouflaged combat jackets, sub-machine guns, hand-grenades and vehicles. To me they appeared as men from another world, deeply bronzed and obviously very fit and highly trained.' At this time the prisoners were not ill-treated. One German in fact patted Dyson on the head in an unmistakable gesture which said 'Cheer up!'

After the first heady days of *Blitzkrieg* victory in the west until shortly before the collapse of Germany's resistance in 1945, her troops generally behaved correctly towards their prisoners and there was a mutual respect which front-line soldiers often develop for each other.

When that respect was missing, soldiers were exploited as soon as they were taken into captivity. Many Germans, while displaying little mercy towards Russians taken on the Eastern Front, openly showed distaste and contempt for their Italian allies for whom immediate looting of rings, watches, money, documents, cigarettes and other personal effects was part of the legitimate spoils of war.

The very young *SS* Panzer troops who captured Gunner Harrison were, however, very different – 'highly trained in brutality and arrogant, drunk with success and momentary power' – they soon sorted out their prisoners. 'I think it is the same for everyone when the unexpected happens,' he wrote, 'one first goes numb, then devastation sets in, sometimes bravado, but soon all this was knocked out of us . . . and we were sure we were going to be shot until a senior officer arrived.'

After coming straight into the army from civilian life, much of the BEF had been pitchforked into battle having received only poor training with inadequate equipment. In a war which suddenly came upon them they surrendered to an enemy over whom they had constantly been misled by propaganda at home. Like most of his mates, Private Drysdale knew hardly anything until he was captured: 'I was pretty naive as all we young soldiers were from working class homes at that time, who were influenced in thought as regards the war by the news media and had very little intelligence of our own to fathom out what it was all about. I was so naive . . . that, after being captured, I went up to some German tanks and rapped them with my knuckles to see if they were really made of wood, as we were led to believe from our propaganda machine. I can assure you that they were not made of wood at all.'

Officers found the act of surrender could be just as traumatic. Captain Loder was forced to surrender after weighing various possibilities in the knowledge that men's lives were in the balance. After his platoon was spotted by a German patrol he decided that it was useless to hold out any longer in the farm near Hazebrouck where they had set up a defensive position: 'We were completely isolated and had no food and very little ammunition. We could not possibly last long as the farm was already on fire and it would only be an unnecessary sacrifice of life to resist further. We therefore surrendered. . . . The enemy was round us on three sides and well in the rear as we afterwards learned.'

Despite the fact that surrender took a variety of forms it was, then, generally not something over which the individual had much control.

On the other hand, there was a fundamental difference which marked off soldiers from sailors and airmen when they actually gave in to the enemy. Thinking about this, Corporal Bell commented: 'Air Crew were invariably captured after being shot down or after bailing out of damaged aircraft. Sailors were captured after being taken off a sinking ship and felt relief at being saved. In both cases these Servicemen had very little direct contact with the enemy and felt only relief at being still alive after some long-distance bombing and, possibly, shelling. For the soldier, particularly the infantryman, it was a totally different state of affairs entailing the actual laying-down of arms and raising of hands before handing over his shocked and outraged person to an armed enemy. It was personal, usually undignified and exceedingly depressing and bore with it a tremendous feeling of guilt, a feeling very difficult to throw off. It took me years to shake off the feeling and I think this is why so many soldier-prisoners engaged in rather dangerous games with their captors.'

Among the many thousands of British soldiers taken prisoner few were to escape the enormous weight of depression and guilt that accompanied their act of surrender.

The combination of shock and kaleidoscopic rush of events was often so great on Allied aircrew as they came tumbling out of the skies over enemy territory that they knew very little of what was happening to them until they stood on enemy soil.

This was certainly so in the case of Pilot Officer Sidwell who escaped from the shattered rear-gunner's turret of a Stirling after the aircraft had been hit over Hamburg, killing four of its seven crew.

His reactions on hitting the ground in one piece were typical of many aircrew: 'I shared the numbing experience of most RAF POWs who were shot down. I think the mind took time to adjust to such vastly-changed circumstances in a short time. Suddenly from a comfortable Mess (to which you returned if your luck held out) and the trappings of normal life, you were placed in a situation where you only had what you stood up in, and you thought back to the things you'd done or hadn't done at home.'

Later on, in a POW camp, Sidwell thought back to his capture and remembered he had received no briefing about the numbing of the senses suffered by captured aircrew – nor had anyone else in the compound. As he remarked: 'I was like the others. I hadn't really thought anything about being shot down and certainly nothing about [being a] POW.'

Some aircrew, like Flying Officer Griffiths, knew even less about their escape. The first sign of trouble over Berlin came when he heard a loud bang and saw flames shoot from the starboard wing. After members of his crew bailed out at 18,000 feet the aircraft went into a spin and blew up, knocking Griffiths unconscious. He recounted what happened next: 'I awoke falling through the air, pulled my 'chute and hit the ground seconds later. Four of my crew were killed. With three lumps the size of hens' eggs on my head and many superficial cuts on the face, I thought I was bleeding from the ears. I rolled myself in my parachute and using my "Mae West" as a pillow went to sleep until dawn.' During the next day he was spotted by police who were combing the area and taken prisoner.

Sergeant Roberts had an even more painful experience over Berlin when he was badly burned on the face and one hand after his Lancaster was hit by flak. He managed to get out of the aircraft but nearly died before the police picked him up. 'As I reached the ground my parachute caught in a high tree and I was left suspended about forty feet up. In an endeavour to evade [capture] I released my harness and fell to the ground – my leg was injured and my shoulder dislocated – I had to lie in the thick snow until I was found . . . and during this time I caught pneumonia.'

In all kinds of strange ways aircrew managed to survive by the skin of their teeth. Blasted out of the sky, colliding with each other over heavily-attacked targets, lost on faulty instrument bearings, beaten by foul weather conditions – whatever the cause, the toll on bomber and, to a lesser extent, fighter crews ensured a steady stream of airmen into the big prisoner of war camps set up specially to receive them and this did not slacken until almost the end of the war.

One of those shot down during the final struggle in Europe was Flying Officer Brittain. Returning from a high speed raid his Mosquito was hit by flak over the Dutch coast. Together with his Royal Canadian Air Force pilot, Flight-Lieutenant Guy Hackett (later killed in a civilian flying accident) he crossed over the coast north of their projected flight track when disaster struck:

'At that instant the port wing caught fire. What a dilemma. The situation was pretty bad as the flames were close to the empty petrol tanks. Guy tried to dip the wing in the sea and at the second attempt the port engine cut dead. In we went. It happened too fast to realise the danger, if any. After trying desperately to carry out ditching procedure, Guy discovered we'd come down on a sandbank in only a few inches of water. I thought the kite was sinking slowly.

Making an exit through the emergency hatch, we lugged our "K" type dinghies to the end of the sandbank, and stopped to enable our heartbeats to become normal. Guy returned to the 'plane and threw in an incendiary shell, then beat it back to me quickly. Verey cartridges exploded . . . and machine gun and cannon shells whizzed off in all directions. I lay in the water behind my parachute. Guy pulled out his cigarettes and we drew in the smoke as if it was the last cigarette we'd ever have. Lucky? I'll say we were.'

Luck – either good or bad – was the key to most aircrew's survival and the common element which ruled their lives and sent them into captivity.

In this sense, every man who found himself behind barbed wire might think himself fortunate to be there. His colleagues whose luck had run out lay in their graves in enemy soil. When they had recovered from the traumatic experience of being shot down, survivors did not forget that grim reality.

In the case of men of the Royal Navy a rugged determination to stay alive and, like aircrew, a large slice of luck decided whether or not they would end up in a POW camp.

It was only good fortune which saved Leading Stoker Reading's life while he was serving on the destroyer HMS *Sikh* when she was sunk off Tobruk harbour. A flying piece of shrapnel furrowed across his neck, permanently scarring him. Immediately behind him stood a ship's cook who was watching the action. The red hot piece of metal tore through his stomach, effectively spilling out his guts. After that, covered in blood and entrails, Reading was almost glad to abandon ship. Some five hours later he was picked up after clinging to a Carley life raft and landed on the mainland where he was sent into Italian captivity.

In April, 1941, HMS *Voltaire*, an armed merchant cruiser, sighted the German auxiliary cruiser *Thor* in mid-south Atlantic. On board *Voltaire* was Lieutenant-Commander Mercer who described the final engagement of his ship. 'We both opened fire but the shells from our 1906 guns went wild while *Thor*'s shooting was extremely accurate, the first salvo destroying our radio room. We were thereafter hit with almost every salvo until our guns were put out of action, bridge destroyed, engine room flooded with fuel oil, fires everywhere. *Voltaire* eventually sank . . . leaving about 150 survivors scattered in the oily water clinging to bits of wreckage.'

After a few hours the survivors were picked up by a motor boat and delivered to the *Thor* where they were scrubbed down, wrapped in blankets and escorted to the hold. As one of only ten surviving officers Mercer knew he was lucky to be alive; puncture marks from shell splinters in his face and legs was, he thought, a small price to pay.

The realization that he was relatively safe came more slowly to Ordinary Seaman Gant who was serving on HMS *Bedouin* when she was sunk by torpedo-carrying bombers. Heavy damage sustained on the upper deck destroyed the Carley floats and many survivors had to make do with floating wreckage.

Covered in thick diesel oil and hours later as dusk was approaching, Gant was picked out of the water by a German seaplane and flown to Syracuse in Italy. After a medical check he bedded down for the night in a local hospital. On opening his eyes the next morning, 'I heard a nurse singing, saw clear blue skies and a window edged with flowers. Only when I glanced to the other end of the ward where an unshaven armed guard was standing did I realise that I had not been called to the great beyond. For me the war was over.'

During the first few hours and days of capture, knowledge of just how close they had come to being killed dawned on prisoners. As Captain Norwood, the last person besides the ship's captain to leave the *Sikh* before she went down, commented: 'Capture in the sense of being rescued after several hours in the water was a formality. One doesn't resist this kind of arrest!' POWs knew there was nothing they could have done to have avoided capture in the heat of battle when their ship sank beneath them.

This may have been only poor comfort to take with them as they passed behind barbed wire but they realized, like surviving aircrew, that it was providential for them to see the inside of a camp at all.

2
TRANSIT

MANY THOUSANDS OF soldiers plodded their way into captivity in blazing heat under cloudless skies during the first summer of war. With so many prisoners, the Germans had severe problems in coping with the unexpected scale of their victory. Railways and other forms of transport were occupied to such an extent that Allied POWs had to be marched away from the fighting front, often for days on end.

For beaten and exhausted troops this was an added indignity. 'You ought to see us. We look a terrible sight: torn clothes, filthy and scruffy, and as hungry as hell,' wrote Second Lieutenant Heasman. The Germans also had a few special tricks in store for them. They were kept short of food, force-marched up to forty kilometres a day, refused any form of cover at night and made to march several times on circular routes through villages to stamp the mark of German authority on their inhabitants.

Despite such attempts to subdue local citizens many of them did what they could to help the men marching into captivity, though Private Vincent 'had the feeling that was to become common to a lot of prisoners whenever they were watched by civilians – the feeling that one was no longer looked upon as a human being who had once had a life of his own, but merely as something abstract that was only categorized as a British, French or Russian prisoner. If a uniform makes one anonymous,' he added, 'the brand of prisoner-of-war carries one a stage further.'

Private Low, trudging through three defeated countries, observed sharp differences between them:

'French people offering food received a German rifle butt for their pains – such is war!

Crossing into Belgium was frightening – there seemed no civilians, everyone was keeping to their houses.

Holland gave us a boost – the end of the journey on foot and the people impervious to the German rifles giving us loaves, sausage, anything they could get past the guards to us – wonderful people.'

Another British Tommy on the road in northern France, Lance-Corporal Rich, 'walked from dawn to dusk with no food and very little water', and bitterly saw German guards kicking over butts of water put out by villagers for POWs driven almost insane from the heat and dust of their forced journey. Near Maastricht in Holland, nuns set out tables with food as a column of starving prisoners approached. 'To our helpless disgust,' recounted Private Davis, 'the guards forced us at rifle-point to pass by on the other side of the road while they loaded up on "our" sandwiches.'

In some places, civilians suffered more directly. After being captured at Dunkirk, Private Astley escaped back to England and reported that 'Food was scarce. P/W were able to obtain food from local inhabitants but this depended on the guards. In some cases leather whips were used when food was taken from local inhabitants.'

Ravenously hungry, their tongues swollen and lips cracked, clothing hanging in tatters, crawling with body lice and suffering from dysentery, some limping from foot wounds or arms roughly tied in makeshift slings, battered remnants of the BEF wound in long columns away from the Channel ports under the watchful gaze of their German guards. Those who collapsed at the roadside were either picked up later or shot out of hand. Others fought among themselves for scraps of food or risked death by breaking column to dash into looted shops in search of anything to eat.

In fields along the route prisoners clawed at half-rotten mangels, potatoes and anything edible, ignoring the threats and blows from their guards. 'Of course,' wrote Sergeant Tuck, 'some were fired on as they broke ranks,' adding, 'I recall one particular incident when in the distance I could see a group of four men who had broken ranks and were raiding a potato patch. With no shout of warning one of the guards raised his rifle and fired, the whole group got up and turned to race back, and then one spun round and fell. The guard then fired two more shots at him and the poor lad's body jumped into the air twice as he was hit. There were several more incidents of this type. But that particular one I somehow can never forget.'

So hard was the lengthy march into captivity for prisoners already shocked by the fire and storm of the German *Blitzkrieg* that they spent every last ounce of willpower in moving forward, dazed and stupefied, within the long columns of trudging men. As Major Booth found on the march: 'When one reaches an advanced stage of exhaustion, planned thinking becomes almost impossible and all one wants is to stick with one's own friends and to go on, doing what everyone else is doing almost automatically.'

Some things, however, did force themselves about the hazy dullness of extreme fatigue. Corporal Hope recalled 'one outstanding memory . . . during the early days of the enforced march . . . is that of coming suddenly upon a huge pile of British steel helmets (10–15 feet high). I remember precisely my own fearful reaction to this – somehow British propaganda had been so good that I at any rate (& I think too some of my comrades) imagined that the owners had all been shot and similarly, when first we were bedded down in the fields, a vague sense of supreme mistrust came over me because of the maching gun emplacements at ground level. We really wondered how long we had to live.'

One fact which many British POWs also noticed was their position at the very end of the columns of marching prisoners. They thought it was deliberate German policy to teach them a lesson as the only nation not to have surrendered after the fall of France.

What was only too obvious was the high state of preparedness with which many Frenchmen marched into captivity. 'The French were lamentable', complained Lance-Corporal Longmore, 'with little or no intention of making a fight for it, however hopeless and were magnificently equipped for the long walk . . . to Germany. Their packs contained good strong boots, clothes & endless articles of food which the Germans allowed them to keep . . . The "Entente Cordiale" was at its lowest ebb in 1940, as the French responded readily to German efforts to drive a wedge between the Allies.'

Most prisoners who survived usually found their way through a mobile reception camp (*Beweglicher Auffangslager*) to a Front Stalag lying some way behind the fighting lines, as at Lille and Poperinghe in July, 1940, which was capable of imposing a minimum of organization on them. They were then sent on to a staging point.

In 1940 there were a number of these, notably at Brussels and Trier on the Franco-German border, where the city was *en fete* for German victories. Rifleman Porter arrived at Trier where British POWs were paraded 'like a circus' past hostile inhabitants on their way to a massive barbed-wire compound. 'Oaths, kicks and rifle butts helped us on our way,' he related. Overhead fluttered huge Nazi banners celebrating the fall of France.

There were some prisoners who arrived at their staging points at Emmerich or who travelled east to Hemer after sailing up the Rhine. But this was no pleasure trip for men suffering greatly from overcrowding on the decks of river steamers or confined below in the stifling dark holds of barges. During frequent visits on deck to relieve themselves, prisoners had to squat on a pole slung alongside deck level. German guards promptly put a bullet through anyone who lost his balance and plunged into the water below.

When Private Rudd and his mates got to Hemer they were forced to parade through the town where loudspeakers proudly announced the arrival of 'Churchill's beaten army'. Then, as Rudd recalled, even the German officers were surprised when the bloodied, unshaven and ragged British were 'suddenly called to attention and ordered to march in fives . . . by our own NCOs. I don't know how it was done, but I found myself getting into step with the rest of them and marched through the town as if we owned the place. This is what it seemed like to me; probably the Germans said it was pathetic although it was noticeable some of the jeering died away.'

To French POWs watching this defiant display, the effect was inspiring. 'It was almost a victory march,' related Robert Guerlain, 'a march by men who were sure of themselves and of their cause, and not the least bit affected by their status as prisoners. They marched down the street, heads held high . . . bearing their dirt and rags magnificently.'

At staging points, POWs were packed in batches of fifty, sixty and even more into cattle trucks and sent on to their first permanent camps. There were grim smiles and muttered oaths as they saw the wording on the boarded high-sided wagons with their barred window-slits: 'For 8 Horses or 40 Men.'

What was to follow was so terrible that men never forgot it. As well as dreadful hunger, thirst and mental torture about relatives at home there was the claustrophobia of a dark and airless wagon, freezing by night and unbearably hot by day. These conditions were made even worse by the all too infrequent stops for men, bent double from the agony of dysentery, to relieve themselves and the scant rations of black bread and potatoes or thin potato stew.

After three days and nights without ever seeing where they were going, men squatted and crushed together in an overpowering stench of excreta and unwashed bodies. Those who were ill lay suspended in strips of blanket lashed to the roofs of trucks. Some died and remained where they were – their bodies swaying in time to that of the train – until the end of the journey. Holes were gouged out of solid plank floors through which urine and faeces were scooped.

Some trucks were so packed that men temporarily lost all use of their limbs. 'Still hot, trucks stink,' scribbled Gunner Scott on his fifty-six hour rail journey into Poland, 'Some of boys dying. God it is terrible to see ourselves, we cannot stretch our legs – too many in truck.' In later years anything that could happen to them seemed bearable when measured against that horrific journey. The very fact that they had survived toughened them mentally and physically.

Not every soldier captured in 1940 was transported to a prison camp in the same way. Under Article 4 of the Geneva Convention officers were separated from Other Ranks and sometimes sent off under more bearable conditions. Captain Loder, for example, arrived at Trier by lorry and train, only three days after he was captured and observed that 'we were lucky in our journeys as some prisoners had marched 200 miles.' Afterwards he was sent to Oflag VII C/H at Laufen by cattle truck in a group of 200 officers, all of them feeling the strain of their journey by the time they got there.

Captain Irwin also journeyed to Laufen by cattle truck after marching part of the way, finding it 'not very gruelling' but Captain Lyon got there the following month only after foot-slogging through France and Holland and so by various stages to Bavaria. He also witnessed a punch-up between the Allies. French officers were separated at Doullens from British prisoners and sent off by another route after feelings between the two groups rose to a dangerous level 'due to a pro-German faction among the French officers'.

There was also a roving remnant of the BEF which was not picked up after Dunkirk. These evaders tried to get back across the Channel or to Marseilles.

For a while, about 150 British soldiers who had struggled southwards were allowed out on parole in the town until ugly fights with members of the German garrison led to their removal inland. Under the armed control of their Vichy guards they worked among the vines of southern France until they were transported to Italian, Austrian and German prison camps; 'Not entirely a Cook's tour,' remarked Gunner Taylor.

The second great influx of prisoners into German camps came in September, 1943, following the surrender of the Italians when Winston Churchill had what he termed 'an objective of the highest importance.' This was to liberate British prisoners in Italy and prevent them being transported into Germany. 'I regard it as a matter of honour and humanity', he wrote in his sonorous phrases to President Roosevelt, 'to get our own flesh and blood back as soon as possible and spare them the measureless horrors of incarceration in Germany during the final stages of the war.'

Unfortunately for the 80,000 POWs trapped in camps in northern Italy, Germany had other plans. Before Churchill's 'red hot rake' could be drawn from southern Italy through the German *Winterstellung* – their holding line south of Rome – German troops began moving them northwards over the Brenner Pass into Austria and on into prison camps throughout the Reich.

When the Italian capitulation became known a secret order from London was received in all camps: 'Stand fast – no attempts must be made to induce or provoke mass breakouts.'

Prisoners fully expected to be free and were ordered in nearly all camps to 'Keep fit and stay put' until arrangements could be made by the Allies for their release. It is difficult to imagine their sick disappointment on being taken away to a second captivity in the Reich. Sergeant Nell, one of the victims in September, 1943, felt 'rather depressed. I had so hoped that I might spend a part of the Autumn in England . . . Everything comes to he who waits. We waited and the blasted Germans came. It is Major P——'s fault for not giving us permission to evacuate ourselves if we so wished; now we are properly in the soup and will have to wait until Germany is absolutely crushed before we are free again. Major P—— ought to have known that they wouldn't leave us alone. Germans aren't so easily routed.'

The 'stand fast' policy seems to have been ordered by General Montgomery. There were genuine fears that prisoners might be carted off *en masse* to concentration camps if they showed signs of resistance, ominous reports were received of armed POWs on the loose being massacred by German troops and it was thought they might become entangled in the Allied front line as it fought northwards.

At any rate, the directive came from the top and, after muddled staff work, was transmitted as a direct order to camp leaders. In some places they had the unhappy task of using British bayonets to prevent British POWs leaving camp as the Italians crept away and the German troops arrived.

Yet thousands of British prisoners did manage to get away from their camps and evade German search parties until they drifted into Allied forces in southern Italy or crossed the border into neutral Switzerland. In camps where the senior man was strong enough to disobey absurd orders and often with the direct assistance of the Italian Commandant, all the prisoners took off for the mountains as at Campo PG54 where Staff-Sergeant Cowie noted on 11 September: 'Evacuation of camp ordered by Camp Commandant. At 5 p.m. Camp Leader advised to travel south through the mountains. The party moved off at 5 p.m. and travelled 3 kms along the valley. Stopped for the night, everything quiet.'

After many hair-raising exploits some of them eventually reached the safety of Allied forces or were interned in Switzerland. Often, they were only successful through the courageous efforts of Italian civilians and partisan groups. Without their assistance it is certain that numbers of them who eventually reached safety would never have made it.

But POWs who remained at large were hounded relentlessly by German army units and bombarded with propaganda leaflets with messages like the following example carried out of captivity by Corporal O'Loughlin:

'*War prisoners who have evaded from concentration camps. Foreign-
ers who are wandering in the impervious regions of Italy*

REMEMBER:

The Italian army has been thoroughly reorganised and you will
soon discover what a frightful fate is hanging on your heads.

Should you be caught while in possession of arms, or should
you have joined a gang of 'partisans', you will be considered
franc-tireurs and as such you will be tried in accordance with
the laws of war.

Why, then, will you still put up with hunger, defy danger
and suffer all sort of discomforts? Why should you prolong
your suffering for the sake of what is a hopeless cause?

Surrender to the Italian Military Authorities who will treat
you as well as they did formerly and will again recognise you as
war prisoners.

Only following this course will you be able to avoid being
condemned and to hope to see again your Fatherland and the
dear ones who are anxiously awaiting your return home.'

Not at all impressed by this, Corporal O'Loughlin and the rest of his
group struggled against freezing temperatures and deep snow across
the Alps into Switzerland where they were interned for the rest of the
war.

For the great majority of prisoners there was, however, no escape
from the search parties. By acting swiftly and adopting a number of
cunning tricks German troops forced the majority of British POWs
onto trains bound for a new captivity. These were men who had
originally been brought mainly from desert fighting in North Africa
where German forces had handed them over, almost apologetically, to
the Italians.

One successful German ruse was recorded by Sergeant Prosser:
'Major W—— gave us a lecture . . . and told us he didn't think the
Germans would move us out of the country. The Germans took the
camp over in the evening, they said they would only be here for a few
days and that they have only taken over to keep order and to prevent
the prisoners roaming the countryside.'

Another deception which kept POWs quiet enough to be moved
was that witnessed by a Fleet Air Arm pilot, Lieutenant Cambell. He
remembered at Campo PG136 in August, 1943, that 'We were . . .
shepherded into a fleet of trucks, all one thousand or so of us. The
trucks were swelteringly hot and the Germans let us have the covers
down. We proceeded towards Modena, very excited, as we were sure
we must be released soon as the fighting in Italy collapsed; "V" signs
to all the Italians, laughing and waving. We got to Modena, drove
through the town to the railway station, into the station yard and there

they were, dozens of cattle trucks. The whole atmosphere changed – in almost silence we clambered out and in due course we were herded into cattle trucks. The one thing we had dreaded was coming to pass – we were heading for Germany.'

Determined attempts by prisoners to hide in camp or escape while in transit met with swift and often drastic German action, as Captain Nicholls quickly found out. On the way to Germany he passed through Campo PG78 and tried to escape from there:

'I thought I would hide up in the loft of our building, above the plaster ceiling. I was by no means the only one with the same idea. When most of the officers were being loaded into trucks to go to the station we got up into the roof and hoped to stay there until everybody had gone. But the Germans were not that stupid. They sent a few troops firing up through the ceiling up into the loft. Not being very brave I came down pretty quick[ly] as did the others.

It was very depressing being carted off in trucks to the railway station . . . A couple of brave chaps tried to make a break by jumping from the trucks but they were shot to discourage the rest. It certainly discouraged me.'

The prisoners who were rounded up by the Germans soon discovered they had to cope with a different régime. 'With characteristic thoroughness, they counted, recorded, tabulated and grouped us,' wrote Private Ayling of the motor-cycle unit which took over his camp while Trooper Stopford began his journey north 'under the most uncomfortable conditions we had yet endured and with superior and stricter guards.'

Yet despite strict German discipline on the journey over the Brenner Pass there were many POWs willing to risk everything on escaping. This was a difficult and exceedingly dangerous task and only very occasionally successful.

Even with long odds against it, however, men repeatedly tried to avoid a second dose of captivity. One of them was Lieutenant Freer Roger who managed to break through planking to release the pin of the door catch on a railway wagon taking him to Austria. At the bitter hour of four in the morning he jumped from the train as it slowed down with at least five other POWs close behind. 'The train was doing about 20 m.p.h. We went out one by one like parachutists. A—— and I just missed a telegraph pole and landed softly half way down a steep railway embankment. The best sight I have ever seen was the tail light of the guard's van disappearing in the distance. No shots disturbed the silence of the night as we picked ourselves up.'

Steering south-east by the stars they linked up with hundreds of other escapers only to run into a German patrol as they attempted a make or break effort to get through to the British lines.

This was typical of the stories told by most POWs who attempted to escape while in transit. They ended up in captivity with little chance of getting away again. Lieutenant Moody was one prisoner who had nearly reached Allied safety once before when he was picked up by a German patrol in December, 1943, after getting away from a train taking him to Austria. 'After that,' he wrote, 'I'm afraid I gave up . . . I felt as though I could break down and cry I was so disappointed to be so near to safety and so confident and then, when I least expected it, to be taken prisoner again. I made at least two other attempts before I arrived in Germany but I'm afraid they were only half-hearted as I think my spirit was broken after the second attempt.'

While most British prisoners in German camps were captured in 1940 or came from Italy in 1943 there were others who arrived from Greece and Crete between June, 1941 and April, 1942. Among them was Gunner Peacock, one of thousands of British and Commonwealth troops taken from a collecting point for prisoners at Corinth and transported by rail and on foot through Yugoslavia into Austria and Germany. This march had a 'strange, dreamlike quality' which was heightened by the sight of 'three sailors from one of our sunken ships dancing triumphantly barefoot on the rocky road in front of two middle-aged German guards who were sitting exhausted by the roadside.'

After the fall of Crete another large batch of POWs found its way to German camps. After being rounded up on the island men were battened down in the stinking holds of small Italian freighters for the sea journey to Salonika. From there they travelled through the Balkans and Austria under primitive conditions.

Lance-Corporal Morley was one of many Royal Marines who suffered a tough journey to Stalag IVB at Mühlberg, north-west of Dresden, on the River Elbe: 'Toilet and washing facilities were non-existent on the train, but we were fortunate in our wagon in that the open windows were only covered with barbed wire to prevent escape, so we were able to use empty food cans and throw urine and excrement through the windows, retaining the tin for future use.'

When they eventually reached Mühlberg, Morley and the others were confined to their huts because of a violent outbreak of diphtheria. Afterwards he went to a work camp and remained their for the rest of the war.

There was a trickle of arrivals from the bloodily-opposed Dieppe landings in August, 1942; most of them were Canadians. A number of British prisoners also began to arrive in Germany after getting ashore at the Anzio beach-head in January, 1944. They were usually taken to

Rome where they were interrogated in a former film studios and afterwards, by way of a transit camp at Laterina near Florence, were sent in filthy cattle trucks to various prison camps in Germany.

From the many thousands of soldiers who stormed the Normandy beaches on D–Day and pushed on against bitter resistance the Germans collected another haul of prisoners. Private Sudworth was one of those captured and was fortunate to survive when, as he recounted, a German *SS* unit 'took us into a field, deprived us of all valuables and lined us up to be shot. Fortunately, three of our fighter 'planes came over at that very moment, waggling their wings in recognition. The Germans scattered for cover, but we stood there waving, whilst the 'planes flew round us in a protective circle. After a while, when it was obvious what they were doing, the Germans came back, gave us our possessions, and herded us off towards their HQ.'

Eventually he was taken to Rennes in the Brest Peninsula but on the way he only just managed to survive Allied air raids and had to be protected from angry Frenchmen by the German guards. 'We were,' said Sudworth, 'glad to complete our journey all in one piece.'

What was to be their final group of British prisoners was captured by the Germans at the 'bridge too far' – Arnhem. One soldier who fought in that epic encounter, Corporal Goodrich, fell into the hands of *Waffen SS* troops who were 'entirely correct' and even shared out tobacco and cigarettes they had looted from nearby shops.

He was taken to a church in the town suburbs where a machine-gun had replaced the altar crucifix. One thing which he remembered above all was the metallic clatter of altar candlesticks and chalices bouncing on the stone-flagged floor as the altar table was swept clear for its deadly load. After undergoing interrogation he was sent by rail under *Wehrmacht* guard to Germany.

These soldiers who surrendered on the battlefields of Normandy or in the killing fields of Arnhem had one considerable advantage over men who had been captured earlier in the war. Unlike them, they knew they would not be spending the rest of their lives behind barbed wire.

They were also at an advantage in that they were spared the long walk into captivity. The prisoners who had suffered from it later recalled that grim trek with mixed feelings of hatred and pride in having survived at all. 'The long march was only possible once in one's own lifetime,' concluded Corporal Walker, 'drawing on your past training and bodily resources to keep moving and dodge the rifle butts.'

Once in a lifetime was certainly more than enough for most men as they entered their prison camps. But whether they arrived at a German prison camp early or late in the war, however, they were troubled by the same doubts and uncertainties as to what awaited them there.

Unlike soldiers who had been captured by the Germans, surviving aircrew were all brought to the same place. At the small town of Oberursel near Frankfurt the authorities had established, in a small barbed-wire enclosure, a central Air Force Interrogation Centre officially named *Auswertungsstelle West* but commonly known as Dulag Luft. This was the principal centre for the whole western theatre of operations.

Durchgangslager Luftwaffe – or German Air Force Transit Camp – was located in permanent brick buildings and received its first prisoners, thirteen British and French officers, early in December, 1939. New huts were erected in mid-1940 to accommodate increasing numbers of aircrew shot down so there developed an interrogation centre with three barracks, one of them housing the British Permanent Staff.

Associated with this was the Hohemark Hospital of fifty to sixty beds which dealt with wounded POWs. The orthopaedic specialist there was *Oberarzt* Ittershagen: 'he seemed a man who practised medicine in the highest traditions of the profession, without partiality whatsoever for rank, creed, nationality or religion,' commented Air Commodore Ivelaw-Chapman who spent some time at the Hohemark with a badly smashed shoulder. Also connected with Dulag Luft was a transit camp at Wetzlar to which prisoners were sent as soon as possible after their interrogation had been completed.

There was a set procedure for dealing with incoming aircrew. Each man was put into a separate cell which was sparsely furnished with a bed, table and chair. Prisoners could not open the double window and individual heaters, rather too powerful for the small space, could only be operated from the corridor outside. Insulating material filled the cavities of the walls and doors to prevent prisoners contacting each other, though some managed to communicate by tapping out Morse code on heating pipes running through their cells.

Every prisoner was introduced to what looked like a Red Cross form. It was headed 'Arrival Report Form' which is precisely what it was but the reception officer usually told them that if they filled in all details their family could more quickly be notified of their captivity or, more rarely, that they might be shot if they refused to co-operate.

Many prisoners refused to fill in this form, however, because, following various non-important questions covering name, rank and Service number (which the Geneva Convention required them to give anyway) there were a whole series about their Service squadron, group station number and so on. Later in the war, Bomber Command

aircrew were warned of this fake Red Cross form and knew some of
the interrogation techniques that would be practised on them at
Oberursel.

Knowing what was likely to happen to them, new prisoners were
reassured when things went according to plan. 'I felt as if I was some
minor actor playing a role in a play which had already been worked
out,' said Sergeant Bruce of this time though he was shaken by the
interrogator's detailed knowledge of his squadron, names of pilots and
aircraft recognition markings.

Another member of Bomber Command who had been 'well
briefed' by RAF intelligence before being shot down was Sergeant
Banfield: 'I knew what to expect when I arrived . . . at Dulag Luft –
where I was subjected to solitary confinement for seven days. During
three sessions of interrogation they gleaned no more than my Rank,
Name and Number!!'

On those prisoners who refused to fill in the fake Red Cross form
the Germans had considerable information although they invariably
gave such prisoners extra time in solitary confinement. Even when the
form was only partly completed useful snippets of intelligence were
often gathered by *Leutnant* Heinrich Eberhardt. In addition, he wrote
up assessments of each prisoner and submitted them to the chief
interrogator, Major Heinz Junge.

Junge had been a POW in the First World War and arrived at Dulag
Luft in 1942 at the Kommandant's request. Each day at noon he
briefed his interrogators and evaluation experts and impressed on
them the need for consideration and courtesy when dealing with their
prisoners.

Most POWs were only interrogated once at Dulag Luft. After a
reception officer had seen him the initial assessment and fake Red
Cross form were used by Junge to match up an interrogator to the
prisoner.

From this point on the interrogator, who invariably spoke excellent
English and wore Luftwaffe uniform (though most of them were
only attached to the Service and carried the nominal rank of *Leutnant*),
made full use of the resources open to him which included access to the
Beute und Nachrichten Abteilung, *BUNA* for short, which meant 'Information through Booty'. Into *BUNA* went every scrap of material
recovered from aircraft shot down and from their dead and surviving
aircrew.

Pilot's maps, some burned or torn, streaked with grease and blood,
letters, newspaper cuttings, theatre tickets – down to every seemingly
insignificant item – were carefully filed away. In addition there was a
complete and continuous history of each air force unit in every Allied
country which was kept up to date by information from the Press

Section, which received material from German agents all over the world, and from exact transcripts of interrogators' conversations with prisoners. Information about other aircrew was speedily available from the Casualty Recording Branch.

Having co-ordinated all the available evidence the interrogator was at a distinct advantage when meeting a newly-captured prisoner and was sometimes able to lead him on to give new information. Sergeant Wareing was 'unfortunately persuaded to fill in a Red Cross form' giving his station and squadron because the interrogation officer told him that many others had co-operated. 'It is to my shame that I did reveal my squadron,' wrote Sergeant Peachey many years later, adding, 'I must, however, point out that before doing so he [the bogus Red Cross official] told me the squadron and where it was situated.'

Sergeant Tomblin, who flew a glider into Arnhem after surviving the D-Day landings, arrived at Dulag Luft and was kept in a cell on short rations. Exasperated by his refusal to give any operational details his interrogator gave up and told him: ' "O.K. You win, I will arrange for you to go to a permanent Stalag. Before you go I will tell you that you flew with Alec Johnston, your Flight, 'E' Flight, was commanded by Major Jackson. You came here from RAF Down Ampney and you have other airfields at so and so." His knowledge amazed me, and I could only think that someone had done a lot of talking for a hot steaming dinner.'

Many aircrew at Dulag Luft who were surprised and dismayed at the accuracy of German intelligence thought that other POWs must have spilled the beans. 'I was quite surprised at the factual information that was repeated to me and hardly prepared for a field service cap belonging to an A/G [Air Gunner] on our squadron being placed on the table before me,' wrote Sergeant Humes. His interrogation was something of an anti-climax because, as he explained, 'Sitting at the entrance to the interrogation room, I ran my fingers through the sand in the fire bucket and pulled out a complete escape kit minus its cover. I hurriedly buried it again.'

Instead of punishing, humiliating or maltreating prisoners, Junge and his staff used a more subtle weapon – what one of the most skilful interrogators, Hans Scharff, called 'disarming amiability'. No amount of preparation, he added, could insulate a man from 'barbed-wire psychosis':

'The very fact of being a prisoner exerts powerful pressure upon the mind and spirit of a man. He is instantly weighed down with a feeling of guilt, even though his capture is not his own fault at all. He feels guilty, because he knows he is on the sidelines from now until the end of the game; that he cannot be in there fighting with his pals. He is, in short, about as unhappy in his spirit as a man can get to be.

Since we, too, were soldiers, it was but natural that we should exploit this state of mind.'

Scharff's psychology was obviously shrewd: 'I had the impression that it might even be dangerous just to talk about the weather with him,' said Colonel Zemke of the United States Army Air Force.

Not everyone, however, was handled with kid gloves at Dulag Luft. Sergeant Spencer was interrogated 'after spending a couple of days in a small cell where the heating was permanently on and the windows wouldn't open. It was uncomfortable (as it was intended to be) but I made the most of it by drying my clothes out. I'd been in wet clothes since we ditched several days before.' Another POW who suffered the heat treatment was Pilot Officer Hancock, though he never knew the reason for it.

After the war, Killinger, Junge, Eberhardt and two others were given prison sentences by an Allied military court for maltreating POWs. Even so, there was a widespread belief that the sentences were unjust, especially since Killinger and Junge appeared before Göring in 1944 to answer charges of being too easy on their prisoners.

At the camp fraternization between the Germans and their prisoners was part of a game of bluff and counter-bluff. By providing many facilities which could ensure a more or less civilized existence, the Germans planned to break the aggressive spirit of their captives and encourage them to talk. In return, the prisoners hoped to put their captors off their guard and exploit every opportunity to escape. Pilot Officer Harvey had this in mind when he joined the Permanent Staff, thinking he might find a way out. 'There was a vacancy in the cookhouse and I was able to transfer to the staff. Security seemed a bit slack and I was hoping to escape, having altered my battledress to look more civilian and arranging regular evening trips to the stores outside the compound with another P.O.W.' Before he could put his plan into effect, however, security was tightened up. After opting out of his staff job he was sent to Stalag IVB.

A number of prisoners who eventually escaped successfully from other camps were highly critical of the set-up at Dulag Luft when they were debriefed on returning home. Flight-Lieutenant Shore was one prisoner who received invitations to drinking parties at the house of Rumpel, the Kommandant. He was determined, however, not to co-operate at all with the Germans and pointedly refused their offers; nor, he decided, would he sign the walks list which prisoners could join in return for giving temporary parole on escaping.

Sergeant James was another POW whose suspicions grew after

being taken to Dulag Luft from the Hohemark where he had been treated for severe burns sustained while bailing out over the French coast. While on walks in the neighbourhood with other prisoners he heard of lavish drinking parties for officers and shoots arranged for them outside the camp. A little later, after his transfer to Stalag IXC, he came to the conclusion that the permanent staff at Dulag Luft had been raiding Red Cross parcels.

Charges such as these continued to be heard in RAF prison camps for most of the war. Pilot Officer Layne, for example, who had flown with a Pathfinder Force, was interrogated by a friendly young civilian. In excellent English he explained that he had been injured while flying for the Luftwaffe and now worked for the Red Cross. 'This, of course, was untrue,' added Layne. 'He was, in fact, an aircrew member of the RAF who had collaborated with the enemy. After the war I heard he had been tried and sentenced for treason.' Sergeant Saunders (RCAF) also came across this 'very handsome' man. 'I heard later on that they lined him up and shot him in the cold, grey light of dawn, after the war,' he said.

There is no doubt that a few RAF prisoners were so softened by the comparative luxury and mildness of the regime at Dulag Luft that they accepted anything the Germans could offer and turned traitor. As Sergeant Wood wrote, 'The distrust felt by transients for the permanent staff here was surprising and complete.' But the truth of the matter, which was necessarily hidden from most RAF aircrew, was very different.

Flying Officer Dilley, like other prisoners, was 'furious to find three RAF officers apparently collaborating with the Germans in administering the tiny camp and enjoying considerable luxury thereby. It was only when we got home that we discovered the three were British intelligence officers "planted" on the enemy by the Air Ministry.'

This arrangement was an extension of the system initially put into operation by the camp's first Senior British Officer (SBO), the celebrated Wing Commander H. M. A. ('Wings') Day, who was sent to Stalag Luft I for leading eighteen POWs out of the first successful escape tunnel in German soil.

Newly-captured naval prisoners were usually taken to German naval headquarters at Wilhemshaven on the north German coast. The authorities knew that really useful information usually came from prisoners still in a state of shock who were interrogated as soon as possible after capture. It was German policy, however, to send there any naval POWs thought to have specialist knowledge, such as submariners and men taken in the St Nazaire raid.

The questioning at Wilhelmshaven was thorough and it was clear

that the interrogators knew a good deal about British naval operations. Prisoners there also had to fill in the same kind of bogus Red
Cross form as that used at Dulag Luft.

Kept in strict isolation, shamed by capture and desperately lonely,
some prisoners fell for a well-used German ploy. There would be a
rough and threatening session, the POW might even be threatened
with death unless he gave operational details. Then would come a
more sympathetic and even apologetic chat – 'It had all been an
unfortunate mistake. Would the prisoner care for a cigarette and
perhaps confirm a few basic points?' Keyed up to face a roughhouse,
the toughest seaman could be disarmed by such tactics.

After being interrogated at Wilhelmshaven, naval POWs were sent
off to a life behind barbed wire. From very early on in the war the
Germans followed a policy akin to that adopted for surviving aircrew
by bringing together all captured naval officers, petty officers and
leading hands in a single camp, first of all at Sandbostel and then at a
permanent camp for naval personnel set among tall pine trees in flat,
sandy countryside at Westertimke near Bremen, called Marlag und
Milag Nord.*

One of the greatest strengths the ordinary prisoner could have was
the ability to get on with life behind barbed wire, or, in a popular
saying, 'To see things through'. As Private Yapp wrote home from
Germany in October, 1943: 'This has no doubt been a bitter disappointment for you . . . but at least the capitulation of Italy was a
great success for us. It is also a great step towards the final victory
which cannot be so very far off now. I am very thankful to be out of
Italy for they are a despicable race and my contempt for them grew
with the length of my stay there. The Germans on the other hand have
a code of honour, look, think and eat like us and treat us like soldiers.'

It was this sheer, bloody-minded determination to find something
positive in the most disappointing and miserable situation that undoubtedly helped many British prisoners to survive when they
reached permanent camps in Germany and the occupied countries.

---

* *Marlag und Milag*: abbreviation for *Marinelager* and *Marineinterierenlager* = naval
camp and merchant navy internment camp

3
ARRIVAL

T HE MOMENT A POW entered a camp would be etched on his memory for ever. Many tried later to explain this and found it was not easy. 'A prisoner-of-war camp is a difficult place to describe,' wrote Terence Prittie, 'probably even more difficult to visualize for those who know of it only by hearsay.'

At first sight the appearance of German prison camps was uniformly bleak, especially those situated in the Polish corridor to which most prisoners from the BEF were sent. They had, recalled Lance-Corporal Longmore, 'an overall smell of rotting potatoes, disinfectant and open cess pits.' On entering such places, he added, one's main thoughts were 'fear of the unknown, degradation and "where is the next meal coming from – and when?"'

Despite the fact that their first dismal impressions were soon confirmed, men were glad to arrive after the hardships of their journey, as Private Mason discovered. After being made to surrender while trying to fight his way back to Dunkirk, he was force-marched through Belgium, arriving eventually at Stalag VIIIB with 'mixed feelings of utter dejection and relief that the long march was over'.

This was a common reaction as prisoners dragged themselves into dusty compounds: 'I was tired, dirty and ravenously hungry but the predominant feeling was one of thankfulness at having arrived in a permanent prison camp,' wrote Lieutenant Harwood when he got to Oflag VII C/H, 'as we had been led to believe conditions would be better and we would be allowed to sleep in comparative comfort.'

The tabulation and documentation of their prisoners was carried out with typical bureaucratic efficiency by the Germans. It took place usually when they arrived at their first camp although sometimes men's lives were reduced to a few lines of ink on official forms after interrogation at transit camps. Lance-Corporal Farrer went through the system and recorded the time that was needed to adjust to a life in captivity after he was captured in Norway. On arriving at Stalag XXA in Poland he found that 'while the documentation was completed it gave us time to come to terms with the fact that this was our future – captivity. Usually, a man knows why he is imprisoned . . . but as a POW there is a strange feeling of having been abandoned. That is the initial shock, and when you have time to think things out, you wonder what right people had [to] put you in that hopeless position. I resented being put in that hopeless predicament in Norway.'

So did many other soldiers and they would soon discover how powerless they were to do anything about it.

Every man captured by the Germans came under the control of the High Command of the Armed Forces – *O.K.W. (Oberkommando der Wehrmacht)* which made policy decisions at the highest level and drafted regulations for their captivity.

Further down the chain of command the *O.K.W.* made use of the system of military districts (*Wehrkreise*) which were administered from strategically important centres throughout the Greater Reich.

All main POW camps were numbered according to the *Wehrkreis* in which they were situated. By March, 1943, there were seventeen from where each Stalag or Oflag was administered. For the actual custody of POWs the *O.K.W.* made use of work groups from military districts (*Wehrkreiskommandos*) who ran the camps.

Registration at one of these camps as a POW imparted a new confidence to men who knew something about the Geneva Convention. Private Ayres went through this registration process late in the summer of 1940 and concluded that 'Once this procedure was over our papers and all particulars were sent to Switzerland and this made us feel a little more secure as the Germans had to account for anything that happened to us.' But prisoners had no idea how little security this actually offered them.

Many thousands of prisoners passed through German camps without ever seeing a copy of the Geneva Convention, despite Article 84 which laid down that a complete text be put up, wherever possible in the native language of POWs, 'in places where it may be consulted by all prisoners'.

Even when they knew of its regulations, the rule of the gun was still far more powerful, as Major-General Fortune, CO of the ill-fated 51st Highland Division, captured *en masse* at St Valéry, found when he complained to the Kommandant of Stalag VII C/A about the ill-treatment of his officers. He was told quite bluntly that the Germans 'had no intention of keeping to the Geneva Convention, which was drawn up by a lot of old women and not by soldiers'.

A complete lack of interest in the protection of prisoners under the Geneva Convention stretched to the very top of the Third Reich. Hitler himself certainly never visited a POW camp – nor a concentration camp for that matter – but, like others in his circle, he was brutally indifferent towards their sufferings.

In a rare comment about POWs during one of his lengthy after-dinner monologues in September, 1942, Hitler told his admiring guests: 'I make no secret of the fact that in my eyes the life of a single German is worth more than the lives of twenty Britishers.' After threatening to make British prisoners live with the Russians he added, 'This would make an excellent measure, to which their only counter would be to make our prisoners live with the Italians!'

No doubt this raised a few laughs among the Führer's entourage. But there was a deadly edge to his humour.

After German forces smashed their way into Russia in June, 1941, both sides killed the greater part of their prisoners with complete disregard for human life. Neither side had come to any agreement under the Geneva Convention.

Allied POWs like Private Maggs were appalled at the savage treatment handed out by German guards. While working on a new camp to house Russian POWs at Stalag XXA he was warned against any contact with them for fear of catching typhus. From this camp he remembered, 'They were bringing the dead Russians out all the time in a cart pulled by prisoners and burying them in long trenches with quicklime. I saw them throwing the bodies in the cart and if they could not get the right number in they had to jump on top and tread the bodies down.'

There is a numbing effect caused by mass slaughter such as this which dulls the senses. How can we imagine tragedy on such a scale? Single events sometimes have a more telling effect, as Corporal Rowley found when he was at Stalag IVF. There the German Kommandant constantly referred to 500 or so Russian POWs as 'animals' and his bestiality obviously rubbed off on members of his staff. The events of Christmas Day, 1944, remained vividly in Rowley's memory since, as he explained, 'I was in the compound when I saw two German guards carry the dead body of a Russian POW into the camp and dump the body on the floor of the wash house. I asked the Russian interpreter what he was going to do about it and he said "leave well alone". I went into the wash house and examined the body. He had been shot through the chest. There was also a bullet embedded in his elbow; it appeared that he had been shot by a drunken guard.'

Such treatment explains why some sixty-five per cent of all Russian POWs failed to return home – as did forty-five per cent of Germans captured on the Eastern Front.

Regular German officers were often genuinely horrified at this barbaric treatment of the Reich's prisoners, but could do nothing for those not covered by the Geneva Convention.

At the centre of Germany's POW administration late in the war (*Chef des Kriegsgefangenenwesens*) was *Generalmajor* Westhoff. Allied officers who interrogated him after his capture in May, 1945, found him 'an efficient administrative officer, correct, almost severe, but with a redeeming sense of humour'. Here was a man who openly blamed the Nazis and the weak-kneed opposition of some of his own superior officers to breaches of the Geneva Convention and 'genuinely tried to see that the spirit and the letter' of the Convention was maintained.

When the Allies picked him up, Westhoff was ready to talk. Every care, he told his interrogator, was taken to avoid passing problems to higher authority. When reports came in about German POWs being locked in their huts, deprived of food or knocked about in American, Canadian and British camps, he kept the files in his own office to avoid what he called 'unnecessary friction' from his superiors. All officers working with him had to undergo courses in Vienna to acquaint them with the Geneva Convention, but, 'as everyone interfered in matters relating to PW', he said, 'our life was made extremely hard. That was the two-year-long struggle which I carried on.'

Although Westhoff undoubtedly managed to avoid many of the really drastic measures which merciless *SS* officers would have been happy to inflict on POWs, his power to do so was strictly limited. Various decisions which violated the Geneva Convention were demanded by Hitler, Himmler and Göring, with the willing agreement of *Generalfeldmarschall* Keitel.

Without any knowledge of that struggle, many thousands of Allied prisoners owed their continued existence to the raw nerve and courage of Westhoff and others like him who resisted Nazi orders. 'They [the Gestapo] could do as they pleased,' Westhoff said. 'None of us had any say in matters, and fear of the concentration camp was always at the back of our minds, as they'd put us in their black books.'

'Oh, you know, one became such a blackguard,' admitted Keitel before paying for war crimes with his own life in 1946. Unlike the Nazi leadership, other men attempted to protect prisoners when they were put behind barbed wire; it was fortunate that some people of honour and principle, including Westhoff, could still be found in the nightmare of Hitler's Reich.

Stalag XXA, to which large numbers of Other Ranks were taken in 1940, was a vast camp of several nationalities at Thorn in eastern Poland. Different kinds of accommodation used there revealed the hasty improvization forced upon the Germans by their unexpectedly rapid military victories.

A disused balloon hangar was the first stop for many men, where they were briefly interrogated. Afterwards they were usually accommodated for a while in one of the large tents which had been erected around the hangar or in one of several fortresses in the area,

built by the Prussians nearly a century earlier. Massively constructed
from stone and brick and only partly visible from ground level, these
forts were approached across a drawbridge which spanned a deep, dry
moat, leading to a small central courtyard.

They looked dismal and forbidding to newly-arrived prisoners as
Private Dyson found when he got to Thorn. 'We eventually arrived at
our destination about 8 June [1940] well after dark. The train drew to a
halt, the doors opened and we struggled out into a clear starlight night,
the only lights visible were from a circling 'plane and from the mast of
a radio tower. After much shouting by the guards we were assembled
and made our way along a sandy track hoping our journey was at an
end. . . . First a pair of heavy iron gates opened, then a drawbridge
was crossed and after descending a flight of steps we entered a
vault-like room, the door closed and we were left in total darkness
lying on some straw. Was this to be our fate, confined in what
appeared to be a dungeon?'

The feeling that the world had forgotten all about them was so
overpowering deep inside the fort that prisoners easily became prey to
their worst-imagined fears. What if everyone at home thought they
were dead? What if the Germans decided to kill or torture them? And
even if they survived would they ever see home again?

These same fears and an overwhelming sense of isolation were
experienced by Private Bowers when he saw Stalag XXA for the first
time. He remembered that, after crossing the moat, 'We seemed
completely cut off from the world outside, wandering about down the
dank corridors with water dripping eternally from the roof and down
the walls, dimly lit with low wattage bulbs in places. The hollow echo
of voices and footsteps and a mournful dirge called "Stalag Blues" that
someone was playing on a trumpet all . . . contributed to what seemed
to be part of another world. One could almost imagine that one had
already died . . . . All the time there was an earthy smell mixed with
the smell of the latrines and the lime . . . used to disinfect them . . . .
We simply lived from one soup time to the next. There was nothing
much else to think about.'

A German officer barked at the prisoners: 'Those among you who
will listen to the voice of reason will one day perhaps be allowed to go
home. The others, the stupid ones, the stubborn ones, will remain here
for the rest of their lives to put right all the damage they have done.'

Yet, despite the grim surroundings of Stalag XXA, prisoners like
Gunner Joyce soon found that 'conditions were a slight improvement
on the past . . . if only for the nightmare of those never-ending roads
being past, and it was easier to drag weak and aching limbs around a
prison compound.'

Along with the other new POWs, he was interrogated and was soon to discover the advantages of knowing next to nothing about the wider conduct of the war.

A 'most benevolent' German officer interviewed him and over a friendly cigarette he was reminded that any information he could give would certainly go a long way toward smoothing his life as a POW. It was, said Joyce, comparatively easy to resist this offer and remain silent since 'the alternative to . . . dumb insolence was also quite simple, in that you just did not know [any answers].'

German Intelligence officers based their interrogations on a rather basic army questionnaire until a much more sophisticated one was produced for the Eastern Front in 1942. But in the early days they had not fully realized the need for speed in questioning POWs and men who were interrogated had already begun to come to terms with their captivity.

Unlike detailed information extracted from prisoners at Dulag Luft, Intelligence material sifted from 50,000 soldiers of the BEF and from 30,000 later POWs from Greece, Crete, Italy and the campaign in northern Europe only concerned battlefield units and weapons. This was low-grade stuff and of limited value to the Germans outside their operational zones.

After their interrogation prisoners were fingerprinted, photographed and numbered. Since they were also crawling with lice, their bodily hair was shaved off and their clothes put through a steam machine. This clever process simply killed the adult lice and hatched out a whole new generation which reinfested the POW as soon as he received his – or more likely someone else's – slightly damp clothing back. A favourite POW trick was to leave a potato in a jacket pocket and find it nicely cooked on its return.

There then followed inoculation and documentation. Grim photographs of each POW, often showing the strain of capture, were taken and affixed with his personal number to a *Personalkarte*. This double-sided card listed various details including a physical description, civilian occupation and a home address. A print from the index finger of his right hand put directly next to his photograph completed the prisoner's record.

Armed with a set of these documents, the German authorities thought they could check the exact identity of every Allied POW and established his whereabouts. In this they were, however, hopelessly optimistic because they reckoned without their captives' devilish ingenuity which frustrated every effort to establish a foolproof system.

Each prisoner wore a small metal tag which was perforated in the centre. His personal number and base camp number were stamped on both halves. If he died, the tag was snapped in two; one piece went with the body for burial, while the other was sent home with his few personal belongings.

In the first winter of captivity prisoners found a different use for them, however. In order to achieve the high standard of accuracy demanded by starving men, the width of a tag was found to measure out exactly five portions of a German loaf. After cutting, individual portions were decided by drawing lots so that no man could regularly have a gram more than another.

The same miserable surroundings and sense of isolation experienced by prisoners at Stalag XXA also affected men taken to other German camps. Stalag XXB was in course of construction at Marienburg in East Prussia during the winter months of 1940 when the first British prisoners arrived. The single, large, sandy compound perched on the banks of the River Nogat was surrounded by barbed wire and an internal electrified fence. The inevitable watchtowers reared up at each corner of the outside perimeter wire which was patrolled by armed guards day and night.

Private Rudd got to this camp while Polish workers were still building it and thought it a 'godsend' when put to work with them because they smuggled in food for British prisoners despite drastic punishments if they were discovered. 'I can well recall sitting on the sand,' he wrote, 'and watching the sun set in the west just where I wanted to be most.' Private Low thought he was lucky to be put in a hut mostly completed apart from window-glass. There was no furniture of any kind but the wooden floor made a far better bed than open fields.

Many early British arrivals at Stalag XXB were sent off on working parties or to other camps after a month or two and were replaced by a large batch of POWs who arrived in the late autumn of 1940 from Stalag XXA at Thorn. After the tough conditions at that place the prisoners' first impressions of their new camp suggested still harder times ahead and, as Private Dyson soon discovered, they were not wrong: 'The camp was a rectangular compound . . . with lines of wooden barrack blocks on three sides. Some of these were called "*Erdhutten*" which implied that they were half-buried in the ground. The whole area was exposed to the winds and had a bleak appearance. The town of Marienburg was visible about a mile distant with its thirteenth century castle built by the Teutonic Knights dominating the sky-line.'

The wooden barracks were designed to combat the bitterly cold Prussian winters but a general lack of heating and rough bunks almost on the floor caused numerous cases of frostbite among many nationalities in the *Erdhutten*. It was, thought Corporal Hope, 'quite a hell-hole and seemed to house half the armies of Europe.' Fights between

POWs, mingling freely in the main compound, were frequent. 'In human behaviour,' thought Lance-Corporal Farrer, 'the French were the most courteous, the Serbs and Croats the gentlest and the British the toughest.'

As time went on, NCOs and men turned up in many Stalags in Germany, East Prussia, Poland and Austria. Official Red Cross sources pinpointed at least seventeen camps in 1943 and thirty-four the next year, although this was nowhere near the true number where Allied prisoners languished behind barbed wire.

Naturally, there were fewer Oflags than Stalags but at least a dozen housed large numbers of British officers. Many of the early captives in 1940 went to Oflag VII C/H at Laufen on the German–Austrian border.

In earlier times the camp had been a country palace of the Archbishops of Salzburg. The main four-storey buildings, which were ranged about two courtyards, dated back to the eighteenth century and, despite extensive modernization, retained something of their former magnificence with wide stone-flagged corridors leading to large airy rooms topped by ornate plaster ceilings.

Newly-arrived prisoners were more concerned with the general overcrowding, however, than fine surroundings. When Captain Lyon arrived he found himself crammed into a room with twenty-two other officers. Each man had about fifteen sq.ft. of sleeping accommodation; by way of contrast the British army's regulation forty-five sq.ft. seemed positively generous.

Outside the main block several hundred Other Ranks, who were kept there as general orderlies and cooks, were housed in a long range of stable buildings and beyond them an upper field surrounded by a high barbed-wire fence was overlooked by a watchtower.

From this field and another smaller enclosure prisoners could drink in the magnificent sight of distant snow-capped mountains and Alpine scenery. But this could be a demoralizing view of freedom, as Lieutenant Roberts discovered in July, 1940: 'The feeling of being caged in is only increased when from our paddock we can see a river and hills around us. On fine days, we can catch glimpses of snow-capped mountains, many miles distant.'

While tantalizing visions such as these were hard to bear for the newly-captured they were preferable to the desolate surroundings at Oflag VIB, near Warburg, which became the main camp for British officers from October, 1941, when Laufen was disbanded. To Warburg came men captured in France and Greece, together with their orderlies, who had been at Biberach, Oflag VB, set up in August, 1940. At Biberach conditions were certainly no worse than Laufen with one-storey brick-built huts, complete with inside latrines and running water. The whole complex was situated on a pleasant, high plateau with good views of the surrounding countryside.

The conditions at Oflag VIB were, however, very different. For a start, it was a large camp. According to Captain Sewell, who was interested in precise figures and made a note of them, the inside of the wire perimeter measured 1,650 yards. In November, 1941, he recorded 2,466 Allied POWs incarcerated there, of whom 1,733 were army officers and 246 RAF prisoners; the camp also contained 472 British orderlies.

In addition to the size of Oflag VIB, it also looked depressing to new arrivals. Major Booth noted in his diary some first impressions of the place in November, 1941: 'In the early days, VIB resembled exactly my worst imaginings of a prisoner of war camp; a flat, bleak landscape, cut across by the barbed-wire fences; mud inside, a few bits of tattered washing flying in the wind, the grey dilapidated huts and dreary figures walking round and round, round and round.' During a wet autumn the arrival of men from other Oflags turned the whole place into a quagmire: 'Mud abounds all over the camp,' wrote Sewell in October, 1941.

A great many officers stayed at Oflag VIB until, in turn, it was disbanded in August, 1942; others moved to new camps before then. Sewell got to Spangenberg, Oflag IX A/H, when Warburg closed after passing through another camp housing British officers – Oflag IX A/Z (the Z standing for *Zweilager* or branch camp) at Rotenburg. There were 363 of them here in August, 1942, together with eighty orderlies, living in what had been a girls' school set in attractive, wooded countryside. The main problem was the very limited exercise ground with a perimeter measuring only 220 yards, but it was still, considered Sewell, a 'great improvement' on Warburg.

At Spangenberg he met officers who had been there almost since the war started. In fact there were two camps: the ancient castle atop a rocky hill to which many of the very earliest Allied prisoners were sent and the *Unterlager*, situated in the small village of Elbersdorf about a mile away, properly termed Oflag IX A/H.

Standing guard over the old highway from Thuringen to the Main and Rhine, this fortress housed over twenty British prisoners in December, 1939. Originally, the castle's rooms were reasonably dry and warm but the plumbing collapsed and since there was no adequate ventilation the whole place was soon reduced to a grim, chilly dampness even on the sunniest days in the summer of 1940.

The serious over-crowding left far too little space for the prisoners to get reasonable exercise. Some men thought of using the deep moat below the ramparts but it was strewn with rubbish and occupied by three wild boars, nicknamed by the prisoners 'Gustav and his two wives'. Attempts to flatten them with the aid of coping stones tipped from the battlements proved wholly unsuccessful. Meanwhile, the stench that arose from the moat was indescribable.

In order to ease the problems of overcrowding a group of half-timbered buildings in Elbersdorf was commandeered by the German authorities. To this *Unterlager* were transferred all army officers from the castle, now known as the *Oberlager*, leaving behind men of the Royal Navy and RAF.

For a time there was plenty of space for everyone but by the end of 1940 both camps were filling up, each with some three hundred prisoners. Overcrowding was again serious, despite the fact that all French POWs, who had originally been at the castle, were sent elsewhere.

Both camps were closed by the Germans between February and July, 1941, when most officers were sent to Stalag XXA at Thorn or to Stalag XXID at Posen in retaliation for what the Germans claimed was the ill-treatment of their own men in Canadian prison camps. They returned to Spangenberg only to be sent very quickly to Warburg. Oflag IX A/H did not receive British officers again until January, 1943.

Eight months later, after Sewell arrived at the *Unterlager*, he recorded 219 British officers and thirty-two orderlies living in three buildings. A courtyard in two parts with grassed plots and a garden at each end allowed POWs to stretch their legs – but not to much purpose. The whole area was bounded by a perimeter only 255 yards long surrounded by a veritable forest of barbed wire, nine feet wide and just as high. Sewell stayed there until March, 1945, although senior officers were transferred to Oflag XIIB in May, 1944.

There were a number of Oflags containing substantial numbers of British officers, particularly at Weinsberg (VA), Eichstätt (VIIB), Tithmoning (VIID), Mährisch-Trübau (VIIIF), Lübeck (XC), Hada-mar (XIIB) and Schubin (XXIB), while the one that became best-known to the British public after the war, Colditz (IVC), was reserved for repeated escapers.

Many prisoners remembered the first and last winters of war as the worst time in captivity. Those men who arrived in prison camps after the first great surge of prisoners in mid-1940 normally walked into compounds which at least had some kind of discipline and organization. But for much of the BEF the German prison system was a shattering and unexpected end to their fighting days.

Physical maltreatment on the long journey into captivity left many officers and men unable to withstand the terrible conditions of that first winter's imprisonment. Deep in the massive stone depths of Stalag XXA during the turn of the year of 1940–41 men survived appalling cold like creatures from another age. They scraped ice twelve inches thick from the inside of small windows that allowed only a fitful light into their cell-like rooms. Once outside, the very mucus froze in one's nose. Frostbite was an ever-present danger.

In the bunk below Lance-Corporal McKechnie in the fort lay a young soldier, barely eighteen years old, coughing his life away with tuberculosis and so wasted in body that he could not get to the cookhouse for his meagre ration of thin soup. With temperatures well below zero the Germans refused permission for anyone to collect his rations and so, recalled McKechnie, 'he had to beg from others and as he could not get to the toilets, he used his mess tin for that purpose. I reported his condition and was told "What can we do about it?" He died a few days after reporting [himself]. The only way to survive was to get out on parade in the morning and report sick.'

For this young man the effort to do so cost too much and came too late; and so it was that for some the first winter of captivity was also the last they would ever see.

In June, 1940, the first transport of 2,726 British army POWs arrived at Lamsdorf in Upper Silesia and were immediately sent to work in the Siemens factory in Labedg. Four months later over 7,500 British prisoners were being administered from Stalag VIIIB and, after the German invasion of Russia, the number of prisoners there grew rapidly until the second half of 1943 when it had become the largest POW camp in the Greater Reich.

Sergeant Bruce arrived at Stalag VIIIB with three other members of his crew from Wetzlar in July, 1942. Under normal circumstances, they would have gone to Stalag Luft III at Sagan but new NCO's huts in the centre compound had not been completed and so over 1,000 RAF aircrew eventually ended up at Lamsdorf. Many stayed there because the increasing number of prisoners passing through Dulag Luft outstripped the accommodation available at Sagan. 'Little did I know,' said Bruce, 'I wasn't to see that outer gate for nearly another three years.'

On being taken to the camp's RAF compound he saw before him a classical prison-camp layout. Four long blocks of single-storey white-painted board huts, divided internally in the centre by ablution areas, formed eight separate living quarters. Just inside the compound a single tree crowned a large mound; to one side was an outside latrine block.

Beyond the wire fences the prisoners could see other compounds, broken only by internal roadways running between them on two sides. There was no access for the RAF men directly to the outside wire until they were allowed eventually to mix with other prisoners, mainly army NCOs. These 'permanent army types' were, thought Sergeant Saunders, RCAF, 'very tough characters'.

The thousands of prisoners who ended up at Lamsdorf were amazed at the sheer size of the place. Private Strudwick, who arrived in November, 1940, 'cold, hungry, lousy,' thought 'every nationality in the world was there'. Morale was very low and the prisoners were subjected to constant German propaganda from loudspeakers set up all over the camp.

What impressed Private Davies most was the symmetrical rows of buildings and 'miles of barbed wire and lookout towers' around the compounds. As for Private Howe he could hardly believe his own eyes: 'At last we filed through the gates of Boredom, Misery and Hunger, with the German Eagle and Swastika looking down on us. For a moment or two we stood still with the amazement of what was in store for us . . . [and] we were then interviewed by an inter-preter. . . . We were then given a lecture on discipline in the camp and what the consequence would be if we disobeyed.'

A short spell behind wire soon convinced him that he would be better off outside on a working party. From other POWs there came rumours of extra food, and even money to be earned, and so, despite never even having seen a pit head before, Private Howe decided he was a collier. He was destined to toil underground in the Hermann Göring coal mine.

Most British prisoners sent from Lamsdorf on various working parties were glad to leave that camp. Not so for the RAF, however; they were not given the chance.

There were ways in which they could get out on working parties but RAF prisoners were not officially employed outside their camps. The Germans had no wish for them to find their way home and fly again against the Reich; indeed, they were not even meant to be in prison camps with soldiers at all. It was only force of circumstance which caused the Germans to change that policy.

One of the most ruthless and successful men in the struggle for power within the Nazi Party was Hermann Göring. Among the many ways in which the *Reichsmarschall* attempted to maintain and improve his position was to insist that camps for RAF prisoners were placed directly under his control. Their staffs were appointed directly by the *Chef der Kriegsgefangenen der Luftwaffe, Oberst* Ernst Wälde, and, in practice, Göring himself decided on the appointment of Kommandants.

As head of the Luftwaffe's POW organization Wälde had full responsibility for the establishment and administration of Stalag Lufts; they were built by the Luftwaffe's own construction branch, starting with one at Barth in Pomerania on a sandy, forested, inlet sheltered

from the Baltic. It was completed by July, 1940, and run entirely by
Luftwaffe personnel administered by the Territorial Administrative
HQ of the Luftwaffe (*Luftgaukommando*).

After Stalag Luft I had opened the German authorities continually
faced problems of over-crowding. Barth was finally evacuated in
April, 1942, when most of its inmates went to the massive new camp
at Sagan, Stalag Luft III, where the Germans intended to hold all RAF
prisoners.

In time this camp also became full and, while some NCOs returned
to Barth, the great majority were sent, in April, 1943, to another new
camp at Heydekrug in East Prussia, Stalag Luft VI. Sergeant Wood, at
this camp after spells at Kirchhain (Stalag IIIE), Sagan and Luckenwalde (Stalag IIIA), found it to be a different can of worms' from
anything he had previously experienced.

Single-storey brick-built barracks were still being completed by
Russian POWs on a flat, sandy, cleared site when Wood arrived there.
'They were,' he recalled of the Russians, 'in a very sorry state and since
the guards used to shoot them if you got too close we used to throw
them things. Many of the things confused them. Soap, however, was
different. They knew what to do with that, all right. They ate it!'

Later in 1943 Barth became for a while reserved exclusively for
officers; NCOs were sent to Heydekrug where they remained until
the Russian advance caused that camp to be evacuated in June, 1944,
when they were sent to Stalag Luft IV at Gross Tychow in East
Pomerania or to Stalag 357 at Fallingbostel. At about the same time
Stalag Luft VII opened at Bankau in Silesia to accommodate RAF
NCOs from Stalag VIIA at Moosburg and new prisoners from Dulag
Luft.

One other camp also contained large numbers of RAF officers and
NCOs. Oflag XXIB, in the buildings of a former girls' school at
Schubin some 150 miles west of Warsaw, received men sent from
Dulag Luft. In March, 1943, they were all sent to Sagan where they
were forced into the east compound.

Since RAF POW camps were laid out on the same lines and built on
wide, cleared sites to make escaping difficult, they presented much the
same picture wherever they were. Sergeant Eeles remembered Stalag
Luft III at Sagan, an important railway junction in south-eastern
Germany, as a camp 'built in a vast clearing in a pinewood forest'
where the inmates had 'no outside vision beyond a vast impenetrable
panorama of coniferous trees.' The first view that Flight-Lieutenant
Philpot got of the camp was when 'we turned a corner of the wood. I
looked up. Among the pine trees – almost up in the branches it
appeared – a large wooden sentry box could be seen, with a uniformed
man in it. He had a gun and was walking slowly about, staring all over

the ground below from time to time. His box was on wooden stilts and as we came closer I could see long straight stretches of barbed wire, and coils below, and beyond that a parched sort of wasteland, flat and featureless except for some raw-looking wooden huts in the middle.'

Philpot did not stay over-long behind the wire. He got clean away in October, 1943, in the famous 'Wooden Horse' escape and made a remarkable run to safety.

The outlandish reception committee which greeted new arrivals to POW camps often unnerved newcomers. Many were coolly received by resident prisoners, as Sergeant Spencer discovered when he got to Stalag Luft I, 'feeling rather scruffy'. After German guards had shoved them into some semblance of order they were marched away from the railway station at Barth: 'Eventually we saw the camp in the distance and weren't very impressed. When we went down by the side of the camp towards the main gate and Kommandantura we saw lots of villainous-looking characters staring at us. Most of them had long beards and long overcoats . . . they were the cream of the RAF on one of their off days! After being pushed around and finding out the hard way that the guards knew the meaning of "square-headed bastards" we finally got allotted to our huts.'

A suspicious welcome reserved for newcomers to prison camps was, of course, the result of a need to guard against German stool-pigeons and, very occasionally, traitors.

On one famous occasion, however, the tables were turned completely when many of the 3,000 or so RAF POWs, taken from Heydekrug to Stalag 357 near Fallingbostel, (formerly the camp was two miles away at Thorn) were shaken rigid by an unexpected arrival. Among the prisoners pressed against the wire of their compound on that autumn day in 1944 was Sergeant Dominy who later recounted what happened: 'We all knew . . . of the incredible fight at Arnhem and were at the wire to watch when the prisoners from this epic fight were marched along the road past our camp by Sergeant-Major Bill Lord. He had all the swagger of a Guardsman on parade. They were carrying their wounded and their guards were a shambling, dishevelled lot, just about keeping pace with the steady Praetorian tread of the finest soldiers in the world. We did not cheer. We came instinctively to attention and Bill Lord, noticing our two medical officers standing with us, gave his party "eyes right" and snapped them a salute which would not have been out of place at Pirbright or Caterham.'

When Regimental Sergeant-Major Lord got to the nearby Stalag XIB he brought order to the British compound within a week and then set about the task of pushing the various nationalities in that huge, dirty and ill-organized camp into shape. The man was irresistible. Bombardier Stonard met him and never forgot the Sergeant-Major's bellowing command at 8 o'clock parade: 'My name is Lord! J. C. Lord. Jesus Christ Lord, the only holy man in the British Army and don't you forget it!' A scourge of idle Americans in Stalag XIB, bringing discipline to the British, he was a man before whom even the hardest German guard commander was known to quake.

There were a few other British POWs who by sheer force of personality dominated the German prison system wherever they went. Among them were Major-General Fortune and Lieutenant Mike Sinclair, known by the Germans as 'the Red Fox', (*der rote Fuchs*) who repeatedly escaped until he was shot dead at Colditz late in 1944; others were 'Wings' Day and Warrant Officer 'Dixie' Deans, who led many thousands of RAF POWs through captivity with spirit and determination. Warrant Officer George Grimson was an escaper extraordinary, making various illicit exits and entries of RAF POW camps while setting up escape lines in Occupied Europe. He vanished at the very end of the war, probably to a lonely, painful death. Such men as these achieved a truly heroic stature while in German captivity.

For them imprisonment seemed to hold few personal terrors, but for the great mass of RAF prisoners their entry into full *Kriegsgefangenshaft* (POW captivity) was a traumatic and depressing experience. Most of them came to terms with it, however, once the early shock of capture had worn off. They even managed to turn the German term for their plight to good account; they called themselves, with proud independence, '*Kriegies*'.

There were two main routes by which prisoners arrived at Marlag und Milag Nord. Men saved from a watery grave in the North and Baltic Seas and in the North Atlantic generally ended up at Stalag XB, the huge camp at Sandbostel near Bremen, which was overcrowded and dirty and housed about 2500 prisoners of many nationalities. In this camp a compound some 250 yards square was allocated to them.

The conditions at Sandbostel were poor until the German navy took over from the army. With *Kapitänleutnant* J. Spiehs in charge, matters rapidly improved: 'Nothing, however, could better the driving sand storms in dry weather, or the sea of mud under foot after rain,' observed Captain Wilson.

Able Seaman Clark got there from a working party at Bad Sulza. 'We were marched through the main gates of this new Stalag; lots of huts and other POWs. We were halted at the sick bay . . . and greeted by a German Naval officer. "Good afternoon gentlemen." We looked in amazement. "I am your Camp Commander; Submarine Captain in the last war – any submarine men here?" We said "yes" – and he replied

– "Is there anything you want?" We said, "Something to eat, we are hungry" – telling him that [for] four days we had only had four loaves and four tins of meat for forty men.'

Soon the POWs were tucking in to a good, hot, vegetable soup before they settled in to their world behind barbed wire in the naval compound. Here they stayed until the new camp at Westertimke was ready for them.

Another prisoner who travelled the same route to Westertimke was Lieutenant-Commander Mercer who found life at Sandbostel 'reduced to a basic routine' of interminable food queues. In June, 1942, he was sent with other officers to the new camp of Marlag Nord where the Germans had tried to make sure no one escaped. 'The perimeter was a double barbed-wire fence spaced about six feet,' said Mercer. 'Outside was a deep, wide trench and detectors were buried at intervals to register any vibration in the guards' hut. There were, of course, the usual elevated sentry boxes equipped with searchlights and patrolling sentries around the wire. The entire perimeter was floodlit at night except during the passage of Allied 'planes overhead.'

If the Germans thought that such precautions would deter their prisoners from attempting to escape they were to be sorely disappointed. Lieutenant-Commander Moran, who spent some time at Sandbostel after surviving twenty-one days in an open lifeboat drifting in the North Atlantic during June, 1941, was one of twelve prisoners who dug what was probably the longest escape tunnel (330 ft) during the war from a German POW camp.

Getting away early in March, 1942, he travelled half-way across Holland before recapture. He nearly got away, too, from Westertimke, but was sent to Stalag VIIIB with other repeated escapers and finally ended up at a camp where, the Kommandant at Lamsdorf assured them, 'You will be safe until the end of the war and you will cause no more worry to your relatives at home.'

After a carefully guarded journey one day in September, 1942, the prisoners were taken to a floodlit castle perched on a rocky hill. Inside, a noisy and enthusiastic reception welcomed the first group of RN POWs to their new home. Then the new arrivals lowered their trousers and were given an embarrassing and somewhat inexpert medical examination for venereal disease. Only later did they realize that the 'German doctor' and his 'staff' were part of an elaborate joke played on them by the inmates. 'We wondered what sort of place we had come to,' said Moran.

Early next morning they found out. During their official documentation events quickly reached an alarming conclusion when other prisoners perched high above the castle's courtyard began to water-bomb the proceedings. The guards reacted promptly and furiously and soon bullets were flying everywhere. Oflag IVC – Colditz – was living up to its notorious and well-earned reputation.

Only those men considered the cream of escapers were sent to Colditz. They were proud of getting there and lived up to their hard-earned reputation. But most RN POWs remained in small groups in transit from camp to camp before arriving at Sandbostel and finishing up at Marlag Nord.

The prisoners at this camp thought that it was easily the best they had seen. As the only camp organized and administered by the *Kriegsmarine* some inter-service rivalry no doubt played its part in persuading the Germans to put up a good show of running it. So far as the inmates were concerned, the camp was run tolerably efficiently and correctly.

This was not, however, true of the whole Marlag und Milag Nord complex at Westertimke. While Marlag Nord was reserved for RN personnel and eventually comprised two compounds, Marlag 'O' for officers and Marlag 'M' for Chief Petty Officers, Petty Officers and Senior Ratings, there was also Milag Nord for captured merchant seamen.

The two camps, Marlag und Milag Nord, were alike as chalk and cheese, but a few RN men were sent officially to the latter. When they arrived in Milag Nord they were immediately impressed by the 'Wild West' atmosphere which contrasted strongly with the strict sobriety of the Senior Service's own camp nearby.

Tales of wild living in the camp were naturally magnified by RN prisoners and relayed to bemused newcomers. That some of the stories were true, Technical Officer Haddow discovered when he arrived there in 1942.

Haddow was on loan to the Merchant Navy when he was captured off Narvik. He went via an internment camp and Sandbostel to Milag Nord: 'We had,' he wrote, 'all the bad habits such as gambling wheels and so on.' Captain Monckton who reached the camp after the *Empire Starling* was torpedoed in November, 1942, was also struck by the widespread gambling that went on and remarked that, as German discipline weakened, 'the camp was one great "racket".'

Stories of women in the camp and heavy drinking were also established on fact; with over 3,000 interned merchant seamen of many nationalities who were not required to work, their absence would have been little short of a miracle. Nevertheless, they were still prisoners: 'The only drawback to everything that happened in the Camp,' thought Captain Monckton, 'was the eternal fencing-in by the wire and the presence at all times of the Nazi guards. One could never forget that one was cooped up like a lot of hens in a hen-house, and it tended to put a dismal effect on everything that took place.' In retaliation, sixteen MN officers got out of Milag Nord through two tunnels in March, 1943, and September, 1944, and a third one was started but never completed.

Entering Marlag Nord was a much quieter affair for prisoners who travelled the second main route to Westertimke. These were men picked up on operations around the Mediterranean and South Atlantic.

Two large camps, one at Wolfsberg, set in spectacular scenery in south-east Austria (re-designated Stalag XVIIIA shortly before the first British prisoners captured in Greece and Crete arrived there) and the other Stalag VIIA at Moosburg, north-east of Munich, acted as staging camps. Here men were either sent out to work or transported to Marlag Nord.

Some of them, like Captain Norwood who was captured at Tobruk, found the Italian prison camps by no means unbearable and arrival at Stalag VIIA 'a harsher reminder of what war entailed after an almost idyllic period of convalescence in Italy'. Marine Blockley, however, thought he was fortunate to arrive at Stalag XVIIIA after surviving the attack on Crete: 'I consider myself very lucky to be alive and all in one piece. I am very sorry indeed if this incident [capture] has upset any of you . . . but it is better than being killed like thousands [of] others were. I am in a camp with my mates, good food, clothing and excellent living quarters.'

The camp at Wolfsberg was bearable because the British permanent staff and prisoners in transit were housed in solidly-built brick stables formerly used by an Austrian cavalry regiment. After spells working outside and inside the wire at Sandbostel, Blockley was one of the earliest arrivals at Westertimke where he was put to work building roads and planting gardens to brighten the new camp's desolate appearance.

Naval officers and men who were transferred by force from Italy suffered the same kind of difficulties *en route* for Germany as had others who arrived before them, but since they were already hardened by their experience in Italian POW camps they were able to make a quick appraisal of their new captivity.

Among them was Ordinary Seaman Gant who had been imprisoned at Campo PG52 at Chiavari near Genoa. Arriving at Stalag VIIA in September, 1943, he observed a new attitude on the part of his captors: 'The camp at Moosburg had little resemblance to that of Chiavari. There was a certain professionalism that the Italians lacked. Although the huts were similar they were much smaller and there was adequate lighting and a stove. It was the security arrangements that first came to [our] attention. A double row of barbed wire at least 12ft in height not only surrounded the perimeter of the camp, there were also rows through the camp quartering it into four segments. Allowed to run loose at night were Alsatian dogs between the rows.' He soon realized that assembling prisoners was a much quicker process since 'the dogs played a major part [in] ensuring that no prisoner moved from one rank to the other while counting was in progress.'

As an Ordinary Seaman, Gant had no choice about whether or not he would go to Marlag Nord. Those who went there, either because, as Senior Ratings, they chose to do so or, being commissioned officers, they were sent automatically by the Germans, welcomed the chance to be once again among their own, special kind, administered by the German navy. 'In comparison with Italian camps it was,' thought Petty Officer Macey, 'heaven, strange as it may seem.' Mainly, this was because Marlag Nord was 'run on naval lines and as near to a ship's routine as we could. This being so, we were much happier and knew where we stood.'

After entering the camp at Westertimke men began to learn things about themselves in the special atmosphere of POW life. 'Capture shakes a man out of the protective chrysalis of common sense and the semi-transparent envelope of habit,' wrote Lieutenant Morgan who arrived at Marlag 'O' late in 1943 from Italian captivity.

As if in compensation for the loss of their real life prisoners began to experience a new sense of personal freedom. They would also discover that each man's character was to be tested to the full.

PART TWO

GUESTS OF THE FÜHRER

'We as prisoners of war still have our duty clearly before us, we must continue the fight behind the enemy lines.'

Major-General V. M. Fortune, speaking to newly-arrived officers from Greece in June, 1941, at Oflag VB.

Quoted by W. Wynne Mason, *Prisoners of War*, p. 84.

4
BARBED WIRE ARMY

B Y ESTABLISHING A sea-route for sending on parcels of food, clothing and other necessities of life to POWs in December, 1940, the International Committee of the Red Cross (ICRC), based at Geneva, provided their only lifeline during the war years.

That some help was urgently needed soon became clear from letters sent home by captured members of the BEF; one army captain wrote from Oflag VII C/H in the autumn of 1940: 'We get up at 7.0 a.m. and have a mug of coffee, soup and potatoes at 11 and 5 o'clock, sometimes bread, so you can understand that parcels of food are urgently needed. Some arrived today from the Red Cross, they are to be shared one between ten officers. No parcels arrived yet for me, my clothes are worn out and in holes.' Despite all the efforts of the ICRC, such was the state of affairs for most POWs in that first winter of mass imprisonment.

It was only with the greatest reluctance that the British Admiralty agreed to open a loophole in the blockade of Occupied Europe to allow ICRC-chartered ships to ferry vital foodstuffs, clothing and medical supplies between Lisbon and Marseilles. The *Julita*, sailing just before Christmas, 1940, began a regular service controlled at all times by the Red Cross.

From these small beginnings a huge enterprise grew, with vessels flying the flag of the ICRC sailing into Lisbon and Genoa from the Dominions, the United States and South America. Later in the war a northern route to Gothenburg was established from where stores were ferried across the Baltic to Lübeck and other north German ports.

Inspiring as this great undertaking undoubtedly was – 'through a besieged continent blockaded and impenetrable, we had to open the gateways of the ocean,' wrote an ICRC delegate, Marcel Junod – the shipment of essential supplies was made possible only by very close attention to detail.

Each timetable of sailing and information about routes had to be agreed simultaneously between the nations at war and every ship's captain knew that any deviation from his agreed course could be fatal. Even so, despite the most careful planning, there were a number of incidents including the sinking of the *Embla* in 1944. Nor was the onward transmission of supplies guaranteed when they were unloaded because Red Cross delegates had to argue continually with the German authorities over their use of precious railway trucks.

Despite everything, relief for POWs rapidly became the biggest, costliest and most extensive of the ICRC's many activities for helpless victims of war. It was a real success story and general opinion among prisoners when they emerged from the shadow of captivity was that it had saved many of them from certain starvation. As Sergeant Taylor wrote: 'If it had not been for the Red Cross and Order of St John with their food parcels and clothing I am certain lots of POWs who eventually got home would never have "made it".'

Knowing that his family would have received news that he was missing and were unaware of his survival, many newly-captured prisoners suffered great mental anguish, like Second Lieutenant Heasman: 'What we are all most anxiously awaiting is a letter or some indication that you know at home we are prisoners and not dead or wounded.' Flight-Sergeant Bulmer had the same worries: 'My one thought . . . was that M—— [wife] and mother would know I was missing and the fact that I was powerless to inform them seemed to me the biggest trouble I had ever had to bear.'

Information was often received in cards and letters addressed to relatives because official arrangements were rudimentary at that time as POWs tried to get news of their survival and imprisonment back home as soon as possible. It was on the long march into captivity that many of them first demonstrated the art of making something out of nothing which served them so well in the years that followed.

Private Perry learned quickly while on his way to Stalag XXA, scribbling his name and army number on a scrap of paper torn from his army paybook, addressing it to his wife in England. This message was to arrive in an envelope from the Belgian Red Cross at Dendermonde together with a cyclostyled slip of paper: 'From your husband-son, which [sic] passed here as a war prisoner in good health – The 20th July 1940.' An official note was enclosed; the information had just been received from Germany and his wife was asked to confirm the news with the War Office's Casualty Branch. 'I am more than surprised,' wrote Perry from his prison camp, 'that the communication from the Belgian Red Cross reached home.'

Another soldier who found a way to get news of his survival home was Private Bowers. 'Somewhere on that march, I think it was in Belgium, some Red Cross nurses were accepting hastily scribbled messages on odd bits of paper addressed to our families. It was rumoured that by some devious means they were being sent to England. That rumour happened to be true. Two of mine did get home long before my mother received official notification that I was a POW. She had received the official telegram to say I was missing of course. . . . She took them to some official in St James's [Palace]. . . . There she was told to ignore them as they were probably forgeries and that our Regiment wasn't in France anyway. Blind bureaucracy of course.'

Blind bureaucracy, however, was not the only reason why both the War Office and British Red Cross War Organization treated unofficial reports about POWs very cautiously. Having accepted information from sources which could not be checked and then subsequently to have to inform relatives of the death of a much-loved husband, son or brother when reliable details came to hand would have been devastating for those who waited so anxiously at home. Unofficial reports about men in captivity were, in consequence, often disbelieved.

In helping prisoners to get news of their capture to their families, courageous civilians often ran enormous risks under the Germans' very noses. Private Phillips was one prisoner who gave his name and address to young girls of the Dutch Red Cross at Heerlen. After the war he learned 'that my family had in fact received a card from these excellent people. I shall always be grateful to them for it,' he added, 'as it could not have been easy for them.'

For most POWs, however, the only means of getting news about their fate to loved ones at home was through regular, official channels. But many things could go still wrong, leaving both prisoners and relatives anxiously out of touch with each other. 'I'll probably see you myself, before this card gets home – they only take about a year,' wrote Private Little in the summer of 1940. And the mailing operation was, of course, a two-way process: 'Thank the Lord you are safe, my darling,' wrote Lance-Corporal Clark's wife to him, 'I never want to go through another three months like I have done again.'

Of the greatest importance in helping prisoners face up to their imprisonment and to bear its tedium and boredom was reassuring news from home. 'I received your first letter on November 16th [1940],' wrote Private Aldous, 'and it has eased my mind a great deal to know that you are all in the best of health.' Major Booth also noticed their morale-boosting effect: 'These letters have made a tremendous difference to the spirit of the camp; they are all most reassuring and speak of life at home continuing in the usual way with no alarms and excursions, and apparently no irksome restrictions.'

Some desperately unlucky POWs remained out of touch with home for long periods. It was nearly a year before Sergeant Tuck's relatives knew that he had been captured at St Valéry, eighteen months for Sergeant Lawrence at Stalag XXIA before he heard anything from home, and a complete absence of news of any kind for Sergeant-Major

Hudson, in Stalags IVB and 357. None of the letters sent by his relatives reached him; it was, he thought, simply the 'luck of the draw'.

Many men would have been crushed by this experience but few were able to enjoy the luxury laid down by the Geneva Convention of a 'capture card', to be sent within a week of his entering a permanent camp by each POW and four postcards and two letter forms supplied by the authorities thereafter every month.

The arrival of capture cards from POWs in Italy raised a mixture of relief and alarm because they were all the same, with a printed message which began: 'My dear . . . , I am alright (I have not been wounded (or) I have been slightly wounded). I am a prisoner of the Italians and I am being treated well.' Prisoners had to strike out the part which did not apply. Few thought the last sentence applied to them but crossing it out meant seeing an angry guard tear the card to shreds. The German equivalent said nothing about wounds and so relatives were not left to speculate on just how bad a 'slight' wound could be.

There were two other main channels by which anxious relatives heard news of Germany's prisoners. One was from radio broadcasts and in particular from the lips of William Joyce – 'Lord Haw-Haw' – and the other from Vatican Radio.

The use of German radio to transmit messages home was forbidden to all ranks under any circumstances by the War Office but some prisoners were naturally tempted to use this means of letting their families know they were safe. Their numbers were not large but Joyce and his German masters knew that additional listeners to German propaganda broadcasts would be added by bringing the occasional POW to the microphone at the Concordia Studios in Berlin to retell details of his capture. Prisoners' names were regularly transmitted to keep people tuned in, and, since the smooth-tongued traitor spoke to a massive audience in Britain during the first year of war, his news was passed on even when it was not heard by immediate relatives.

Vatican Radio also broadcast the names of POWs, though with more limited success. The fact that its representatives were not allowed to enter German POW camps where the great bulk of Allied prisoners were held reduced their influence and usefulness with officials in London.

Having once managed to dispatch a 'capture card', the other pressing need was to still the gnawing pangs of hunger. 'Grub will keep entering into it, sorry! – at all times, a prisoner's first and foremost thought is of food. He lives and thinks of it, and sleeps and dreams of the sheer pleasure of a big "scoff" or "bash". This longing for food was the main factor in making us all a bit "barbed-wire happy",' said Private Ayling.

Food dominated every prisoner's thoughts in permanent camp because there was never enough to go round. Lance-Corporal McKechnie soon discovered this and had the unenviable task of trying to ensure fair shares for all as section leader, responsible for looking after twenty-one men, in Stalag XXA. 'Collecting and distributing the rations was the worst job, deciding by lot who was to have the ends of a loaf, and counting out the biscuits individually into hats around a table.'

Typical German rations consisted of *ersatz* tea (made out of strawberry leaves) or coffee (burnt barley) without milk or sugar which passed for breakfast. At midday a bowl of soup, thin and greasy, usually potato or swede but sometimes to be seen with small lumps of horseflesh floating in it, was followed by one-fifth of a potato-flour loaf or thirty hard-tack biscuits together with a portion of margarine in the afternoon. That was all until the next day – and so on for months on end. Suffering from such an inadequte diet there was more force than humour behind Private Aldous's letter to his mother in August, 1940: 'When I come home, you had better be ready to do some overtime on your cooking.'

Allied POWs should not have starved in German prison camps had the Geneva Convention been correctly observed. Under Article 11 it had been agreed that prisoners' food rations should be equivalent 'in quantity and quality' to that of depot troops – in Germany members of the *Ersatzheer*, the reserve army guarding POWs.

This rule was rarely followed and certainly not in the big, permanent camps. Logistical problems for the Germans in feeding thousands of unexpected mouths made the first year of imprisonment a time of permanent hunger and things were also very bleak in the last winter of war. In some instances POWs were deliberately kept short of food in order to prevent them escaping or to make them easier to handle by their guards.

Food parcels, sent from Britain, America and Canada, together with bulk supplies from Argentina, became essential in making up the deficiency in prison rations (something which those who signed the Geneva Convention never intended) and prisoners came to rely on them to prevent the worst effects of malnutrition. But the poisonous results of lack of food on starving prisoners and the power it gave to those who could manipulate their rations could be seen in most camps.

Some POWs disintegrated completely under the harsh effects of extreme hunger. They stole food from their fellows, compromised themselves with the German authorities for better rations and adopted a policy of 'every man for himself'.

'Hunger makes you do many things,' wrote Lance-Corporal Tibbitts. 'It brings to the front many things you never thought possible in a person. I saw this in our early camps and hunger did make the odd one or two, who let the Germans bait them with a few bits of bread, do things they never thought possible. But punishment meted out to them by their colleagues was very severe indeed.'

At Stalag XXA, Rifleman Porter experienced the lengths to which starving men will go to steal food. While out on a working party one day he was offered two loaves of black bread in return for his shirt. Wolfing one down immediately he smuggled the other back into camp. That night he rested his head on his precious loaf but discovered next morning that someone had neatly sawn off both ends while he slept, leaving only the centre portion. 'In future I always ate anything as soon as I got it,' he said, 'as many men had no hestitation at all of stealing anything they could lay [their] hands on.'

The punishment inflicted on their own colleagues for this worst of all 'crimes' was swift and often brutal. In Stalag XXB Private Low saw thieves flung into the camp's latrines – an evil-smelling deep pit – from which they were rescued coughing and retching after being forced to take several gulps of the stinking mess. Every camp had its own refinements on the same theme.

Another form of summary justice was witnessed by Private Sud-worth at Stalag VIIIA. After trial by a POW court, an Irish guardsman was found guilty of stealing food and punished by his colleagues: 'Every day at mealtimes, for four days he would be strapped face down to the table and flogged, with ten lashes. At the end of four days, he was in a pretty bad state. He had been posted as missing in his own hut. It was thought he had escaped. When the punishment was complete, he was quietly returned. The Germans never found out the reason for his condition and gave him a long spell in hospital to recover.'

Not all the punishments were quite so drastic as this. Another case of food-stealing at a work camp near Munich was resolved by sending the culprit to Coventry and placing him on iron rations after the Man of Confidence had refused to allow him to be flogged.

In virtually all main camps some prisoners operated fairly harmless 'rackets' – meaning anything shady or 'fiddled' – but a wicked form involved stealing from other prisoners under the pretence of provid-ing them with food. Company Sergeant-Major Soane saw some of this during his early days of captivity at Stalag XXA where he met a number of Regimental and Company Sergeant-Majors. Captured early in the German advance across France and Belgium and sent to Thorn by train, they had organized themselves before the main bulk of prisoners arrived. 'These men were working all kind of rackets, promising the starving lads bread for watches, cigarette cases, gold rings and many other things; after these things had been handed over they would give the boys a small portion of bread, not even enough for one meal.'

Stalag XXA was notorious for the number of 'rackets' run by senior British NCOS, but other camps also had their share of men who looked after themselves, regardless of others.

After arriving at Stalag XXB, for example, Sergeant Tuck met 'the only NCO, an R.S.M., who was really disliked by the thousands in that first big camp – he was in charge and seemed to live like the Germans. He was smartly dressed and looked well fed.' Later in the war, while imprisoned at a small camp in Rennes on his way to Stalag XIIA, Private Sudworth came across a Paratroop Sergeant who, as he found out, was working a steady 'racket':

'He was originally with us in the camp, but volunteered for duty at the French-run hospital. He got himself the job of receiving wounded prisoners as they came in. He would meet them at the door and persuade them to hand over their watches and rings for safety. This, he said, would prevent them falling into the hands of the German orderlies, and the owners could have them back later on when they were settled in the wards. Unfortunately, this did not happen, and he kept the lot; selling them to the townspeople and the Germans and living like a Lord on the proceeds.

We awaited his ultimate return to the camp with some degree of anticipation. What was going to happen to him was nobody's business. But we never saw him again.'

The stores of food which arrived in Red Cross parcels were rarely stolen by prisoners (because there was a general agreement against this kind of theft) nor by their guards, though there was a steady loss of some items like cigarettes and at least one consignment of 30,000 parcels in transit went missing altogether. Guardsman Adams heard a strong rumour in Stalag IVB that most of the parcels which failed to reach him never even left the British dockside. Angry and sickened by this, he wrote telling relatives not to bother to send him any more.

Since they knew that if Germans were discovered raiding Red Cross parcels they would be severely punished, prisoners sometimes turned this to good advantage in getting their revenge on particularly-hated guards or officials.

At a camp attached to Stalag XVIII A/Z a vicious road foreman was to discover just how effective this form of revenge could be. Following another day's brutal overwork, the prisoners stole his satchel just as he boarded the train for home. After packing it with Red Cross foodstuffs they spirited the satchel back onto the station platform knowing that it would be found and traced to its owner. 'We derived some satisfaction,' said Private Cocker, 'from the belief he would almost certainly face prison for trafficking in Red Cross goods.'

The supplies of food reaching Oflags and Stalags had a marked effect on how well POWs coped with their captivity. One man who registered this connection was Corporal Welland: 'Our morale tended to vary according to the arrival (or non-arrival) of Red Cross parcels. Often we were told that parcels had reached a railway station some miles away and in order to get a local farmer to bring them by tractor to the camp we would be asked to give perhaps 1,000 cigarettes, say ten each, to make this possible.'

After a lifeline with home was established and German rations could be supplemented from the all-important parcels, prisoners had to come to terms with other aspects of their new lives. As Major Whitcombe wrote about the early days at Oflag VII C/H: 'Morale was low enough as it was; the thought of having been taken unwounded emphasized one's failure and being surrounded by barbed wire guarded by armed Germans was depressing in the extreme – and we were faced with a long time to contemplate it. Although we always talked about being home for Christmas [1940] we, in our more realistic moments, knew that we were in the same position as those to whom the same thing happened in 1914.'

One of the hardest things that POWs had to bear was the feeling of being trapped behind barbed wire with no end to their captivity in sight. The only way they could cope with this was by never allowing any doubts to creep in about the eventual defeat of Germany: 'Most of us throughout our captivity were sustained by a blind faith that sooner rather than later the war would end in our favour,' commented Trooper Wilson. 'I feel sure that prisoners taken in the early days of the war would not have survived undamaged mentally and spiritually if they had not had this protective shell.'

'You know I gave it [the war] at least 2 years from the start and thus I am resigned to at least another 12 months in durance,' wrote Lieutenant Roberts in September, 1940. 'It is not a thought – to be caged in – that fills me with pleasure but I consider it worth while to carry on in good spirit.' On the same topic, Private Aldous penned a letter to his parents in July, 1941: 'I don't know what your opinion is in England, but I myself think I will be home soon.'

The enemy of hope in a prison camp was the monotony and utter boredom of a life which suddenly had no purpose or pattern. As Major Munro Fraser found at Oflag XIIB, 'Prisoner of war life is an interminable weekend, an endless Saturday and Sunday that never succeeds in getting round to Monday. This impression is given by the fact that there are no workaday duties in the bag. We have no offices to attend from nine till five and few jobs that must be finished before we can turn to some more congenial task. All our activities belong to Saturday afternoon – or they are Sunday affairs.'

The same thoughts occurred to Major Booth: 'Day follows day, as like as two pins; the procession of them stretches out of sight, forward and backwards, with no indication or turning.' This was too much for some prisoners who lost all hope of ever getting out again and simply turned their face to the wall and died in their bunk, went raving mad or ran for the wire, tearing at it until cut down by a hail of bullets.

In order to mark the passage of time POWs reacted in two ways. They started on various activities and set themselves precise targets which they could look back on with satisfaction when they were achieved. At some camps prisoners worked by a different clock from the 'standard' German time so that when they were called out on parade at 7.0 a.m. their watches actually registered 8.0 a.m. In this way they enjoyed an 'extra' hour in bed. At such times, standing in all weathers while their guards went up and down the rows, counting and re-counting them, many prisoners thought how artificial is the usual divisibility of time by which our lives are given shape and purpose.

The second way in which men marked off their time in captivity was by following the war's events. While they had no influence on its duration and they could make no deals with the Germans to reduce their imprisonment, POWs picked up clues about what was happening from their guards' behaviour. During the final year of their captivity, with the Reich dissolving into ruin, the signs were there for all to read.

From the earliest days of captivity rumours of an early release, like the seasons, blossomed and decayed. Major Booth reported a fine crop, 'of amazing variety and ingenuity', including the widespread belief that the Germans had failed in an invasion attempt. It was said they had lost 80,000 soldiers drowned in The Wash and the sea about the English coast had been set on fire. News of an armistice was heard by Private Lusted soon after arriving at Stalag XXA: 'They say there are peace talks going on,' he wrote, adding, 'I hope so.' Later in the year, President Roosevelt's re-election was greeted enthusiastically by prisoners like Major Booth who thought 'it will be a prelude to a peace drive.'

Early in 1941 Corporal Hope and his mates at Stalag XXIA were 'all convinced that the war will be finished this year' and then came news that 'Gerry in cook house expects a Revolution here in one month and the war to end in 3 [months].' Soon after this came an 'amazing rumour about Hess being in England' – for once the POW grapevine was correct – and news of Operation 'Barbarossa': 'At last Russia is *indeed* in the war!! Great news today,' wrote Hope on 23 June.

'Have decided War will end on Aug. 17th 1944 i.e. length of last

War as from May 10th 1940 (German attack on France). This is 279 days from now,' concluded Captain Sewell with more confidence than he felt on 13 November, 1943. But even if things failed to work out as anticipated, POWs were cheered by the fact that they were relatively better off than many civilians. They also knew that the Allied nutcracker was closing inexorably about the Reich as Major Casdagli recorded in February, 1944: 'I am heading for one thousand days in the bag – what an *age* and what a waste of an active life. *Tant pis!* It might be much worse, we are anyway WINNING.'

The worst times were birthdays, wedding anniversaries and at the turn of the year when the bleak prospect of endless captivity particularly sapped morale. There was not much seasonal cheer for Sergeant Nell, in Stalag IVB, on Christmas Day, 1943: '*Perhaps* I shall be home next year at this time,' he wrote, 'I can't stand much more of this existence. It will drive me mad. Even now I get fits of deep depression which would end in suicide if I had the means for such an act at my disposal. I look behind me and see an endless arch of wasted years. Looking ahead I see no release – just a tunnel of time broken by rollcalls and meals which have become so automatic that they have insidiously become time. The monotony and futility of it all is maddening. When will I break out of the darkness into the light?'

British army psychologists wanted to discover if there were any common characteristics among POWs. When they probed into the problems of survival they found what they called a 'vintage mark' which applied to groups of prisoners who exhibited the same kind of behaviour connected with their fighting experience and capture.

At its most extreme it was seen in the 'Red Devils' of Arnhem who stuck closely together. 'They did not', stated an official report, 'have time to adapt to Stalag life and they have been aggressive and difficult. They keep together and resent discipline.' Such comments were meat and drink to the 'Red Devils' who would have regarded them as a compliment to their own special *esprit de corps*.

The way in which men reacted to captivity was also dependent on rank, service and age. Under the Geneva Convention officers could not be required to work outside their Oflags. So they were almost entirely dependent on their own resources for building a community from which they could finally emerge with some self-respect.

Matters were made more difficult, however, by the German practice of separating senior from junior officers, and by the hostility which developed between regular and non-regular officers.

By removing senior from junior officers the Germans thought they could intimidate the younger men. But they failed miserably and this led to a breakdown of discipline within some camps which threatened their already fragile peace. At Oflag VIB, for example, when Major-General Fortune and other senior officers were shifted to Oflag IX A/H in January, 1942, parades degenerated into riots. The Kommandant was forced to put on armed guards to prevent prisoners fooling about, reading and smoking on *appell*, and slipping away to their huts.

The punishment cells became filled to overflowing with a waiting list which grew ever longer as discipline inside the camp virtually collapsed. Battalion Commanders did not see why they should help the German staff and there was nothing to bring bloody-minded officers to heel beyond the somewhat remote threat of a court martial after the war: 'Discipline really depended in the long run,' thought Second Lieutenant Baxter, 'on the personal strength of character and tact of battalion and company commanders and on public opinion.'

Those prisoners who came from the British regular army were products of a rigid military discipline which governed their lives far more than it affected men who had volunteered or were called up for the duration. The non-regulars often showed their intolerance of barbed wire and stupid guards and were generally the wilder spirits. For their part, regular officers believed that their pre-war training made them more fitted to withstand the rigours of POW life.

This division between regulars and non-regulars extended to men from the ranks. When he was captured, Private Hayden, a regular soldier, had just returned from overseas. Imprisonment as a POW was for him merely 'another foreign station. I had only been back from India a few months before war broke out. I think for this reason if no other I, like so many more regulars, was able to adapt to the situation far more readily than the territorial – plus the fact of the rigid discipline of the pre-war army for which I thank God, for [it was] this discipline that saved me on many occasions.'

There were many hardened veterans who shared this view: 'As I was a regular soldier and had served two years on [the] North-West Frontier of India as well as in the Libyan desert and was used to discipline and rough times,' commented Staff Quarter-Master Sergeant Ovens, 'maybe I did not notice the hardships of POW life as so many of the others did.' In return, volunteers were often highly critical of regulars.

Sergeant Dexter, who was called up on the outbreak of war, considered that morale in camps was generally very well maintained once the first shock of capture had passed. However, he was ashamed at times of the way in which the British assumed they were superior to other POWs – 'having to see Indian soldiers pushed roughly away from water taps and I noticed that Guardsmen and regular soldiers (compared with T.A. and volunteers) were less amenable to discipline.' And at a concert held for officers in Oflag VIB, Second Lieutenant Baxter heard the speaker begin, 'Now, gentlemen, if you will just sit and think for a moment – er – regulars will just sit.'

Regular soldiers who had served in the general mayhem of 1914–18 were regarded by many new prisoners as 'antediluvian half-wits' and were told so. On the other hand, since the British army had been forced out of Norway, France, Greece, Crete and parts of North Africa with some rapidity, older officers resented the limited experience of younger men who were sometimes field officers while they remained subalterns or captains.

Many men called to the ranks had, in the words of one President of the Board of Education, 'minds dulled and senses blunted by four generations of urban over-crowding and two of agricultural depression'.

Since they had been brought up in poor housing, often hungry and poorly clothed with nothing to spend, they expected little out of life and were able to adapt extraordinarily well to the not entirely unaccustomed hardships of POW life, determined, as many said, to make the best of a bad job.

'My opinion of camp life [depended on] . . . what kind of person you were – did you give in and moan all day long or did you make the best of things and forget all about your life back in England,' said Lance-Corporal Musson. 'I think I was the latter.' Similarly, Private Taylor determined to make the best of his uncomfortable lot: 'I, as a regular soldier, did what I thought was the right thing. I wasn't for staying in one camp playing football and watching concerts, waiting for the war to end (that would have sent me barmy). In all my escapades I met some very great men, an elite company who never forgot their heritage – their country.'

Youth, too, had its advantages because the younger prisoners like Lance-Bombardier Larke tended to be more optimistic about their imprisonment. 'Morale was always fairly high so I thought. Being very youthful I think had a lot to do with it, as one tended to adopt a more carefree attitude. Barring accidents in bombing raids I never doubted that I would one day come home again.'

It was not surprising that single men without family ties also adapted better to POW life than prisoners with wives or relatives to worry about. A highly-educated character who tended to stand out in the ranks and was a misfit in the army might, against all expectations, settle down well in a prison camp and even appear to revel in that kind of life. As a seasoned regular Lance-Corporal Hancy, however, claimed he could always spot the hardest and most bloody-minded POWs; they were regulars like himself who relied more on training and inbred discipline than sheer brain-power to get by. They were the ones who 'were not the intellectual type,' thought Private Drysdale, 'and they seemed to have more initiative than the scholarly type'.

The War Office selection teams who were interested in how men had adapted to imprisonment and interviewed large numbers of them in August, 1945, discovered some general kinds of behaviour. After capture they found that most POWs had become apathetic and listless, their feelings very often relieved only by outbursts of anger against their officers and other prisoners. This was witnessed by Private Vincent while he was at Stalag VIIB: 'Hunger, black despair, and the bitter lessons we had learned on the march had changed us. Fear of the future and a mistrust of everyone poisoned all our thinking, and often led to violent quarrels.'

Later on, when they began to hate the enemy, men became mentally more balanced but, if their aggressive feelings turned inwards, they might suffer from an ever-deepening depression at being cut off from the outside world. The result could be madness and suicide.

This is what happened after prisoners arrived at Stalag XXA as Private Dobbins recalled: 'Some of the lads committed suicide, others seemed to will themselves to death. Others suffered acute depression – going mad.' There were many forms ranging from a mild pre-occupation with their bleak surroundings – 'barbed wire fever' as POWs called it and which was a common complaint – to full-scale breakdown.

Due to the physical hardships and mental pressures of a prison camp some POWs behaved in an extraordinary fashion. This happened to a good friend of Lance-Corporal Hancy's at Stalag XXB who confided that he would never accept German imprisonment and had decided to feign madness. He made a small wooden horse on wheels which he dragged everywhere behind him. Standing in the ranks on *appell* with his toy at his side, he swore and shouted at the guards who repeatedly battered him to the ground. Eventually he became genuinely mentally ill and was taken away by the German authorities for early repatriation.

Another form of delusion occurred at Stalag Luft I where Captain Vietor, USAF, came across a Canadian pilot who became a fanatical reader of religious tracts. 'Six months of rapt concentration loosened his marbles and he came to believe he was Christ. To keep the peace, his roommates solemnly agreed with him.'

When prisoners were fighting to retain their own mental balance such behaviour could be particularly difficult to handle as Signalman Jevons discovered while acting as *Vertrauensman* (Camp Leader) at a work detachment attached to Stalag IVB. In the summer of 1944 a South African POW began to act very strangely and matters came to a head when the deranged prisoner attacked a British first-aid orderly. Jevons was forced to ask the Kommandant to place the man in a cell for his own safety. When the guards arrived the prisoner flew at them in a crazed rage and eventually they shot him dead. 'Since that day,' Jevons wrote shortly before his own death, 'two thoughts have plagued me. If the South African hadn't made such a fuss and if I hadn't asked for the Kommandant's help that man might have survived the war and recovered.' Such were the matters of life and death forced upon POWs by their imprisonment.

Precise figures of general breakdown and mental illness among Allied POWs were not kept but it was certainly very rare. Most prisoners managed to come to terms with their imprisonment by channelling their anger and frustration in different ways.

There were, thought Gunner Peacock, three types of prisoners. First came those who by some means managed to stay in Stalags for the whole of their captivity. These men were employed in the sick-bay, clothing and parcel distribution, and a whole variety of other jobs.

A second group went out on working parties and stayed there either, like Peacock's brother, because they found a farm with the possibility of extra rations which suited them or they were employed in a mine or factory. Lastly came men who were known as 'Cook's tourists'. 'We were the ones,' Peacock wrote, 'who couldn't settle for the humdrum life of the other two groups and managed to keep moving between the Stalag and any one of scores of working camps.'

A move could be engineered in one of two ways. A prisoner could escape, which was relatively easy from many work camps and when recaptured would be returned to his main Stalag, or he might report sick and hope for the same result. After the big escapes from RAF camps the latter became the safer and preferred method as word got round that escapers might be shot on sight or handed over to the Gestapo.

Any prisoner under the rank of full corporal could be made to work for the Reich under Article 27 of the Geneva Convention but, on both sides, there were many ways of getting round this.

There were men like Private Page, who was warned on arrival at Stalag VIIIB to tell the Germans that he was a corporal, who promoted themselves – termed 'Stalag promotions' – claimed to have lost their army paybook and were not found out until details about them could be transmitted from London. Others demoted themselves or, when questioned as to their usual occupation, gave fanciful replies which sometimes landed them in trouble.

This was the problem faced by Private Randall who claimed to be an electrician in order to stay with a mate after being transported from Italy. The plan worked until his first job when his lack of training quickly revealed itself when he ruined valuable electrical goods.

Things appeared very sticky for a while because he was suspected of sabotage and was threatened with a firing squad. Fortunately, he was given the benefit of the doubt and transferred to a labouring gang.

Since they were desperate for manpower to keep their war economy functioning, the Germans failed to notify soldiers of their rights under the Geneva Convention and put a good deal of pressure on NCOs to go out to work as Staff-Sergeant Harling discovered at Stalag VIIIB. 'To try to encourage NCOs to go on work parties, our water supply was turned on at 6 a.m. for half an hour when one washed, or washed one's clothes and collected any drinking water for the day and when the Red Cross parcels arrived they were placed at one end of the hut for a week before they were opened and issued.'

Prisoners who were already employed in work gangs were not told of their rights either. Company Sergeant-Major Soane was one NCO who laboured on a farm for several years before finding out that he could not be required to work. Taking advantage of this he returned to Stalag XXA where he was extensively quizzed by the Germans and sent eventually to what had been Oflag IIIC where, among new inmates, were men from his own home and battalion: 'I sincerely hope that now we have found each other we can remain together until the end,' he wrote.

From October, 1942, the Germans collected most NCOs who refused to work from all over Germany and concentrated them at Stalag 383, previously known as Oflag IIIC. POWs who got there found a pleasant enough camp set amid heavily-wooded countryside at Hohenfels in Bavaria. The accommodation was in small huts and there was provision for recreation, sport and theatre. After the hardships of many work camps there was not a great deal to complain about apart from food shortages.

Men who went out to work camps or *Arbeitskommandos* looked forward to improved food rations and the avoidance of boredom but there was a clear pecking order in the desirability of jobs. Farm work on *Landwirtschaft Arbeitskommandos* was considered the best option, since this almost certainly involved more food by legal, or illegal, means and there were stories (not all of them entirely fanciful) of nights spent in bed with the farmer's wife or even, in some wilder cases, the farmer himself.

Generally it was reckoned by prisoners that living closely with a family could only lessen their hardships and this was especially true of the many small, scattered farms in Austria where they worked. Next in order came work on railways and various building jobs, followed by labouring in one of the big industrial concerns, termed *Gewerbe Arbeitskommandos*. The least favourable of all was pitwork in Polish or German mines which was often reserved, though not exclusively so, for POWs who had previous experience or whom the Germans singled out for punishment.

In addition to *Arbeitskommandos* the Germans formed *Bau und Arbeitsbattalionen* (Building and Work Battalions), referred to as B.A.B. Organized early in the war as pioneer battalions for hard pick and shovel work, they were supposed to be moved rapidly about the Reich to wherever an emergency building programme was started and were equipped with field cookers. In practice, however, these B.A.B.s eventually became indistinguishable from regular *Arbeitskommandos* but still retained a separate administrative identity.

Every Stalag acted as a centre around which satellites of *Arbeitskommandos* were administered. From some of the bigger ones large numbers of work camps were run with prisoners constantly travelling to and from them. In March, 1942, Stalag VIIIB for example had more than 260 *Arbeitskommandos* of varying size dependent upon it. NCOs not required to work because of their rank were expected by senior officers in the main camps to take turns in acting as Camp Leaders at them.

Early in the war forced labour was considered an important factor in Germany's war effort, but the apparent advantages of this were almost outweighed by the disadvantages of employing POWs.

Many thousands of reluctant prisoners certainly contributed by filling some gaps left by the recruitment of German civilians into the armed forces. However, there was the long-term economic burden of maintaining prisoners in terms of transporting, feeding, guarding and housing them. They were also highly inefficient workers, often completely unfitted to their work through their lack of experience or poor physical state and often making determined efforts to hinder the Reich's war effort.

Since these drawbacks to the use of prison labour were not entirely understood at the time, the conclusion of Germany's western campaign in 1940 marked a further extension from agriculture and forestry to all branches of industry.

At each Stalag a Labour Office organized work detachments in batches of twenty prisoners with two guards. The employer was expected to provide and take care of adequate housing for them, including 'proper' security measures, and was compensated by the Reich. Prisoners were supposed to be provided with the same food and work the same hours as civilian employees, although nightwork was avoided where possible to prevent them escaping and they were not unconditionally entitled to Sunday or holiday rest. The general rule was twenty-four successive hours of rest in any seven days but they were often forced to work without a proper break for weeks on end.

Payment for work done was made by the employer – not, of course, directly to prisoners but to their Stalag – at the rate of about sixty per cent of that earned by German workmen in the same categories with special regulations covering those in some industries, including agriculture, forestry, and construction work. Credits, which most men never received, or *Lagergeld* (currency specifically for use only inside prison camps) were the only financial rewards for much heavy and unpleasant work. Both of these forms of payment were a source of considerable dissatisfaction at the time and after the war.

When prisoners volunteered or were conscripted for work they had very little idea as to where they would be sent and what type of labour awaited them. As they set off from their permanent camps in the winter of 1940–41 they were dressed in a ragged variety of clothing. Stripped of their army uniform and worn-out boots they struggled into various bits of Belgian, French, Jugoslav and Polish uniforms and bound rags around their feet (*fusslappen*) or stuffed straw into newly-issued Dutch wooden clogs to prevent frostbite and chafing. Under their thin shirts men fixed cement bags to keep out the bitter cold while morale sank to its lowest ebb. Parcels of clothing, which did not begin to filter through until 1941, news from home and food were all scarce.

When information that British soldiers were working in salt and coal mines reached England there was an outburst of public anger and demands that German prisoners should be forced into similar work. The real reason, however, why they were not made to work underground was because guards for them could not be spared in sufficient numbers.

In order to reassure the public, the Foreign Office released news of 639 men from Stalag VIIIB working in four coal mines, all of whom were volunteers and were 'apparently glad to work as they receive relatively good pay', though it was admitted that the state of 136 men from Stalag IXC in salt mines at Dorndorf and Vadra was 'not entirely satisfactory'.

A spell in the mines might have opened the eyes of officials safely esconced behind a desk in London. Many thousands of prisoners were forced against their will to work underground and even then the Germans had to trick them into going there, as in the case of Private Rudd, who refused to believe he was being sent from Stalag VIIIB to a pottery factory. 'I soon realized how right I was when the cattle trucks opened [and] we saw the winding gear of a coal pit.' Most working parties were advertised as biscuit, chocolate, or other desirable factories, to encourage POWs to volunteer for them. As Private Ayling found to his cost, his 'biscuit factory' turned out to be a gypsum mine where he spent nearly four years in backbreaking toil.

From the latter half of 1942 all working parties in Silesian mines were administered from Lamsdorf in the same way that the Germans arranged for every *Arbeitskommando* in Austria to be run from Wolfsberg – Stalag XVIIIA. Regardless of where the mine was situated, however, working conditions were harsh, as Signalman Trewin soon discovered at a pit near Brüx in the Sudetenland: 'The hills should look lovely in the Spring with so much wood about. What a contrast to the grim black skeletons of pit heads all along the valley reminding us of our daily scuttle underground, dim lights and tired trudging back to the lager – which up to now has been one long mess of snow and slush, numbing feet and making us filthy. However, even an indifferent warm shower which in our tired state needs some self discipline to effect, gives us sufficient energy to brew a cup of coffee and tumble into bunks to be wakened immediately it seems by another shift either coming in or going out!' He added wearily, 'Such is Deutschland.'

Some prisoners knew precisely where they were going and, though they tried to fool the authorities, ended up in mining just the same. 'Despite my efforts to appear half-dead, I was pronounced by the German doctor to have a strong heart,' recalled Private Davis who duly found himself sent to a mine at Königshütte in Poland. Not only did the place appear ghastly – 'drizzling rain and tips of slack coal and rusty wagons' – the work of shovelling coal was heavy and made doubly hard for POWs in their weakened state. Before long, Davis was trying to 'work his ticket' back to Lamsdorf like most of his colleagues and, after making himself a 'first class nuisance', eventually returned there.

In some work camps prisoners remained for nearly the whole of their captivity. Working underground with Polish miners, Private Ward was one long-term prisoner who exchanged all kinds of goods for items from his Red Cross parcels. Despite the regular searches after an eight hours' shift, many were never discovered, including eggs packed 'fore and aft' in his forage cap or carried in trouser legs held up by puttees.

Normally a prisoner began work underground with an experienced civilian who showed him the ropes. Sometimes a close friendship developed between them – usually Poles were far friendlier than Germans – though in the case of Gunner Harrison things were not too easy for a while. As he explained, at *Arbeitskommando* E88, 'Your day started about one hour before we were due on the coal face. After leaving camp we were taken to the bottom of the mine in a cage – in winter we were pleased to get down as it was so very cold outside. We then walked about two miles to the work centre where we were collected by the civilian gang. . . . The first six months we were on the coal face the civilians did not like us and showed it. This came to a head when I had a fight with one of them, as I could not take it any longer. The other men did not come to his help and the next day and every day afterwards he shared his lunch with me . . . and from that moment I received respect from all the civilian gang.' The harsh penalties imposed by the Germans on those who fraternized in this way were never enough to prevent many friendships developing.

The relationship between Allied prisoners and the civilian population was, however, a complex one. Writing in August, 1940, a German authority on labour affairs offered some guidance in this matter: 'When dealing with POWs, strictness and justice, caution and reserve must be observed. The POW can expect to be treated with respect regarding his personage and his honour. Bad and degrading treatment is not compatible with German dignity. Nevertheless, the POW, while in confinement, remains Germany's enemy and cannot be granted the same treatment as a German civilian. To disregard him is the best form of dealing with him. He who seeks association with POWs, or even cultivates it, is giving offence and loses honour and respect.'

The reality of their treatment as prisoners belied this pompous official advice. Many POWs were forced to walk in the gutter when they were escorted on foot by German guards through towns and cities but it was almost impossible to work for months or even years with civilians without striking up some kind of relationship with them.

This was especially true of the prisoners who were chosen for work on individual farms from groups taken under guard to small towns and villages. Driver Hall was one of those sent from Stalag XVIIIA to Pisselsdorf in Austria. Each morning and evening he was collected by guards and billeted in the village with other POWs working on farms in the area. At first the work was hard but he got used to it and, with much better food than before, 'I found this sort of life made me healthier and happier.' Time seemed to pass quickly, he got on well with the farmer and his wife and managed to contact them again after the war was over.

If Austrian farms were at one end of the scale for POWs the other lay in the huge industrial works which fuelled the German economy and where the largest number of *Arbeitskommandos* were situated. One of the biggest was at Blechhammer, near Ehrenforst in Upper Silesia, which occupied some 20,000 prisoners of all European nations and a high proportion of slave labour, including Jews. 'Dressed in their striped suits, the poor things could only shuffle to work they were so weak,' recorded Private Ayres, 'and their bodies were just like skeletons with a skin pulled over them.' British POWs could do little to help in the early months because their parcels of food and clothing had not yet arrived and Jewish prisoners were strictly segregated.

For eleven hours a day and six days a week prisoners worked to clear the twelve square kilometres of the *Baustelle*, as the area was called, where a series of factories turning out synthetic products of all kinds, including oil, petrol, and coke were built.

Many men, spending all their days at Blechhammer, knew the Kommandant of the British camp, *Rittmeister* Prinz zu Höhenlöhe, who protected the prisoners from their Nazi employers, the *Bauleitung* of the *Oberschleisisches-Hydrierwerke* (Upper Silesia Hydroworks) which housed them as cheaply as possible and paid them about 11d a day for their labours. Eventually the German authorities became aware of this and dismissed him; Höhenlöhe was, thought Lance-Corporal Tibbitts, 'every inch a gentleman . . . a real soldier.' So highly was he regarded that former prisoners invited him to a reunion in London after the war.

On such a large site there were, inevitably, many opportunities for Allied prisoners to mingle with civilians and slave labourers. Apart from some notable exceptions, the guards were fair and some could be bribed, either to bring items into camp themselves, to overlook bartered goods which POWs brought in, or to allow them outside the wire.

One of the greater ironies of Hitler's Reich was the fact that, despite all the many and varied ways devised to keep POWs securely in captivity, the weakest link was the German guard himself. Prisoners could invariably discover a few who were prepared to accept Red Cross goods in return for favours; their willingness to compromise themselves was the foundation of 'rackets' in the camp system and more of them became involved as the war turned in the Allies' favour.

Among the many deals struck between guards and British POWs at Blechhammer was one which allowed prisoners out through the wire at night from where a swim across a canal, bar of chocolate firmly clamped in mouth, brought them to a civilian brothel.

POWs who had the nerve and wanted sex could certainly find a way, as Gunner Magill recalled at an *Arbeitskommando* attached to Stalag XVIIIA. In the centre of Graz was a brothel and British prisoners managed to slip away from the camp and even travelled openly by tram, their absence covered by other POWs. The unit of currency was a whole and *unbroken* bar of Red Cross chocolate. Such was the bartering power of food and cigarettes in the Greater Reich as it was destroyed by the demands of total war that virtually anything could be obtained in return for them.

Prisoners naturally made full use of their Red Cross goods, as

Sapper Beard explained: 'These parcels were a great source of propaganda; we would open them in front of the "civvies" and pull out each item saying out loud in German what it was.' However, the young women with whom they worked made few efforts to contact the prisoners through fear of the Gestapo 'and others who may have been jealous of a workmate getting a bar of Lux soap'.

Despite the threat of dire punishments if they were found out, numerous secret liaisons did take place between POWs and local women at other camps, especially in Poland, but the passionate affairs which sometimes blossomed nearly always ended in heartbreak and, sometimes, in tragedy. This happened to Corporal Bell who met a lovely Russian girl while working on a farm near Danzig. She had been captured and transported to work as slave labour for the Reich. Their affair grew but was ultimately destroyed. The sequel is best told in Corporal Bell's own words: 'From the farm we were sent to other places and I saw her only once more, in the final stages of the war after I'd finally escaped − I finally made it! − but it was rather late to do anything because, you see, they'd killed her. She finished up in Belsen and was among the thousands who were shot before the place was liberated. I knew she was there, the grapevine had been busy, but I was too late, she was dead.'

The memory of that tragic episode remains vivid; 'I still think of that golden girl even after so long a time.'

The chances of mixing with the civilian population and even living with a family was greatly increased for those prisoners who worked in the occupied territories, though even inside Germany it was not unknown. Private Drysdale was one British Tommy who took his chance of liberty while working at maintaining tram lines in Posen. There he struck up a friendship with a young Polish-German conductress. By bribing various guards to cover for his absence the liaison was kept alive until, late in 1943, Drysdale simply walked out of camp and joined her in the city. After enjoying a relaxed social life and even receiving German medical attention, he was only discovered when trying to help a colleague escape who, becoming too nervous, gave the game away. Drysdale's punishment was announced after his court-martial − nine months' imprisonment in a punishment camp.

Prisoners found it more difficult to strike up relationships with German women because intercourse with them could result in their appearing in front of a firing squad. Nevertheless, some POWs did have affairs as the Russian front drew able-bodied young men from the Reich even before a secret *O.K.W.* Order, dated August, 1941, reduced the punishment for this offence by a 'realistic amendment' to general regulations. British prisoners found guilty of associating with

German women in future were moved to another *Arbeitskommando* and not subjected to draconian penalties, though the sentence could still be as much as four to six years.

Although POWs still believed that the death penalty could be imposed, Sergeant Dexter clearly remembered some prisoners slipping out at night from his *Arbeitskommando* to visit girls evacuated from Berlin. 'Other fellows had girl friends in our village where there was a male age-gap of 15 to 50. One was discovered in bed by a nonplussed mother who could only say, "Whatever are you doing?" The P.O.W., equally nonplussed, could only stutter, "I am waiting for a bus"!!' The most peculiar behaviour, he thought, 'was by some local girls, and even some mature women, who came up to the camp with a blanket over their arms – ready to counteract the cold snow on their bottoms.'

Under the Geneva Convention prisoners could not be required to work on military projects which directly helped the enemy, though the Convention was not very specific in this area.

Many POWs who went out to work on *Arbeitskommandos* were highly ambivalent towards working for the Reich. They believed that labouring for the German war economy was often not far removed from aiding her militarily and the dividing line was so narrow that prisoners felt ashamed at what they were doing. So they maintained their self-respect through sabotage and strikes.

Private Ward, working in his Polish coalmine, was one prisoner who thought he had given too much help to the German war effort after assisting a Polish miner to re-start production after a stoppage underground: 'I operated a steam winch, lowering coal trucks down a slope and the finding of the fault and . . . getting . . . production going again troubled me. I felt I had helped the Germans so I arranged for all the men to be out of the way at the bottom of the slope then let four or five wagons smash their way down without the check of a brake. The wagons tore down wooden pillars and a fall of coal blocked production for some while. I said the brake had failed and felt I had made amends.'

That part of the German economy which depended on forced and POW labour suffered some disruption through acts like this, though the net effect was not very great – apart from the satisfaction and self-esteem it gave to those involved.

The possibilities of committing sabotage depended also on where one was forced to work. For prisoners labouring cheek by jowl with a peasant farmer it was hardly possible to damage crops or machinery without being found out. But on industrial *Arbeitskommandos*, and especially on the railways, opportunities were always available.

One of the most effective ways of causing havoc was to switch round direction cards on trucks. Sand and gravel in wagon grease-boxes, over-weak mixtures for cement foundations, pick axes driven through power cables as they were laid, nuts, bolts and tools dropped into machinery, wooden supports sawn half-through, metal spikes driven deep into tree trunks so that they tore the teeth off sawmill blades – the varieties for ingenious POWs were endless.

One example which involved Gunner Palmer labouring near Munich was, like all the best form of sabotage, highly effective but very simple: 'Our party delayed the working on an underpass for the railway by moving the wooden pegs so that when the walls met they were about two feet out of position. Out came the drills for a second operation, to knock down what we had built. We were threatened with all sorts of punishments.' Later, while working at a Polish coal mine, he was involved in a second line of attack.

Conditions were so bad in the partly-flooded pit that the prisoners went on strike and were lined up and given ten minutes to change their minds; failing this, every seventh man was to be shot. 'We didn't put it to the test,' wrote Palmer, 'as we knew some excuse would be given to carry out the threat.'

In this desperate game of bluff and counter-bluff the Germans held all the cards and yet POWs sometimes stood their ground in the face of terrible pressure. Despite shootings and beatings the strike weapon could have a surprisingly powerful effect.

There were times when strikes were tinged with humour, as Lance-Corporal Luckett discovered, when the prisoners who were sorting iron ore from rock stopped over what could be termed war work. After a guard fired over their heads and following an angry confrontation with the Kommandant, the whole shift was locked in a large building – soon to be joined by the relieving shift which also refused to work.

After two days in the cooler on bread and water, all the prisoners were paraded and addressed by several senior German officers: 'Through an interpreter they wanted to know why we refused to work, etc, etc, and were told that we considered it "war-work" – back came the reply that, although we were sorting iron-ore, it went to the home front to make railway lines, and spoons and forks! – a slight pause, then a very English voice said, "We don't —— believe you, we think you're making knives as well"!! The lads started laughing – Gerry didn't know what the joke was so we were bustled in the cooler again.' Early the next morning they received an ultimatum – work or starve – and were forced out again.

The threat of suspending food supplies was the quickest way for the Germans to beat the strike weapon and they employed it regularly.

But some acts of sabotage and strikes received a more drastic and immediate response.

At one *Arbeitskommando* Signalman Hoare called for a strike in the lead mine where he worked: 'I was young, certainly naive and not yet disillusioned by the questionable behaviour of the leaders of the human race.' It was, however, short-lived; Hoare and another prisoner were sent off to a *Straflager* or punishment camp and the others were driven by flailing rifle butts to the mine. 'They were finally "persuaded" to go back to work again – except the ones who needed medical attention,' he concluded.

For committing minor offences, prisoners ended up in the 'cooler' – punishment cells in a wired-off section in prison camps. Those found guilty of more serious ones such as strikes, sabotage, assaulting their guards or sexual intercourse with German women, went to *Straflager* Fort Zinna at Torgau near Leipzig, which was used until the end of 1942 or to *Wehrmachtgefgangis* Graudenz, a military punishment centre near Thorn.

In April, 1943, Corporal Bell was committed to Graudenz for six months after being court-martialled for stealing grain, 'property of the Reich'. Inside the prison, there was a strict régime and food was short:

> 'There was only one meal each day – a litre of soup – the morning and evening meals being quite ridiculous and consisting of one slice of bread cut so thin that the bloke who cut it damned near missed it
>
> In this prison we lost all POW rights and were subject to German military law and spent most of the day being drilled by a screeching German "drill-pig" who never let up. All commands were in German . . . If one committed a misdemeanour one's meal-ticket was promptly confiscated for the day.'

At the end of one particularly hard time, Bell's meal ticket showed only fourteen punch-marks when he received food after attending sixty-two mealtimes: 'August [1943] was,' he recalled, 'a very hungry month!'

After trying to escape from an *Arbeitskommando*, Driver Jones also experienced the inside of a *Straflager*. He found life there was largely policed by Liverpool and Glaswegian razor gangs. The result was that 'if anyone with a Glasgow accent admired a solid gold watch and offered half a loaf for it, the owner parted with it gladly.'

Prisoners who were in any way a particular nuisance could lose their POW status under the Geneva Convention. To do so could mean being committed to a concentration camp or even worse. This is what happened to the men who crawled through the 'Great Escape' tunnel at Stalag Luft III, to members of the Special Air Service Brigade, and to any Commandos who were unfortunate enough to be captured –

they were summarily executed under Hitler's 'Commando Order' of October, 1942. The deadly effectiveness of this policy resulted in the survival of only six out of over one hundred SAS members taken prisoner.

Fortunately, few Allied prisoners ever saw the inside of a concentration camp but rumours about them were widespread. One prisoner who knew some details was Sergeant Lawrence who caught glimpses of the Jewish ghetto in Lodz and was told by a Polish slaughterman of the existence of death camps. At another *Arbeitskommando* one or two German guards furtively handed round atrocity photographs of Polish girls. But a German guard whom Private Low met was clearly sickened by the treatment of women at a concentration camp near Lamsdorf. He turned a blind eye when POWs gave them Red Cross food and even sent his own can of soup. 'Like us it could have been the first concentration camp he had seen; what conflicting loyalties he felt are hard to imagine.'

The awful smell of burning flesh occasionally drifting over work camps close to Auschwitz used to puzzle POWs in the early months of 1943. It was not until the end of the war that prisoners in various *Arbeitskommandos* attached to Stalag VIIIB knew what went on there, although they were forced to look on horrified as 'kapos' and guards kicked, whipped and beat defenceless concentration camp victims.

At the other end of the line Trooper Jameson, clearing snow in a Viennese winter, saw Jewish civilians – some in fur coats and many well-dressed – loaded by *SS* guards every day into the last carriage of trains where they were locked in and wired up. 'We knew from our foreman . . . that their days were numbered.' Some of those trains went through Nordhausen where Sapper Dickinson was working at a tobacco factory; he witnessed their arrival and the tearful, harrowing scenes as the women were singled out and sent off to their deaths.

Allied POWs were powerless to help these prisoners beyond occasionally slipping food to them and even that was a highly dangerous gesture. After seeing them many POWs realized that, bad as it was, their own treatment was infinitely better.

It was much to the Germans' annoyance that men brought together in punishment camps struck up a defiant comradeship which guaranteed they would cause a great deal of trouble. Private McIntosh discovered this at Gielchenberg in Bavaria where he was sent after trying to escape from an *Arbeitskommando*. The work there was hard and monotonous – quarrying rock which was poured downhill into a stone crusher – but there was real compensation in the company of a fine bunch of POWs: 'Morale was very high here and most of the time was spent planning future escapes; there was more singing and laughter in this camp than in many of the work camps.'

At Heuberg too, where Private Handley was sent in November, 1940, morale remained high among prisoners set to clearing snow for long hours in a rock quarry. Undernourished and overworked as they were, from their own pitifully small rations the POWs still fed one of their number who had been singled out for extra punishment; there was 'an unshakeable belief in the outcome of it all,' thought Handley, which the Germans could never destroy.

In order to be returned from an *Arbeitskommando* which some prisoners found too tough they either feigned illness or were desperate enough to inflict wounds on themselves.

Eating soap was popularly supposed to produce symptoms of heart trouble but Rifleman Hill had endured enough work camps by the end of 1944 to try a harsher method in order to give up coal-heaving. After pouring boiling water over his left hand he placed a small piece of caustic soda in the wound and reported to the British MO that he had burnt himself on a carbide lamp while underground. He got a few days in hospital, as did Private Copland. Boiling water over his left arm was, he reckoned, a relatively light price to pay.

Other self-inflicted injuries, called 'krankers' by POWs – taken from the German word *krank* (sick) – included raw and festering wounds from sandpaper rubbed continuously against the shin; a knee or wrist bruised and filled with fluid from constantly tapping the back of a spoon on the affected part and serious mutilation by crushing or breaking fingers or toes.

One of the worst incidents of this kind that Gunner Peacock came across was when another prisoner decided he must get back to Stalag XVIIIA at Wolfsberg. Other prisoners agreed to smash one of his fingers with the back of an axe: 'It may be an indication of the state of our minds after four years' captivity,' wrote Peacock, 'that, on seeing his determination, we calmly agreed to carry out his wish.' After reporting sick, however, the victim was taken straight to hospital to have his finger amputated. Later came news that gangrene had set in and he was likely to lose his entire hand.

Since the Germans allowed only five per cent of a camp's inmates to miss work through illness, POWs who were genuinely unwell were forced out to quarrying or mining and the self-infliction of 'krankers' became a matter for heated argument. None of the POWs whom Sapper Dickinson saw deliberately wound themselves at a rock quarry, to which he had been sent for persistently escaping, received treatment, including one man who placed his hand under a moving truck and suffered agonizing injuries. Nevertheless, a determined prisoner could sometimes get away from his *Arbeitskommando* and a steady flow of human traffic entered and left Stalags which became well-organized and developed a life of their own despite such changes.

The permanent staff at each Stalag, mainly senior NCOs, was responsible for the internal discipline of the camp. An elected 'Man of Confidence' dealt with the Germans on a day-to-day basis and liaised with visiting delegates of the Red Cross and Protecting Power. Other prisoners were responsible for administering Red Cross supplies and correspondence. In the larger camps matters were further organized through compound and hut leaders.

The most senior ranking prisoner, who was usually the British or Dominion medical officer, acted as the Senior British Officer and worked closely with the Man of Confidence, which required a man of tact, understanding and a steady personality who could apply rules and regulations intelligently. 'They did a wonderful job of looking after the interests of the prisoners in their relations with the Camp Commandant,' considered Sergeant Suckling. 'They "pulled" no punches.'

From the low point of defeat POWs managed to exist with hope and with their basic faculties unimpaired – as Major Whitcombe determined to do in Oflag IX C/H: 'It is one of my ardent desires and I consider it my duty to come out of this hole as I went into it, or better; not bitter, still young, still cheerful and ready to share a young and happy life with my family whatever outside things may be like. I am also trying to keep my brain working and to put something into it. But like others I find the brain not very receptive here. We put it down to diet.'

The Germans soon realized that prisoners in Oflags and Stalags were likely to give less trouble if they had something to occupy their time. They encouraged various activities, therefore, while restricting the outlay on camp maintenance to an absolute minimum.

In organizing themselves, prisoners took advantage of the huge diversity of talent locked away behind the wire. Men with the most delicate and specialized skills – doctors, dentists, interpreters, wireless experts – were the most useful, but some discovered wholly unexpected uses for their peacetime occupations. At least one burglar found his knowledge very useful in stealing documents from the Germans.

In all the main camps there were facilities for prisoners' recreational and intellectual needs. Faced with unlimited time which had somehow to be filled, some men turned their attention to improving their education or completing studies which they had already begun. A dozen English and Scottish universities made arrangements for their own students who were in captivity to continue with their degree work, like Second Lieutenant Varley, who had started a law degree at

Birmingham. While in Oflag VIIB he completed his studies and sat for his Finals – his father collected his degree while his son remained *in absentia* – and also his Law Society examinations.

There were enormous difficulties in completing a course of study in prison camp, as Captain Irwin found at Oflag VIIIC/H. Sensing that he would be in captivity for a long time, he 'at once started to learn and teach languages. I studied History – Military History – was even able to attract quite a large audience who came to hear my military history lectures. Books started to arrive after about nine months. I read a lot of philosophy. . . . I used to rise as early as 5.30 to 6 in the morning to take my place in the "silence room" – where we used to study, and where I used to dish out early morning tea – especially for the silence room.'

An early start to the day at Oflag VIIIC/H was necessary because of the strain on limited resources when over 600 prisoners attended classes in languages, art, agriculture, sciences, law and other disciplines at the short-lived Laufen University. Every corner of the camp was occupied, from early morning to late at night. One Padre there gave three reasons why it was thought to be unique: 'There were no women in it, the syllabus contained the widest possible range of subjects and it was easier to enter than to leave.'

The many delays in obtaining educational materials, especially books, together with a lack of privacy and frequent moves from camp to camp caused many prisoners to abandon their studies. Only the most dedicated or, like Varley, those who were used to advanced study before landing up in a prison camp had the background and singlemindedness to overcome such difficulties: 'I stave off the boredom by my efforts at reading and study but it is very difficult – or so I find – to concentrate on any one subject for long periods,' wrote Lieutenant Roberts from Oflag VIB.

In Stalags conditions were even worse as Sergeant Nell discovered at Stalag IVB. In January, 1944, he was beginning a London Matriculation course: 'I wonder if I can do it?' he mused. 'It is a large mouthful. Can I chew it? Anyway the studying cannot do me any harm and if I should pass it may do me a lot of good.' One week later the prisoners were on the move again and all plans for educational courses and mail had been upset. 'How much longer is it going to last?' he asked. 'I could put up with fighting but this endless turning over of days in a POW camp: waiting – waiting – waiting. When is it going to end?'

While they were endlessly spinning out time behind barbed wire, prisoners found any form of effort with a long-term aim in mind difficult. For many like Private Little learning was a means of forgetting one's bleak surroundings: 'There are plenty of opportunities for studying here. I have done quite a bit – I don't suppose it will do me much good. I have just learned things I want to know and I'm afraid they won't forward me any way [at home].'

Writing in a battered exercise book during one overcast afternoon in November, 1944, Bombardier Mordue recounted the noise, muddle and confusion of men forced to live in over-close proximity to each other at Stalag 357:

'A would-be tinsmith is banging lustily away at some empty biscuit tins in an endeavour to manufacture a blower . . . just about a yard away a Canadian is squatting on his bed, native fashion, peeling potatoes and a turnip acquired no doubt in the rackets . . . now two beds away I hear the twisted strains of "Home Sweet Home" played by some budding Larry Adler on his out-of-tune harmonica whilst a would-be violinist succeeds in making a noise . . . 3 or 4 South Africans converse in their guttural Afrikaans . . . 2 Geordies prognosticate the end of the war to the room in general. An Oxford chap and a Kiwi are holding a debate on the agricultural propensity of New Zealand. On the tables different games are in progress; draughts, chess, cards, crib. . . . An Eurasian speaks to a Frenchman and a Welshman – all three gesticulating with their hands and legs, the latter to keep warm, the former to emphasize some particular point or other. In the far corner the discordant notes of a cracked piano accordian are being literally forced out; occasionally someone starts singing, others insist on whistling, more tin-bashers make tin lids for tin boxes or tin trays for frying [with] – another makes a pair of clogs to fit over his boots. A German enters and shouts something; he will probably want five men to clean the washhouse or something. He is followed by a couple of R.A.F. chaps, running a raffle – "2 cigarettes a time for this gold watch" – others are cooking, some are smoking, sewing, stitching, writing. An argument starts about the speed of the latest bomber. . . . Outside can be heard the shouts of gambling schools – "20 more in guts wanted"; "pick where you like and where you fancy"; "you'll never accumulate if you don't speculate"; "who fancies the old corner pub?". . . . On the field, the shrill squeal of bagpipes is distinguishable between the hills . . . air raid sirens wail every half hour – the blowing of whistles denotes Roll call so I pull my boots on . . . off I go to be counted.'

The only escape from this kind of life was during the hours of sleep, in hospital, or in solitary confinement. Some camps had such pressure on space that a rota was organized where men signed up in advance to perform simple crimes, guaranteed to give them a standard sentence of a few days in the cooler away from their fellow prisoners. One POW was reputed to have written home: 'No, I'm not lonely – there are 1,000 men in this camp and most of them live in my room.'

With unlimited amounts of time and ingenuity, prisoners embarked on ambitious productions of musicals, comedy shows and serious theatre which would not have been out of place in the West End. Elaborate scenery and costumes were created and programmes professionally illustrated by hand. A big production could bring together a large number of diverse talents including electricians, carpenters, tailors, writers, artists and musicians.

Female roles were filled by young, good-looking prisoners. Things got out of control, however, during a showing of G. B. Shaw's *Pygmalion* at Stalag VIIIB when one prisoner, playing the part of a flower girl, was not only subjected to the usual barrage of wolf-whistles and ribald comment from the male audience but also to an attempted sexual assault by POWs who invaded his dressing room.

While sexual problems were not, so far as the War Office could discover, common among POWs, between prisoners suffering constantly from fear and hopeless boredom as, for example, at Blechhammer, homosexuality grew more open. Couples got 'married' and shared a single bunk while young POWs were relentlessly pursued by some older men. In the end the Medical Officer had to ask the Kommandant to move one of each pair of homosexual couples to another camp because of fights and the hysterics of those involved.

While he was at Stalag VIIIB, Private Mason heard of POWs admitted to the Lazaret for treatment after inserting objects into their rectum to gain sexual satisfaction and also of a 'mystery man' who supposedly visited barrack rooms by night explaining to younger men how to gain relief through masturbation.

This was one of many fanciful rumours and generally treated as a joke, as was the whole subject of sex inside camp. While there was plenty of explicit comment about the 'five-fingered widow' and 'one or two unpleasantly deranged instances' of sexual talk overheard by Second Lieutenant Baxter in various Oflags, together with much rough horseplay, there was little open homosexuality. Indeed, as Private Vincent pointed out, 'Homosexuality was not so common an occurrence as it might be thought in the circumstances. There had been no evidence of it on my . . . working parties and by all accounts it was rare on all working parties,' though some POWs had sexual encounters with Polish youths in the darkness of coal mines which was considered by their friends as 'a rather amusing and daring experiment'.

'Belly empty think of food, belly full think of women,' summarized one soldier accurately. 'Two years without beer or women or good food,' noted Gunner Robinson; when full, which was not very often, he certainly missed 'the feel of a few silk-clad legs'. But dreams of a sexual nature were not, thought the Reverend Naylor, any more common than in normal times; the most persistent dreams concerned lashings of food. 'On the whole a very realistic attitude seems to have been adopted toward this side of life,' concluded interviewers who saw POWs on their return home in 1945.

'It will probably be thought that kriegie life must have been a pleasant mixture of picnics, theatres, cinemas and general enjoyment,' wrote Second Lieutenant Baxter, adding, 'It was not. Kriegie life was a dull, dreary existence of meaningless monotony and frustration. Escapes and entertainments were simply the cases of excitement in an otherwise exceedingly dry mental and physical desert.' He might also have added the regular 'sport' of baiting the Germans.

Prisoners developed this to a fine art and found they could take surprising liberties without getting into real trouble. There was also a serious nature to their antics as Major Whitcombe observed: 'As you can imagine when one is on the wrong end of the gun one is not in a very strong position and everybody had to exercise the maximum amount of cunning and ingenuity in order to adjust the balance and seek out the weak spots in our opponents' armour in order to carry the war in the enemy's camp and thus get some consideration from them if nothing more concrete.'

A prime example of how POWs could infuriate the Germans was seen at Oflag VIB during the visit of an official neutral delegation, all of whom could read English. Tank wagons were used for pumping sewage into recently-discovered tunnels and just before one of them crossed their path a British POW chalked prominently on it 'GERMAN KULTUR'; the escorting Germans were not amused.

Allied prisoners everywhere enjoyed nothing better than taking a rise out of their captors. British POWs sweeping the streets of Munich taunted sentries posted outside the Nazi Party's 'Brown House': 'When the guard wasn't looking, the sweepers would stop sweeping, lean on their brooms and mutter and gesticulate to each other and at the same time stare fixedly at the unfortunate sentries; point to items of their equipment and generally go through the motions of deprecatory comment. I was assured,' wrote Bombardier Tonkin, 'that one could actually see the veins on the necks of the sentries stand out in frustration.' Standing stiffly to attention, they never knew how to cope with this kind of behaviour.

One had to be careful, however, because a single miscalculation could spell disaster. A young guard whom Private Low came across was genuinely compassionate towards his prisoners – perhaps earlier service and a wound suffered on the Russian Front had something to do with it. On the other hand, his colleague was shot dead by another guard without warning after he genuinely misunderstood an order. 'So we can see the two sides of the German – always there, always to be assessed,' said Low.

Every opportunity was taken to 'acquire' something at the Germans' expense, as at Stalag IVB when an unfortunate civilian came to do some work inside the wire. While he was in one of the huts his bicycle disappeared and could not be found, despite dire threats from the Kommandant and a thorough search. What the Germans never knew, said Bombardier Robinson, was that 'during the half-hour the workman had been in the camp we had sawn up the bike into small pieces and shot them out of the camp over the wire with catapults made from the inner tubes.' There were brutal Germans, he said, but 'you couldn't beat the mental cruelty, trickery, treachery, of the beastly British. We did everything to make their lives a misery.'

One of the effects of prolonged captivity was to make prisoners expert at organizing passive rebellion against the coldly hostile authority of the Nazis. At the same time, living in close proximity to the enemy, many POWs mentally separated 'good' from 'bad' Germans. In the depths of the War Office, a Memorandum registered alarm about such a shocking state of affairs: 'It is impossible to share with the enemy troops a deep emotional experience such as prolonged existence in combat or in isolated areas without being to some extent bound to them by this experience. It may, in consequence, be even more difficult to make repatriated prisoners of war hate the enemy than it is in the case of other British soldiers.'

The prisoners to whom this could not be applied were those from Bomber Command. They were a true thorn in the German flesh and it is to their experiences that we now turn.

5
KRIEGIES

RIVALRY BETWEEN DIFFERENT departments, muddle inside the War Office and a total lack of any urgency characterized Whitehall's attitude towards POW affairs during the 'Phoney War'. It took the loss of some 44,000 men of the BEF into captivity to startle the sleeping bureaucrats from their slumbers and to form a Prisoner of War Directorate at the War Office in May, 1940.

The organization for dealing with POWs was supposed to operate in the following way. Three sets of lists of prisoners and dead combatants were issued by the German authorities through their *Wehrmachtauskunftstelle für Kriegsverluste und Kriegsgefangene* (Army Information Office for Casualties and POWs). One set was sent to the Information Bureau in London, one to the Swiss as the Protecting Power, and one to the International Committee of the Red Cross at Geneva. The Bureau then notified the War Office's POW Directorate, the POW Department of the Foreign Office and also sent lists to the British Red Cross and St John War Organization.

Very few prisoners knew about these arrangements. As late as March, 1944, an army psychologist commented: 'The existence of D.P.W. [Directorate of Prisoners of War at the War Office] and the intimacy of contact between War Office, Protecting Power and the Red Cross is almost completely unknown to men in Germany, even to those in authority in the Camps.'

Hungry, cold and far from home, it was easy to suspect they had been totally forgotten: nor did relatives have much faith that their plight was being taken seriously, especially since the Government handled questions about POWs in the House of Commons through a junior Minister.

'The public is persuaded . . . the Government as a whole take little interest in POWs,' commented one critic in June, 1941, to which a Foreign Office official added, 'There is much in what [she] says.' But it was mainly through the efforts of the War Office, Foreign Office, Protecting Power and International Committee of the Red Cross that every Allied prisoner had a very good chance of survival while in the grip of an unpredictable enemy. That, at least, was a not inconsiderable triumph.

Locked away inside RAF prison camps were large numbers of young men, mostly aircrew, who had what their C–in–C from 1942 on-wards, Sir Arthur Harris, called a 'clear and highly conscious courage' in facing repeated assaults over Germany. Most of them had specialized knowledge and were much above the average in education.

The result was a volatile collection of types who brought with them something of the defiant attitude towards authority which caused problems for every Station Commander in Britain.

Aware of their elite status, and firm in the rightness of their cause, RAF prisoners developed and maintained an *esprit de corps* which saw them through everything. 'Although at times many messes inevitably suffered from friction through having to live all day and night on top of each other, and re-shuffles were common, I think for me at any rate, there was a sort of (quite unspoken) pride at operational aircrew people being together,' wrote Pilot Officer Sidwell. 'I believe they did an incredible (and perhaps unintended) job in Germany, because wherever they went, they plastered their own RAF humour and ways of life on the bewildered Germans, and helped to undermine their confidence – which was pretty high until late on. The general feeling about lack of discipline in RAF aircrews was largely misjudged, and this showed up in Germany; they were different.'

They made their mark, too, on other prisoners, like Second Lieutenant Baxter who met them in various camps: 'The RAF were always a thorn in the German flesh. They had no respect for anything German, and said so, rudely. They would not be serious. . . . Death for them was a rather futile and blundering adversary which they could play with as a boy plays with a blind bull. Consequently they followed the sport of "goon-baiting" with joy and zeal, careless of German threats and happy over German wrath and exasperation.'

There was, however, another side to all this. Looking back on his years of imprisonment, Sergeant Bruce recalled that, though there was plenty of camp life, 'our daily routine was boring in the extreme' and the depressing tedium affected most RAF prisoners, including Sergeant Harcus who recorded yet another 'normal routine day – quite dull and bored' in July, 1943.

Even writing home became a chore because there was so little news: 'I am sorry,' wrote Flight-Sergeant Bulmer, 'that all my letters must seem alike, but there is nothing to tell after I have said I am fit and O.K.' In filling up the postcards and *Kriegsgefangenenpost* forms which were subject to German censorship, administered for all British and American aircrew centrally at Stalag Luft III from mid-1943 onwards, many POWs settled for letting people know they were 'in the pink', hoping for an early release and telling everyone at home to 'keep your chin up'.

German censors suppressed sensitive information and so a few prisoners used 'dotty' codes – so called by members of the British Intelligence Section of MI9 because they often used rows of dots in the heading or text of a letter to indicate where a hidden message began and ended.

At Stalag Luft VI, as Sergeant Stretton discovered, there was 'contact with the Air Ministry through coded letters sent by a few selected prisoners. The messages and their replies took a long time but much important information was transmitted. By means of these coded letters many items connected with escaping were sent on to us in parcels with printed labels on them – "a present from the Licensed Victuallers' Association". We on the Red Cross staff were of course always on the look out for such parcels and we made sure that they were smuggled into the camp unopened by the Germans.' On one memorable occasion things went wrong and the Germans found themselves with a new portable typewriter and hundreds of forged German banknotes.

Despite the limited usefulness of dotty codes, some camps established a considerable correspondence with officers of MI9. Senior POWs throughout the Greater Reich were always on the lookout for Intelligence fragments which they could transmit to London. This was often extremely difficult, especially in camps where internal security was not very secure. At Stalag IVB for instance, there were eight code-users but only two in regular contact with the War Office: 'Many P/Ws knew that there were contacts with the W.O. which helped the general morale,' noted the official camp history, 'but it had to be kept very quiet as there were so many different nationalities.'

While letters and parcels were of the utmost importance, some prisoners received news which passed the British Postal and Telegraphic Censorship and devastated them. Under the strain of separation women had affairs and 'wellwishers' wrote to tell prisoners about them; some divorced their husbands. POWs who never received mail made a pathetic attempt to hoodwink their mates by pretending that they did. Others received news of relatives killed in air raids. And in every camp it was common for POWs to receive 'Dear John' letters, called by RAF men 'mespots' and sometimes known, with wry humour, as being awarded the 'D.C.M.' ('Don't Come Monday').

These letters were pinned up on noticeboards for the whole camp to see. They included some well-known examples, recorded by Flying Officer Price:

> 'I'm so glad you were shot down, before flying became dangerous.'
> 'Am enclosing a calendar. It will be handy as it has several years on it.'

'It must be nice for you to play golf again.'

'Our engagement has ended, as I'd rather marry a '44 hero than a '43 coward.'

'A POW thanked a woman in England for a sweater received via the Red Cross; he received this reply: "I am sorry to hear that you got my sweater as I knitted it for a fighting man".'

'I am filing for a divorce. Mother and I have discussed it since it is 4 years since you went down and we decided it was best.'

'Don't bother to hurry home as I am living with an American and having a lovely time. I'm having his baby soon but forgive me as Mother has done. Ted is sending you cigarette parcels.'

Here were the concerns which POWs felt most keenly during their imprisonment; a lack of understanding by relatives of their daily struggles and the drabness of their lives, the belief that people at home had forgotten about them or, worse still, saw their capture and captivity as in some way shameful, the pain of separation and worry as to what girl friends and wives might be doing without them.

In addition to the scant amount of news that could be gathered from POWs' letters the first monthly edition of *The Prisoner of War*, which appeared in May, 1942, was sent free by the Red Cross to all who were registered as their next-of-kin and was meant to keep them informed about the Department's activities and of the difficulties which it faced in dealing with the Germans. Two months later, the *Prisoner of War News* began coverage of north-east Scotland.

Neither publication was sent to prisoners because the War Office was against it on the grounds that they contained official reports of camps. The Germans also refused to distribute them since they included extracts from POWs' letters but some information trickled into camps through relatives' letters. 'Don't believe all you read in P.O.W. News,' warned Trooper Hutchings.

The happy faces of prisoners posed in formal groups, talk of good food and extensive entertainments, carefully edited extracts from letters, the overwhelming concentration on permanent camps which seemed to be some kind of Butlins – all told a reassuring story. But even the smart uniforms worn in the photographs lied; they were issued just before the camera was set up and taken away again immediately afterwards. Care, too, was taken to pose groups against German administrative buildings and not in front of the prisoners' own ramshackle huts.

Prisoners were highly sceptical about attempts by the authorities at home to inform their next-of-kin about them. 'See that you have bought a book called "Prisoners of War",' wrote Flight-Sergeant Steele, which claimed to be 'The First Authentic Account of the lives of British prisoners of war in enemy hands.' 'I shouldn't take too much notice of that,' he cautioned 'as I have read a few myself and it paints the picture far too rosy.'

Many relatives also had their doubts over what they read. 'Quite naturally our parents, wives or girl friends, as the case may be, were all anxious to know what life was like,' recorded Sergeant Kelly, 'and, of course, we could not tell them, but one POW beat the system. He advised his girlfriend to read Hebrews, Chapter XIII, Verse 8 . . . that reads "Jesus Christ, the same yesterday, today and for evermore".'

The Germans published *The Camp*, an illustrated newspaper produced in Berlin and distributed to English-speaking POWs throughout the Greater Reich from mid-1940 onwards. In its pages the propaganda slant given to the general news was too obvious to fool anyone but the most gullible reader. From May, 1943, this was supplemented by the *O.K.: The Overseas Kid* for Americans while the French had their own *Trait d'Union*.

While the main spread of articles, contributed mostly by prisoners, covered a wide variety of topics, in *The Camp* the steady drip, drip of poison from a regular 'Weekly Military Survey', based on official German communiqués, which spoke always of 'heavy losses' for the Allies and 'counter-operations' by Axis forces, could be damaging to morale. 'Doubtless contributors to *The Camp* had no thought of assisting the enemy; in fact, that is what they were doing,' considered Flight-Sergeant Younger of the Royal New Zealand Air Force; 'Dixie Deans asked that no one in the camp [Stalag Luft III] should forward material, and no one did.' By October, 1944, when fact and fiction had become too obviously separated, the 'Weekly Military Survey' was discontinued, though the paper was published almost to the bitter end.

The disembodied voice of a German newsreader echoing from loudspeakers rigged up in camps usually involved another attempt to feed POWs with propaganda. This practice was, however, discontinued when the prisoners repeatedly put them out of use and stole lengths of wire. Some of the bigger camps were also shown propaganda films, as at Stalag Luft I in the summer of 1941, where Flight-Sergeant Steele reported, 'Of course the newsreels show only German successes and the only Englishmen we see are prisoners taken on the various fronts.' But many POWs knew how the war was progressing because they had their own sources of information.

The Germans knew that secret radios, variously known as 'canaries' or, in the officers' compound of Stalag Luft III, as 'J.H.' or 'Jimmy Higgins', existed from unguarded comments by prisoners and from material confiscated from huts which gave accurate information about the war. They rarely managed to shut down the 'canary' system for long, however, because more than one set was operating at any one time.

When a big search was mounted a radio receiver was left where it was likely to be found. This usually satisfied the Germans who were then much less likely to carry on with their hunt for another wireless which was carefully hidden. The places where ingenious kriegies could hide one within a big prison camp were legion – inside Warrant Officer Deans's gramophone, within a hollowed-out copy of Hitler's *Mein Kampf*, and inside an accordion (which could still be played), a rugby football and false roof beam at Stalag 383.

Radio officers and technicians were engaged on the highly secret work of building receivers with parts sent from London and carried innocently by the Red Cross. These were detected and smuggled into camp from legitimate food and clothing parcel stores by prisoners on the lookout for them or by bribed guards. Precious valves, condensers and other essential items could also be acquired by direct barter with camp staff and civilians.

If the Radio Padre, Doctor Selby-Wright, began his highly popular Wednesday evening talk on the BBC with the phrase, 'Good evening Forces', a coded message was to follow. In POW camps deep in enemy territory radio operators, crouched over secret receivers accompanied by skilled shorthand writers like Sergeant Aynsley (later to become Chief Reporter on the *Daily Express*), took down the broadcast for later decoding. 'Unknown and unacclaimed,' noted Flying Officer Price, they 'have been working in the cold, in the damp, often hungry to bring in the "authentic news from home".'

On most nights the official BBC news communique was received by a radio which had been rigged up using filched German electricity and transformer wire stretched between the huts as a makeshift aerial. Later, the news would be read out in each of the barracks. Pilot Officer Wilson described how this worked in the officers' compound of Stalag Luft III, where 'a representative would come into each block, in the afternoon usually. . . . We had duty stooges . . . who double-checked – and they would be out watching and making certain that no German approached whilst it was being read. The people listening would come into the corridor where they couldn't be seen from the windows.' So successful did this system become that even friendly guards begged to be given accurate information.

Much of the information received in this way was written up on flimsy news-sheets which were handed on from one prisoner to another. At Stalag Luft I, for example, the first copy of *Red Star* was produced in December, 1943, and Flying Officer Price kept the final one as a souvenir when the Russians liberated the camp: 'The news issued in the Red Star has been compiled from B.B.C. and the Voice of America programmes,' he wrote. 'These have been taken mostly by shorthand experts at all times of the day and up to 3 a.m. every morning. . . . The original radio set . . . is the most extraordinary Heath Robinson contraption ever visualised by the most ingenious Kriegie. It is 70% homemade and contains pencil lead, shaving soap containers, American toothpaste tubes, silver paper, greaseproof paper and condensers made of Healthy Life Biscuit Tins. Its place of concealment has stood the test of every type of search from Blitz-raids to fine-comb efforts by the Gestapo, at a time when von Muller's Abwehr Dept. contained a replica of every type of radio set picked up in prison camps . . . and a complete list of the actual places where they had been hidden, was attached. The Red Star has never fallen into enemy hands, and the Goons never had a clue as to how much we know.'

The prisoners at this camp also fed their news into the most widely distributed underground newspaper in the Reich. *Pow Wow* was produced in three different language editions using carbon paper and a Swedish typewriter. The Germans attempted to stop the paper but copies went to seven other camps and not one issue was missed between March, 1944, and May, 1945. So good was its intelligence that news of the D-Day landings appeared in its pages twenty minutes before it was broadcast in New York.

As well as underground newspapers such as these, lighter journals and magazines also appeared. At Sagan the system was well organized with, as Flying Officer Dilley recalled, '"news hawks" who each week visited every room in every hut in camp asking for items of interest people had received in letters from home. In this way . . . a weekly wall newspaper consisting of typed sheets . . . passed by the German censor, was put up in the recreation hut or classroom. The paper consisted of general news items, an editorial article, sports news, theatrical and film news, perhaps camp nature notes . . . also a collection of interesting or funny personal bits from letters.' What prevented them becoming boring or repetitive was their contributors' variety of experiences before they had been captured.

Magazines like *The Quill* and *Touchstone* at Oflag VIIB, *The Observer* at Stalag IVB and *The Yorkshire Post: Kriegie Edition*, which was the 'House Journal' of the White Rose Club in Stalag Luft VI, were produced regularly and reprinted in souvenir form soon after the war ended.

Others were more transient: the *Daily Recco* at Stalag Luft I was followed by one of the shortest-lived papers of all, *Barth Hard Times* of 5 May, 1945, which sported below its masthead the legend 'Vol 1, No. 1, Last 1' and was taken up entirely with news of the camp's liberation;

Stalag XXA had *Prisoner's Pie*, reproduced by a local German printer, a typewritten weekly newsheet, *Fortissimo*, and a monthly, *Quack*.

At Stalag XXD, there was *Stalag Hot Pot* and at VIIIB *Stimmt!*; the *Clarion* came out at Stalag 344 and *Kelly's Eye*, compiled in pencil and coloured crayon, was brought home inside its cardboard cover by Lance-Corporal Merryweather from an *Arbeitskommando* in 1945. As with others of its kind, this magazine was restricted to subscribers and contained a mixture of articles, drawings, advertisements, quizzes and letters. Typical of POW humour were questions such as, 'How many keys on the lager piano?' and ribald asides like, 'T—— and S—— perform public service: Bore hole in shithouse wall and let fresh air in – let themselves out at same time.'

In addition to 'hard' information there was much gossip – particularly while seated on the communal lavatories where the 'latrinogram' operated. At Stalag VIIIB it was the '40-holer' which Sergeant Harcus found took some getting used to: 'Picture a deep pit with a brick wall around it and a leaky roof. Windows without panes and pardon the reference – seating accommodation for forty – privacy impossible. Imagine one's discomfort in winter with the temperature 30 degrees below.' Just where the prisoners sat a rail ran the length of the latrine. Rats were reputed to scurry along it especially at night and Harcus reported at least 'two cases of serious rat biting in the "40-holer".'

'One can get used to anything,' said Sergeant Bruce about these primitive arrangements though rats invaded the barrack blocks and the stench of human faeces wafted continually over the camp from nearby fields which had been spread liberally with the latrine's contents.

Toilet paper was always in very short supply and Red Cross labels, camp money, and pages from Hitler's *Mein Kampf* were useful substitutes. Prisoners also missed one other thing – being able to pull the chain: 'Not a discomfort exactly,' said Sergeant Kelly, 'but something which we longed to do once more.'

In Stalag Lufts the SBO was assisted by his deputy, the Senior Acting Officer and Man of Confidence, who dealt officially with the Germans. There followed a number of camp 'Wheels', including the Camp Adjutant, Medical Officer, Security Officer and Escaping Committee (whose chairman for security purposes was referred to only as 'X').

An effective system of checking on the movements of Germans inside a compound involved a 'Duty pilot' stationed in a hut nearest the entrance. He kept a careful record of all German entrances and exits. In order to overcome this system Karl Pilz, a security man known as 'Charlie' by the POWs at Stalag Luft I and later at Stalag IIIA, used to climb the wire in some distant corner of the compound hoping to gather some useful intelligence before he was spotted by the prisoners.

It was essential to know the precise whereabouts of German staff or civilians inside a compound because the call 'Goons up' alerted prisoners secretly listening to broadcasts and those who carried this information. Prisoners also got an enormous kick out of monitoring and frustrating the efforts of 'ferrets' in the camp.

Armed with a long steel rod and torch, the overalled German *Abwehr* men responsible for security – known as 'ferrets' from their regular burrowing in RAF compounds – were on the lookout for tunnelling activities and listening for scraps of information carelessly passed between prisoners. At Stalag Luft III Sergeant Eeles noted that one of them had become so aware of the 'Duty pilot' system that he habitually asked that his arrival and departure be recorded. Some camps arranged for anyone coming into the compound to be ostentatiously 'shadowed' by a prisoner. When challenged he simply melted away into the crowd and another took his place – much to the German's annoyance.

Apart from *appell* and barrack block searches the Gestapo sometimes arrived to carry out special investigations. Often the prisoners were warned well in advance by guards who were concerned for their own skins: prohibited items in camp might well lead to awkward questions, even disciplinary action and a spell on the Russian Front.

Camp staff feared Gestapo visits more than did the prisoners, who taunted these hated civilians unmercifully. But their presence caused widespread damage to huts and prisoners' possessions and a long wait on the *appell* ground whilst they searched the camp. 'Spent 8 hours on square today whilst camp was searched by civvy police, for maps, compasses etc,' recorded Sergeant Harcus on 16 May, 1943. 'No food or water, from 7 a.m. until 3 p.m. Kit turned inside out, the ——!' Two days later the prisoners spent another three hours on the square, 'as punishment for laughing at postens'. The effect of this was to strengthen defiance: 'Hell, they can't get us down,' he added.

In winter, with mud and slush everywhere, the prisoners formed a deep and abiding loathing of their tormentors, as Sergeant Wood recalled: 'Finally the Gestapo came in. Their visit was intended to be a surprise but since they had hired a special train and commandeered accommodation in the village they were expected. A Polish guard who had been blackmailed hanged himself in his billet. When they formed up outside the compound, Reveille on a bugle greeted them; this at 2.0 a.m. It was a long, cold and hungry day I remember and when we got back into our huts that evening everything had been destroyed of course. The Gestapo may not have been very bright in this instance but what they lacked in this direction they replaced by nastiness.'

Piles of smashed furniture, bedding, cooking utensils, clothing, books, letters and personal belongings were scattered in the mud. 'Usually after a search the barrack room looked as though it had been hit by an earthquake,' observed Sergeant Stretton, 'clean clothing having been trampled under foot, valuable possessions either confiscated or spitefully broken. A general feeling of hate was always rife after such searches.' They were, he added, 'but a few of the petty miseries which were the usual lot of POWs at this time.'

For prisoners who had so few possessions this was a savage experience, but they lost no time in hitting back. Flight-Sergeant Younger saw an example of this one bleak October day at Stalag Luft VI when, after 'deliberate wrecking' and looting of personal possessions, the Gestapo finished their search: 'Sack upon bulging sack stood outside the doors and nearby, complacently, were grouped the marauders, so accustomed to inspiring fear that they did not think any prisoners would tamper with the sacks. Our guards knew better and turned away, grinning, as they saw sacks disappearing while intrepid kriegies distracted the attention of the Gestapo, one by obsequiously asking for autographs.'

Not content with spiriting back their own goods the prisoners also stole torches and other items; because they were afraid to lose face there were no complaints from the Gestapo. In any case, the reception for them planned by the occupants of one hut must have put them into a state of advanced shock. Flight-Sergeant Bowden and his mates had laid on a series of booby-traps, including a tin containing dissected frogs and mice in formalin labelled 'Food – Don't touch', together with a clock whose figures had been reversed and hands moved anti-clockwise – which just about summed up kriegie life, thought Younger.

When prisoners escaped the cry 'Goon up' was often the first that many knew of it, as German security officers marched into their compound. This sudden increase in activity was bitterly resented – as were any changes which upset the routine of everyday life.

After a while POWs felt safe within the structure and unchanging pattern of camp life. Men hated moving even from one room to another and once outside the wire, on visits to the doctor or dentist, they felt very vulnerable and nervous.

Escapers were as afraid of the unknown as anyone else and many prisoners tried to analyse their motives. But, just as there was no 'average kriegie', but rather a composite of many types, so the reasons for escaping were endless.

Courage played its part as well as boredom, frustration, and a desire to assert a strong personality against the dull uniformity of a prison camp. That, thought Sergeant Wood, 'could explain the "cloak and dagger" manner of some people. Others, the truly dedicated, were there one minute, gone the next.' Warrant Officer Grimson was a prime example: 'For sheer dedication, single-minded purpose, courage and selflessness [he] was unique,' claimed Sergeant Dunphy, who came across him in Stalag Luft I.

One of the best reasons for escaping was the trouble it caused for the Germans. After a successful breakout, tens of thousands of troops might be involved in guarding roads, railway-bridges and frontiers. In March, 1943, for example, 500,000 German troops and police were caught up in the hunt for sixty-five escapers from Eichstätt. If more than five prisoners escaped it immediately became a matter for the German High Command and often Hitler took a personal interest.

Such escapes were not, however, without their effects on other prisoners as Sergeant Bruce discovered at Stalag VIIIB where Wing Commander Douglas Bader hid in the rafters of an empty hut hoping to escape while he was in transit. For several weary hours the rest of the camp stood on *appell* while the Germans searched for the legless airman: 'Of course we all knew where the bloody exhibitionist was but we loyally kept quiet,' commented Bruce.

Only a tiny number of prisoners ever actively dedicated themselves to escaping though many prisoners carried out the various tasks necessary for a successful 'break', from specialists who spent many hours creating forged documents and uniforms to those who staged diversions and confused the count on *appell*.

Attitudes toward dedicated escapers ranged from that of mere tolerance to active resentment. Since the Germans invariably punished everyone if an escape succeeded, which might involve withholding mail, parcels and the closing of the camp's theatre, it was essential that it was well-planned and had some, albeit remote, chance of success. Second Lieutenant Baxter was among many prisoners who thought this was not always carefully considered: 'The spoilt darlings of every "kriegie" camp were the "naughty boys", or officers who were "escape minded". To their activities everything else had to be subordinated. They had the first call on any articles they wanted, they could demand the assistance of the whole camp, and certain stores and food were reserved for them. In fact, this developed to such an extent that many officers who were not connected with escaping efforts felt that the whole thing was an imposition and a racket. At times it undoubtedly was.'

Ordinary Seaman Coward in the naval compound at Stalag VIIIB, where the 'tough element' was a constant nuisance, came across the same problem: 'Escape attempts usually did little more than bring punishment,' he observed, 'not only on those who tried them but upon the whole camp from which they were made.' And among

French POWs there were some who 'were ready to sacrifice their own comrades to their own comforts by denouncing them, and others,' noted Francis Ambrière, 'who without sinking so low still looked upon prisoners who escaped as mere troublemakers.'

Even when there was a successful escape, prisoners who had worked closely on it experienced a sense of frustration and loss. After Flight-Lieutenant Williams, Lieutenant Codnor and Flight-Lieutenant Philpot got clean away from the difficult East compound of Stalag Luft III in the famous 'Wooden Horse' episode, Pilot Officer Sidwell, who had beavered away with them on their plans, felt 'a gap suddenly come in my kriegie life, because we'd had so much in common . . . Now they were gone for good. Although only too glad of their great success, my spirits were a bit low afterwards and there was a gap.'

Contrary to popular belief, escapes and escape activities for most POW were not of great importance in the constant effort to survive prison life. Repeated escapers were certainly dedicated and courageous but news of a successful home run only temporarily boosted morale. The arrival of Red Cross parcels had the same, and most lasting, effect.

There were more successful break-outs from Stalag VIIIB than from any other camp. Despite an undercurrent of ill-feeling between POWs which sometimes led to brawling – as Sergeant Peachey discovered, 'there was no great love for the RAF either by the German guards, who saw in us the people who were bombing their cities, or the British army lads, who, because many were captured at Dunkirk, felt that the RAF had let them down' – many aircrew swapped identities with 'Brown jobs'. Sometimes they remained undiscovered for months or even years.

By assuming a soldier's identity, aircrew could get on to an *Arbeitskommando* which was necessary for most escape attempts. Peachey himself swapped identities with a member of the East Kent Regiment and was sent to a brick works from where he got away. Like most prisoners on the run, however, he was not free for long and arrived back in the 'cooler' at Stalag VIIIB. There, the infamous 'Ukraine Joe' Kissel – a brutal guard nicknamed for his Russian appearance and savage temper – soon came up with his true identity.

Unteroffizier 'Ukraine Joe' had a good memory for faces. Private Whelan, for example, exchanged identities with a RAF Sergeant. Believing him to be aircrew the Germans sent Whelan to Stalag Luft III – a 'far superior' place to Lamsdorf. Eventually, brought face-to-face with 'Ukraine Joe', he was imprisoned back at his old camp though not before one problem had been sorted out. In order to avoid arousing the censor's suspicion, letters had to be sent from prison camps as if nothing had happened and so relatives received them from perfect strangers. The mystified relatives were then contacted by the War Office and asked in strict confidence to write to each other to clear up the fog of misunderstanding.

Despite the very great number of attempted escapes a former prisoner, Squadron Leader Aidan Crawley, estimated that only through one in thirty-five tunnels did a RAF prisoner get outside the wire and only thirty members of the RAF and Dominion Air Forces made a successful escape from permanent camps.

Apart from the occasional train journey following a 'purge' (usually undertaken at very short notice) and other special occasions, most RAF prisoners never saw the outside of their prison camps. While many of them might be engaged in the truly prodigious tasks connected with an escape attempt the majority of prisoners had to find other means of filling their days: 'I think the problems of survival really occupied most people's time,' said Sergeant Bruce.

The basic unit of organization between RAF POWs was a 'combine' in which men came together to cope with everyday tasks of which the most important was getting and sharing food.

One member was responsible for collecting the German rations of ersatz coffee and jam, thin soup, half-rotten potatoes and hard bread for his combine. Red Cross parcels were normally shared on a communal basis and cooking, clearing away and general fatigues devolved upon the 'duty stooge', according to a rota arranged by common consent. Prisoners hated this duty.

During 1944 Flying Officer Bolton and five other POWs lived surrounded by a 'terrific conglomeration of cardboard boxes, old tins, pieces of string, etc on top of the cupboards, along with a thick layer of dust. In the corner by the stove was a pile of coal, brushes and empty tins, and in the unexplored region behind the stove – heaven knows what. Add to this five bods lying on their sacks, continually slanging the stooge, and you have a fair picture of our happy home.'

'Stooge day,' wrote Bolton, was utterly miserable: 'Five hungry, ungrateful bods had to be given breakfast in bed, and fed at various other times during the day. The floor had to be swept in the morning. Washing up to be done after each meal. Rations to collect, coal to collect, and brew-water to collect. It was just one whirl, and all the time the other five were jeering and making all the rude remarks they could think of. . . . At 11.0 p.m. we heaved a sigh of relief and settled in the sack to think up methods of torment for the next five days' stooges.'

One of the jobs that Sergeant Bruce hated most while 'stooging' was emptying the brimming night slop pail because urine often splashed over his trousers and there was no means of getting rid of the stink with cold water and German-issue soap – which had the consistency of granite and about the same cleaning power. 'I intend to watch a washing machine at work for a whole day, when I get back to civilization,' commented Bolton.

The simple chores of life such as washing or cooking consumed vast amounts of time simply because there were so few facilities. 'After lunch had a dhobie bash,' recorded Wing Commander McCarthy-Jones. 'Worst job in kriegie camp. Not enough hot water and a leaky bucket.'

Cooking what meagre rations were available was difficult because German fuel supplies were irregular and coal-dust brickettes or similar substitutes replaced coal. Prisoners responded by burning every available wooden item that was inessential – and quite a few that were essential. One result was that a prisoner would suddenly come crashing through his bunk, preceded by his mattress – built more for staying power than comfort – to land with a crash on the unfortunate victim below. This was caused by a general lack of bedboards; substitute hammock-like supports, made out of string taken from Red Cross parcels, could not always be trusted.

Bedboards which had already disappeared into hut stoves were supplemented by other equally irregular fuel supplies, including coal stolen at night from German stores. Such exploits were dangerous as Pilot Officer Harvey discovered at Stalag IVB: 'Raids took place at night on the German coal store until a POW was caught in the searchlight and shot in the hip. Coal scrounging stopped but by this time we had collected quite a quantity which was hidden under the floor. It was discovered subsequently by the guards in a routine hut check. Russians were ordered in to clear our store but this was chain-bucketed to the top end of the hut from the cart and we kept our coal and the Germans did not realize they were hoodwinked.'

To leave the safety of one's hut at night and venture across a desolate compound, slashed by the sweeping beams of powerful searchlights from search-boxes high above the wire, needed courage and a cool head. Even where white tapes were laid out to guide prisoners to the latrines it was easy to stray off track and end up risking a sentry's bullet or the fangs of a savage guard dog. At least one prisoner was killed in the RAF compound of Stalag IVB when he was caught stealing coal and shot in the stomach. Nevertheless, the magpie-like instincts of kriegies were hard to contain. 'I punish F/Sgt Stuart W. O—— with seven days' severe arrest,' read an Order from the Kommandant of Stalag Luft I on 5 April, 1945, 'because . . . there was found in his property a signboard from a car of the German "Reichsbahn", which he pretended to have found on the floor of the car.' Exactly what the prisoner intended to do with this singularly useless item remains a mystery.

With the growing shortage of fuel in POW camps as Germany's position worsened, prisoners were forced to devise new means of cooking. Various contraptions were put together from old Red Cross 'Klim' tins (they contained powdered milk, hence the name) and wired directly into the camp's electricity system.

Highly efficient 'blowers' were also constructed which, by inducing air through several metal chambers driven by a hand-cranked wheel and utilizing only small scraps of materials, could boil a brew of tea in a few minutes. At night water could be heated indoors by the light of home-made lamps using German margarine for oil and Red Cross string as a wick.

But a general lack of food sometimes made even these primitive arrangements useless. 'Bowls up' was kriegie slang for food on the horizon though, as one POW put it, 'grub up' was a fallacy! Sergeant Bruce could never quite stomach the stinking, fishy slime which passed for German regulation-issue cheese but as bellies distended from hunger and sudden blackouts increased – a man had to be careful when sitting up – so prisoners adopted unimagined survival techniques.

In the summer of 1944 Sergeant Kelly was one of a group of POWs who gathered each day about noon outside the back window of the camp kitchens when staff threw out rotten swedes or potatoes considered inedible even in what passed for prison soup: 'We thereupon dived into this mess in the mud, stuffing what we could into our battledress and taking it back to our barracks to carefully pare off the edible pieces of swede or potato, which supplemented our rations. On one occasion the RSM in charge was walking past and in a loud voice said, "Come on lads, remember you are British," or words to that effect. From the mêlée of bodies a former Spitfire pilot emerged . . . His retort has always lived in my memory. He said, "Sgt. Major, I would have you know I am an officer and a gentleman," and with that he returned to the fray.'

The situation in camps over the quality and quantity of German rations was serious early in the war and became more so with the passage of time. In 1941 the main gripe was lack of variety in the German diet; this soon became part of a general moan about lack of food altogether: 'I'm literally starving,' wrote Sergeant Harcus in December, 1942.

Some weird concoctions were created over hut stoves from parcel rations – especially 'glop', a mixture of practically anything which could be turned into semi-solid form. 'Connie' (condensed milk) and 'Nutty' (bars of chocolate) were both known to stave off the effects of continuous hunger.

Early in 1945 Sergeant Simister crammed details of a week's routine into his diary, recording how everyday matters in camp had become dominated by the general shortage of food. A typical day, 14 March, reads: '0630 Arise and wash. 0700 roll call. 0715 Tea. Make bed, shave, clean boots. Sweep alley. Read and prepare bread crust duff. 1015 coffee. 10.30 to Technical library for book. 11.30 Skilly – French beans and 6 small bad spuds! Stew for dinner. 1400 cut up bread (7 to loaf). 1500 Dhobie. 1530 walk – lovely afternoon. 1630 prepare tea – toast and jerry cheese. 1700 Coffee – real. 1900 Brassed-off – visit Tony. 2000 coffee and bread pud. 2100 Raid, lights out – to bed.'

In bad weather many prisoners could not even get to sleep and so escape for a few hours from the hunger pains which tore at their insides. 'Two blankets cannot keep out the intense cold and even though all available clothing is piled on, one remains awake, shivering and trying to find a little contentment in a cigarette,' wrote Sergeant Harcus, lying stiff and frozen in his bunk at Stalag VIIIB where broken barrack windows gaped openly to searing winds sweeping across the Silesian plain during the winter of 1942–43.

Lacking a decently balanced diet without meat or fresh vegetables, POWs went down with stomach disorders, for which they were given charcoal and sulphur tablets, suffered bouts of dysentery and sickness and broke out in boils and skin rashes. As soon as they received their food parcels, some men tore off the wrappings and wolfed down all the contents. This habit of 'bashing' parcels convinced Warrant Officer Deans and the Medical Officer at Stalag Luft III of the need to pool them and this was started when Deans was moved to Stalag Luft VI in June, 1943.

Medical staff, who were attached to every permanent camp and to some of the larger *Arbeitskommandos*, performed near-miracles despite their inadequate supplies of medicines and instruments. On going to Lamsdorf in March, 1944, Captain Borrie of the New Zealand Medical Corps discovered what he reckoned to be 'the finest P.O.W. hospital in Germany', run with scrupulous fairness by the German *Oberfeldarzt* and staffed with fully qualified prisoners, including a radiologist, anaesthetist and surgeons. They were kept busy dealing with acute surgical cases among the 10,000 men at Lamsdorf and preventing the outbreak of typhus, famine oedema, dysentery and tuberculosis.

Borrie had been at Blechhammer where he had led the Germans to believe that the daily sick rate was ten per cent and had managed to keep many fit prisoners in camp on welfare jobs. Carrying an *Ausweis* and accompanied by an armed German guard, he toured Upper Silesia visiting patients at various *Arbeitskommandos*. Using his privileged position to good advantage he kept his eyes and ears open and transmitted much valuable news by code to London.

Beyond the general symptoms of near-malnutrition about which

Medical Officers could do little was one problem of the utmost seriousness. Typhus, carried by lice – flat, grey and then bloated and red after feeding on human blood – could rage through camps with terrifying speed. Cramped together in unhealthy, often dirty, conditions with primitive sanitary arrangements, POWs were a potential source of plague in the heart of Europe.

At special risk were the vast numbers of Russian prisoners. Systematically starved, beaten and degraded they carried with them, like some dread incubus, the fear of typhus.

'It was the Russian element which opened our eyes,' noted the Rev Douglas Thompson at Stalag IVB. 'They wandered the camp or stood motionless . . . erect like corpses. The other residents passed them as though invisible. Their faces were grey, every sinew of neck and arms stood out in gaunt horror. On their feet were encrusted swathes of cloth. When they moved they hobbled or reeled, some aiding their way with two sticks. . . . A smell of decay preceded them and remained when they were gone.' Dying like flies, they were buried in their thousands. At Stalag XXA Sergeant Wood entered a deserted compound: 'As you walked through the gates the headboard was still in position, "Eintritt Verboten. Achtung Seuche." [Entry Forbidden. Danger of Epidemic] Along one fence, massive potato pies stretched the whole length of the compound. They provided graves for dead Russians.'

A massive outbreak of the disease spread from Russian compounds in December, 1941, to one where several thousand British POWs were held. On receiving information through the ICRC the authorities at home sent urgent supplies of vaccine to inoculate medical and sanitary staff in all camps and followed this up with instructions to camp leaders that heads should be close-cropped or shaved, the use of mattresses discontinued and the body, blankets, and clothing of any infected prisoner thoroughly disinfected after washing.

Careful measures along these lines helped Allied prisoners to avoid the epidemic proportions of Russian fatalities from typhus. Nevertheless, the disease remained a serious problem. Of far less consequence were the unpleasantries of bed bugs, fleas and other pests such as cluster flies which clung to the beams in Stalag VIIIB's huts in great numbers during the winter months. One part of the camp population which was entirely voluntary and thrived on the dismal conditions was comprised of mice. No matter how often they were hunted down they bred like wildfire; most prisoners hardly noticed them after a while.

In setting up recreational and educational facilities there was normally a delay as both the Germans and their prisoners took stock of the situation. When this was settled, the POWs turned to other pursuits.

At Stalag Luft I there was little activity in the first year, apart from some soccer and ice-hockey which was played on a rink made by prisoners and one or two classes started in the autumn of 1940.

By December, 1943, when Morte Doll and his 'Stalag Stompers' gave a Christmas Variety show, there had developed a regular series of concerts, recitals and film shows at the kriegie theatre. They included a German sound film, 'One Night in May', shown in January, 1944, followed by an arts and crafts exhibition and debate in March (after productions had been delayed by an outbreak of meningitis in camp), 'That the ultimate advantages of kriegie life outweigh its disadvantages.' There were even some POWs who voted in favour of this unlikely proposition.

Other activities and productions throughout 1944 included short talks on various subjects, American films, and variety shows by both American and British POWs. 'The standard of performances was very high, and one could really get away from kriegiedom for a few hours,' wrote Flying Officer Bolton, 'even if one was sitting in a converted Red Cross box.' Men who were later to become well-known actors after starting on the rough boards of a POW camp included Roy Dotrice, Rupert Davies, Peter Butterworth, Clive Dunn and Sam Kydd.

Flight-Sergeant Younger heard rival bands which were 'popular props' of variety shows yet observed that 'straight' plays were the most satisfying entertainments according to a camp poll. For many prisoners entry into a world of theatre, music, debating and literature was something exciting and new. Many of them took full advantage of their enforced idleness to explore this strange territory.

An RAF School for POWs – the 'Barbed Wire University' – was formed at Stalag Luft VI from educational schemes started by RAF prisoners who were sent there from Stalag IIIE and Stalag Luft III. By the time the move was complete the camp boasted three classrooms and a general and technical library. In the winter of 1943, 270 lectures were given every week and there were daily examinations.

The educational system at Stalag Luft VI increased continually to meet the demands of many nationalities including American, Polish, Czech and British prisoners. Over a thousand students overcame the lack of space and pressure on facilities to study in a very wide range of informal and formal classes though, as one prisoner commented: 'Those who do try to settle down to some form of study, and the majority do, find it extremely difficult to maintain their enthusiasm and interest. The reason for this lies in the fundamental quality of prisoner-of-war life, which has the likeness of eternity. Thus any work attempted resembles walking up a long featureless hill whose summit is out of sight.'

Nevertheless, the desire for useful qualifications was enough to encourage many men while others enjoyed study because of 'its power to provide a distraction from Boredom and an antidote to Mental Stagnation' which the 'Prospectus of the R.A.F. School for Prisoners of War (Stalag Luft VI)' offered. In this respect the 'Barbed-Wire University', and similar POW schemes, were remarkably successful.

The counterpoint to all educational study was a wide range of recreational activities. In a big camp like Stalag Luft III these were extensive whereas in much smaller places, like Stalag Luft IV, the absence of any sports area restricted POWs to circuits of the trip wire.

Sports meetings were important both to the competitors and spectators because they helped them defeat the slow passage of time: 'One soon forgot . . . one's surroundings,' wrote Sergeant Eeles of the meetings at Stalag Luft III, 'as there happened to be an almost holiday atmosphere about the camp.'

In the long summer days prisoners played golf, basketball, cricket and softball though golfballs were hit out of bounds more often than they could be manufactured from the remains of old football bladders and army boot leather.

Sports such as volley ball, tennis, quoits and badminton attracted a smaller following and in hot weather a static water tank made an impromptu swimming pool. Model yachts, steam vessels, submarines and gliders were remarkable evidence of much delicate and painstaking work since materials and tools were scarce.

During winter months bad weather restricted activities. While the camp's gardeners waited for better weather to plant their greenstuffs and outdoor tomatoes, other men turned to hockey and football. Due to the risk of severe injury, rugby was seldom played but ice-skating was highly popular and groups of prisoners could be seen stamping and calling, their breath vapouring upwards on the freezing air, in high spirits at the antics of novices.

For some activities the changing seasons had no meaning. Communal gramophones ground out their tunes day and night and records in RAF compounds were plentiful. At Stalag Luft III the dance club had a very appropriate signature tune – 'Time on my Hands' – while arts and crafts exhibitions were well attended. Various indoor games were all the rage at times including chess, draughts, dominoes, table tennis, darts, dice and cards.

Harsh reality, however, had a habit of breaking in on POWs and returning them to the darker side of camp life. Sergeant Harcus recorded the outcome of a fight when 'a black refused to let a Scotsman stand on his table to watch Whitsun sports in progress. Fight ensued at which four Scotsmen cut black up with open razors – blood everywhere!' and later on the British MO was forced to stop all dancing due to 'bad habits' – 'What's more, he's right,' Harcus added.

It was known that a few RAF prisoners had their 'winger' and others were dismissed as 'hut benders'. But there was no more homosexuality than among other prisoners and Flight-Sergeant Younger, like most of his colleagues, knew of no single case or even a rumour of one. Naturally, there was rude good humour – a bare bottom poked out at the audience from between drawn curtains at a theatre performance or the lighting of flaming vapours from the backsides of men distended with gas from poor food – but that was about all.

While sudden crazes for various sports and activities tended to sweep through a camp – men might, for example, spend days on end wrapped up in seemingly unending games of bridge – one of the most common of all was 'logging sack time' or 'bashing the pit'. As Flying Officer Bolton recorded at Barth: 'Most mornings at least four bods could be found reposing between the sheets in our room, and one bod at any other time of the day. J—— created a record with 18 hours 50 minutes but doubtless this can be bettered by some of the other rooms.' The door of one room which Pilot Officer Wilson saw at Stalag Luft III had a splendid cartoon showing all the occupants seated in a dinghy without oars and captioned below, 'We know we are drifting – do not disturb.'

Some men discovered that their religious faith was awakened or renewed in a prison camp. They were a minority but the 'God-botherers', as some dismissively termed them, drew comfort from their beliefs. Many prisoners preferred to share their innermost thoughts with a close mate, especially on receipt of bad news from home, though others would seek out the padre for a quiet word.

Although padres occasionally were refused permission to preach, had their sermons censored, and were not allowed to visit camps outside their own area, many of them seem to have been resourceful and popular figures. One Anglican padre whom Ordinary Seaman Coward came across, for example, used to stand at the doorway of his hut when the Americans started their daylight air raids shouting, 'That's right! Let the bastards have it!', completely oblivious of his own safety. His sympathies would no doubt have been engaged by the Canadian who, when asked by the padre if he had any religious belief, drawled, 'Yeah, I hate Germans. Period.'

Being independent souls, some padres managed to fall foul not only of the Germans but also of their own SBOs, as at Westertimke where Captain Wilson complained in November, 1944: 'R. D—— having preached a sermon on Sun. which was little else than rank Socialist party politic, I sent for him & suggested politely that he was taking an improper advantage of his pulpit. He went completely off at half cock

& swore that every word was divinely inspired . . . It is impossible to get any sense into a Welsh fanatic . . . but I don't want to hamper the really good religious work he is doing.'

And this good work was important in helping prisoners to maintain their mental stability: 'The services were a great comfort to those who attended them,' noted Flying Officer Bolton at Stalag Luft I, where the church was 'very well decorated, but the seating accommodation wasn't anywhere near enough so that for a long time the services were held in the theatre.' Yet Sergeant Kelly, who passed through various RAF camps, considered religious belief to be 'sadly lacking.' It is, however, impossible to know just how important religious belief was for most prisoners because the matter remained a strictly personal one.

It was at Christmas time that most prisoners felt the pull of the Church and everything best remembered and most missed with family and friends at home. In addition to the general nostalgia there was the exciting prospect of extra food and drink. Special Red Cross parcels sometimes unfortunately turned up in the following Spring but, even where they arrived late, Christmas Day was celebrated with a better meal than usual: 'Felt really full all day today,' noted Flight-Sergeant Bulmer, 'wish every day was the same.'

Alcohol, generally as fiery and potent as possible, was brewed beforehand: 'In Stalag Luft III and Stalag Luft VI we managed to brew our own liquor,' said Sergeant Kelly, 'mostly from potatoes put into a container with an appropriate lid which was made airtight by scraping bitumen off the roof and melting it down, opening it up after about six weeks and then taking off the scum, leaving a resultant liquid of varying degrees of potency. This happened only at Christmas and the New Year. It was traditional that those who drank at Christmas stayed sober at New Year and vice versa, in order to ensure that the liberating influence of alcohol did not go too far. A refinement of this do-it-yourself "wine"-making was to put your brew into a bucket, put it on the stove, collect the steam into a pipe made from empty cigarette tins, [and] keep the pipe cool by wet towels so a species of pure alcohol dripped out the other end.'

Such concoctions could have devastating results. Strong men were struck down, others went berserk; fortunately, only a few suffered permanent damage. The stuff made by Sergeant Spencer and his mates was so powerful that it stripped the enamel from inside the fermenting bucket; eventually they found a use for it – as a useful fuel in cigarette lighters bartered from friendly guards.

Virtually anything that could be drunk at Christmas time was poured down kriegie throats. For example, Sergeant Wood's combine managed to 'acquire' some embalming fluid from the sickbay: 'The quack found out and, realising the futility of trying to get it back, sent word that we had to stop drinking as soon as our tongues went numb. It was some time before we could speak properly again and longer before we were free of the smell of formaldehyde.' Another particularly evil brew was made by survivors of the 51st Highland Division from boot and button polish.

'What an Xmas!', commented Major Casdagli at Oflag VIB in 1941. 'Seventy-five per cent of our battalion drunk on home-made beer!' No one was hurt but the barracks was a 'shambles'. 'There are,' he added, 'bound to be repercussions about the drunks on evening parade. What a day! Three in our hut were too drunk even to get out of bed.' The Battalion Commander was promptly sacked by the SBO who took a 'dim view' of the proceedings but Casdagli thoroughly enjoyed it all. 'I would not have missed it for anything. Did me a power of good.'

'Rarely has an area of such insignificant dimensions contained so many drunks,' commented Flight-Sergeant Younger of Stalag Luft VI at Christmas, 1943. The guards had returned for a private tasting after making a pretence of searching for illegal alcohol. Some hours later they staggered from the compound hopelessly drunk and this happened in other camps, as in the early months of 1944 at Stalag Luft III where the operation of numerous home-made stills in the East compound had to be banned by the SBO, 'due to rowdy parties and rebellious behaviour'. 'This ban was enforced,' wrote Sergeant Eeles, 'by the simple expedient of removing the offending ingredients directly from Red Cross parcels before collection.'

From the brittle festivities of Christmas, 1943, we shift our attention to an *appell* on the morning of 5 April, 1944, at Stalag Luft III.

In the North compound rows of prisoners stand hunched against a biting wind which swirls snowflakes between their ranks. The German Kommandant, *Oberst* von Lindeiner, gaunt and erect, moves with evident reticence to the head of the parade and the terrible news is read out – forty-one Allied POWs have been shot 'while attempting to escape'. A dark cloud of shock and hate hangs over the camp. Later comes news of more shootings; fifty men in all, murdered while legitimately attempting to reach home.

As if to rub salt into a gaping wound the notorious leaflet, 'To All Prisoners of War', was posted throughout Allied camps on 24 June. It was immediately torn down and secreted away by prisoners and later used in the trials of major German war criminal at Nuremberg. POWs were warned that escaping from prison camps was 'no longer a sport':

> 'Urgent warning is given against making future escapes!
>
> In plain English: Stay in the camp where you will be safe! Breaking out of it is now a damned dangerous act.
>
> The chances of preserving your life are almost nil!

All police and military guards have been given the most strict orders to shoot on sight all suspected persons.

Escaping from prison camps has ceased to be a sport!'

By the time these ugly threats had been made, the next escape tunnel already reached beyond the camp's perimeter wire.

A mutual tolerance between RAF prisoners and their Luftwaffe guards had developed without either side entirely lowering its defences. Flight-Sergeant Steele sensed something of this after being 'purged' to Stalag Luft III where he was 'mighty glad to get away from Stalag VIIIB and the German Army. This is a very fine camp and the Luftwaffe certainly treat us very well indeed, there seems to be a sort of understanding between the two Air Services and the treatment and atmosphere about this camp is totally different from Stalag VIIIB.'

This common respect was shattered by news of the Sagan massacre. No other episode brought relationships between guards and prisoners so near to breaking point, though an earlier matter, the manacling of prisoners in various camps, had caused widespread resentment.

The problem began for British and Canadian POWs in October, 1942, after the German High Command alleged that German prisoners taken during the bloody assault on Dieppe and the British Commando raid on Sark had been bound by their hands. Enraged by this, Hitler ordered the manacling of Allied POWs, though 'protected personnel', together with sick and wounded prisoners, were spared this retaliation.

In Stalag VIIIB about 1,500 British and Canadian POWs were roughly tied with strips of Red Cross parcel string and another 800 were soon added. POWs found by their guards with the string loosened, smoking in the barracks, or even sitting on their bunks, were kept for several hours with their wrists bound harshly together and drawn up tightly behind their back, nose and toes touching a wall.

At Oflag VIIB, 107 officers and twenty Other Ranks were tied with rope about their wrists and remained like that for twelve hours daily. The Kommandant explained that he was acting only on Orders from the High Command and his staff obviously disliked carrying them out: the Germans were 'quite sympathetic and a little disgusted about it all'. A few days later three times the original number were handcuffed. A Medical Officer was in constant attendance but a visiting Swiss delegate reported 'serious effects on mental and physical health'.

Back at Stalag VIIIB, handcuffs with a regulation link chain were substituted for the original bindings after the German MO intervened. Attending *appell* in icy weather and trying to carry on any kind of camp life was, as Sergeant Harcus found, by no means easy. 'Wish these damned chains would come off,' he wrote on the last day of

January, 1943, 'Wrists ache with constant wearing.' Matters seem to have improved in the following month: 'Lost my chains down the "40-holer". Soon scrounged others from Guard.'

As the unresolved dispute dragged on the continued shackling of British POWs took a more relaxed form. A German army representative assured the Swiss Minister in Berlin that shackling was regarded only as a 'symbolic' act and that POWs were invariably handcuffed with a linking chain some fifty to sixty centimetres in length between the wrists, so allowing greater freedom of movement.

During a visit to Oflag VIIB in April, 1943, a Swiss delegate reported that prisoners were officially handcuffed for thirteen hours each day but had some 'liberty of movement' and were able to play baseball in the mornings and hockey in the afternoons. The selected prisoners, kept apart from their colleagues, were always shackled unless they were ill or taking examinations when others were manacled in their place.

Things were not quite what they seemed, however, because the delegate observed prisoners without shackles most of the time and maintaining an alarm system to warn of approaching guards. Even when prisoners were discovered without them and were placed under seven days' arrest they had ropes knotted about their wrists so loosely that they were able to slip out of them. His distinct impression was that 'without actually shutting their eyes to evasions of regulations camp authorities are in general indulgent as regards shackling.'

In some camps the prisoners resolutely refused all attempts to manacle them. At Stalag 383, for example, they burnt cords used for bindings, broke padlocks and threw their chains into septic tanks.

When handcuffs were first produced in Oflag VII C/H, guards were posted outside each room to prevent the prisoners removing them but no action was taken against those who unchained themselves: 'The affair seems to be dying out,' wrote Major Booth in April, 1943.

This was also the case at Stalag VIIIB where a Swiss delegate was able to report that the camp authorities 'appear to connive at prisoners removing their handcuffs and walking with their unshackled comrades,' and the general consensus of opinion amongst over 4,000 Allied POWs still manacled in August was that things could be worse, might be made so by too many protests from home and that their present treatment was 'quite bearable'.

The order shackling British and Canadian POWs was never publicly countermanded but the practice stopped in all camps on 22 November, 1943. By then it had become a mere formality. No announcement was made, however, on the radio or in the Press either in the United Kingdom or Dominions because no one could predict the Führer's reaction to public comment.

There were more isolated incidents of collective punishment as when Sergeant Simister, at Stalag IVB, reported that, 'RAF compound locked up – no one allowed out. Said to be security measure – but we think it is mass reprisal (not allowed under Geneva Convention) as RAF have caused such a lot of trouble of late and many have escaped.' But the manacling of Allied prisoners and the Sagan massacre were the only major ones imposed on Allied prisoners.

With these exceptions RAF POWs could co-exist with the German war-wounded, sick, or those over military age who patrolled their camps. The guards also had their problems: 'To allow prisoners to escape is not only an offence of liberating . . . but in certain circumstances constitutes a neglect of guard duty punishable in the field by death or detention,' read an Order issued by the C-in-C, Northern Russia on 19 February, 1943.

To prevent an escape a guard was supposed to call 'Halt!' three times before firing a warning shot in the direction of the fleeing prisoner – though not with the intention of hitting him or endangering innocent bystanders. Firearms could also properly be used in the case of an attack by prisoners which endangered life or if they impeded a guard making an arrest, for the protection of items entrusted to him and to enforce a direct order. The use of a weapon was forbidden as a form of punishment in itself as was the use of stick-whips and other such instruments. Guards were given powers of arrest only for insubordination by POWs, for insults in word and deed against the State or armed forces, and in all cases of suspected sabotage, escape and crime.

From the catch-all nature of these regulations it is clear that guards could interpret them much as they wished and use their firearms without warning and with brutal effect against unarmed prisoners. Many prisoners knew of such shootings and some witnessed them at first hand.

Often they occurred near the low trip-wire which ran round the compound perimeter. At intervals, warning boards displayed the penalty for stepping into the death strip between trip-wire and main fence, often in an over-literal English translation. At Heydekrug they read: '*Danger of Life! We shoot!* We shoot without warning or call whenever you touch or surpass wire or hole!'; at Thorn it was '*Halt!* Trespassing of warning wire means death', and, at Wolfsberg, 'Do not approach the warning wire or it will be shot!' In every camp there were tragic incidents where prisoners crossed the trip-wire and were gunned down by guards.

At Stalag Luft III Flight-Sergeant Bulmer witnessed such an incident when, 'One Aussie, new prisoner, slightly deranged, ran over trip wire hoping guards would fire at him. Is under impression that he is a traitor.' Two days later he recorded that 'the sick Aussie W/O was taken to hospital last night – he crossed wire yesterday & was fired on twice.' Some prisoners were shot even before they crossed into the forbidden area by a nervous or trigger-happy 'Goon', a universally-applied name for German guards taken from a popular newspaper strip cartoon in which 'goons' were subhuman creatures: prisoners sometimes used the official name of *posten* as well.

On these occasions much depended on the individual Kommandant who might ignore the incident or remove the guard from his duties. Transfer to the East was an ever-present possibility and, as the bitter fighting there drained men from the Reich, many guards were scared even to travel on leave passes because military police dispatched to the Front anyone of military age moving by rail.

'Like any wild animal, no guard could be tamed completely,' wrote Sergeant Wood. 'Sometimes he could be compromised, usually by means of a camera. Then he could be blackmailed. For less serious matters he would sometimes be lured into a state of trust or bribed. This way you achieved little but you gained some knowledge of the outside world.'

At his most dangerous when confused or alarmed he could sometimes be brought into conversation for a little propaganda. 'A dependable opening gambit was to ask the riddle which during the first winter of the Russian war was almost a cliche amongst them. "Which animal most closely resembles a human being?", you asked. If you had chosen the right man he would roar with laughter and say: "Why, a Russian of course." Next, you would ask if he had heard the Russians cut prisoners' windpipes then returned them to their own lines.' It was 'propaganda of a vicious sort,' added Wood, but it worked without exception – not that the Germans were particularly slow in using atrocity stories about POWs to their own advantage.

Prisoners categorized their guards with some precision. In the first instance were those who were uncompromising and often sadistic. They were part of the inhuman face of the Third Reich – the guard commander who would shoot, deliberately and in cold blood, the escaper crouching immobilized in the searchlight's unblinking stare. These were men in whom no sense of morality seemed to linger. But there were others who, though incorruptible and ever-vigilant, displayed a sense of humour and shared a common humanity with their prisoners which led them to small acts of kindness. Many men from Stalag Luft III remember *Unteroffizier* Glimnitz: 'Well, why are you not digging to-day?' he once asked startled RAF men. 'It's bad weather to be above ground,' and on another occasion remarked, 'I hear that the Allies have selected Sagan as the place at which to open their Second Front.'

Another type of German was involved with POWs either through greed or a strongly-developed instinct for self-preservation. At one prison camp an RAF 'contact' gradually wormed his way into the confidence of a 'ferret' named Rudi and reported: 'I had managed to form an estimate of Rudi's character. He was reasonably well educated, cunning enough to keep away from the front line, astute enough to deceive his compatriots, and sly enough to deceive me if someone else should offer him a better bargain.' So long as the price of cigarettes or chocolate was high enough this kind of guard could be relied upon to smuggle in essential goods.

A final group actively helped prisoners, not because they were greedy or wanted to save their own necks but from a revolt against the whole Nazi system. These were Germans of high principle who knew the terrible cost to opponents of the régime and yet were prepared to do anything which might hasten its downfall.

The names of these men go largely unsung except among prisoners who benefited from their courageous help. Their fate is sometimes unrecorded too. 'I hope that Peter Grimm got through the War O.K.,' wrote Sergeant Spencer about a German interpreter he met at Stalag Luft I during the winter of 1941–42.

More is known about a fair-haired *Obergefreiter* at Stalag Luft III, known to inmates as 'Harry', who actively helped in escapes and took quite exceptional risks. He survived the war, unlike two other brave men at Stalag Luft IV, Adolph Munkert, an interpreter, and Sommers, the camp's photographer.

Just after the Sagan massacre Munkert was discovered and probably shot by the Gestapo after giving away nothing about plans for escape down the route pioneered by Grimson, who had been out since January, 1944. Sommers, implicated by a member of the Polish underground of which he was a member, was afraid not of death but that he might give way under torture. He hanged himself in his cell before the Gestapo could break his defiant spirit.

Naturally enough there were few men like these prepared to go to such lengths to assist the Allies. Now and again the human side of German authority was revealed, however, to men like Sergeant Wood: 'One officer that I got to know a little . . . carried a holster. That was mandatory but instead of a gun it held toilet paper. When I thought I knew him well enough I mentioned it. "When things get so bad a Schmeisser and some potato mashers can't help, your need for this type of paper is urgent," he told me seriously and in his immaculate English.'

A similar experience while at Stalag IVB was recalled by Sergeant Nell: 'One day there was a queue of us outside our camp theatre when there was a sudden commotion: a big German holding a pistol was chasing a Russian. The Russian zig-zagged amongst our queue with the German screaming after him. One of the British lads shouted indignantly to the German, indicating the pistol: "You want to watch what you're doing with that, mate, you'll be hurting somebody!" The German paused, looked round and grinned, and said quietly in English: "It's all right – it's not loaded!"'

A more common experience was the crack of flailing rifle butts on bone and flesh as prisoners were driven from their huts, exiting hastily through windows as well as doors and pursued by vicious guard dogs which were allowed to roam at will during the hours of darkness. There were frequent cases of dog bites and MOs often treated painful wounds in the fleshy part of the buttock where guards habitu- ally bayoneted those who misheard their orders or were slow in responding.

For their part, RAF POWs fought back by tormenting their guards unmercifully, though 'Dixie' Deans was against simply baiting them and preferred properly organized and skilful trouble-making. Need- less to say, this was often difficult to impose on masses of young headstrong aircrew.

There was always a question to be asked about the right balance between antagonizing the Germans and the price to be paid for it. As Man of Confidence, with all the worries and responsibilities that his post entailed, Deans was more aware than most of the consequences that might arise from ill-judged actions. Many POWs who were not so involved resolutely set their faces against all things German and hated them with an intensity born of loathing and contempt.

Sergeant Bruce, like many others, enjoyed any indignity or embar- rassment that could be heaped on the Germans and decided to have no contact with them to the extent of deliberately refusing to learn anything of their language, culture or customs. Many prisoners inside the big, permanent camps felt like this and did everything they could to taunt their captors, as a South African, Squadron Leader Calnan, observed: 'Gamesmanship was a closed book to the Germans; they did not know the rules of the game or appreciate its finesse . . . To us it was an outlet for our frustration and an antidote to our despair. To infuriate our captors, to make them look ridiculous, was the best morale-builder we had. The satisfaction of winning a small and temporary victory was very sweet and gave renewed courage, during the blacker days of the war.'

Behind this lay a further consideration because the Germans were forced to use precious troops in administering and guarding POW camps where the inmates were difficult to handle and caused a great deal of trouble. There were few indeed who could better RAF kriegies in such bloody-minded activity.

6

SAILORS IN CAGES

THE CENTRAL RESPONSIBILITY for services to British POWs and their relatives was undertaken by the British Red Cross Society and Knights of St John of Jerusalem War Organization, set up by mutual agreement between these voluntary bodies in September, 1939.

Its functions were often misunderstood by the general public during the war. It was not under any direct government control and like the League of Red Cross Societies and the ICRC at Geneva – together comprising the International Red Cross – it pursued a policy of neutrality and independence.

Despite the absence of any request from the armed Services, the Red Cross War Organization had fifteen departments ready to begin work on the day war was declared. As part of these initial plans a POW Department was established in St James's Palace, put at the disposal of the Red Cross by the King, with Lord Clarendon and, later, Major-General Sir Richard Howard-Vyse as Chairman.

During the war this Department became the largest of all Red Cross and St John activities and its greatest service was in the despatch of parcels to prisoners. Before August, 1940, they were addressed individually to prisoners but in response to greatly increased numbers, and frequent changes of camp location, parcels were later sent in bulk to the ICRC at Geneva for distribution to the camps.

The statistics of Red Cross supplies to British POWs stagger the imagination: over 19,000,000 food parcels, each to the value of 10/- (50 p), packed at some twenty-three centres in the United Kingdom involved the purchase of enormous quantities of raw materials; almost 1,643,000 special parcels for sick POWs despatched between 1942 and 1945 and 39,758 medical parcels sent to camps in the last two years of war together with twelve dental units, each containing the essentials for establishing a dental surgery and laboratory.

Financing these vast quantities of goods was the direct responsibility of the Red Cross. Early on it had been decided that the whole energy of the British people ought to be harnessed for services to POWs rather than relying on a wealthy few. This policy was triumphantly vindicated with over sixty-four million pounds collected in small donations, gifts and grants to the Duke of Gloucester's

Appeal in England and Wales, the Scottish Council of the British Red Cross in Scotland and Ulster Gift Fund.

Many successful ways of raising money were devised. Workers donated voluntarily from their wages to the Penny-a-Week Fund source; flag days throughout the United Kingdom and cinema collections brought in large sums; Joe Davis played exhibition games of billiards and Henry Cotton promoted the Red Cross in golf tournaments; money poured in from sales of produce in village halls up and down the nation, from schools and churches, from darts players – who raised over two hundred thousand pounds between them – and from sources such as Hutchinsons, the publishers, who gave £500 on account of royalties from the English edition of Hitler's *Mein Kampf*.

In addition to the main parcel packing centres every county and most large towns and regimental associations established local next-of-kin parcels centres in the early months of 1941. Staffed by married women with families or the physically disabled and men over sixty years of age, they played a vital part in packing and despatching the four clothing parcels which relatives could send to POWs each year. To every parcel was added a slab of chocolate while prohibited articles were removed and returned to relatives – including, in one case, a pair of underpants with a large 'V', for victory, embroidered on the seat.

Prisoners who received no next-of-kin parcels did not miss out; they were 'adopted' by charitable persons and organizations and so received their share. Special gift parcels were sent to non-adopted prisoners. The men for whom this massive effort was expended were what one Member of Parliament called 'the most depressed British subjects in the world'. They came to rely absolutely upon the precious supplies of food and comforts from home. Among them were the men imprisoned at Marlag Nord.

Morale had remained high at Stalag XB, Sandbostel, though with over 2,000 men of the RN and Merchant Marine housed in the same compound it had been difficult to maintain strict naval discipline. While the Merchant Marine men were, in Captain Wilson's words, 'more or less under the wing of the Navy', he confessed, 'I would greatly prefer to be on our own as a purely naval camp!' Even so, there had arisen occasional problems with his own men, as when he was forced to recommend fifteen days in the 'cooler' for Leading Stoker K—— of the *Rawalpindi* who 'has been a constant nuisance in the camp', and had struck a Chief Petty Officer.

By the autumn of 1941 Wilson and his officers had plumped for the new naval camp at Westertimke rather than going off to Oflags elsewhere and knew that it would be only a matter of time before they would be able to re-establish their RN discipline. Captain Wilson's only problem was the separation of officers from men at the new camp into compounds with guards' quarters and offices between them and little contact between the two. 'I can only assume that the Germans are suspicious of my influence over the Marlag camp, and intend to break it altogether in the new one,' he commented.

He was thus prevented from exercising his full authority after all RN prisoners were sent to Marlag in June, 1942, but Chief Petty Officer Graham, Chief Bosun's Mate at Sandbostel and Man of Confidence in the new men's *lager*, maintained order and morale until various internal dissensions finally saw him replaced by Chief Petty Officer Gissing, from H.M.S. *Seal*, eighteen months later.

In Marlag 'O' the prisoners' accommodation was very reasonable and there was little or no overcrowding until late in 1943 and again during the last few months of war. There were, of course, many petty restrictions but the treatment of POWs by *Kriegsmarine* officers was, thought Wilson, 'distinctly better' than they had experienced in Stalags.

In smaller camps like Marlag Nord it was easier to present a united front to the enemy. 'In this little world of under 200,' wrote Lieutenant-Commander Mercer about Marlag 'O', 'we were fortunate that, due to the high proportion of RNVR Officers, so many walks of life were represented and I have never been in better company in my life. There was a background of self-discipline here, we had little contact with our hosts, and gradually a tolerably stimulating life evolved.'

There were never more than about 1,300 RN prisoners in total in both compounds of Marlag Nord throughout its normal life. Before the influx of POWs from Italy numbers were very small in comparison with many other prison camps with only 137 officers and fifty orderlies in 'O' compound and 488 men in 'M' compound during May, 1943.

The arrival of prisoners formerly in Italian hands increased numbers to 306 officers and 508 men but, after initial difficulties, they were soon assimilated into the smooth running of the camp. In addition, there were a few RAF prisoners who had arrived almost by default, the Germans not knowing quite what to do with them, including fourteen Warrant Officers from Stalag VIIIB who got to Marlag 'O' in August, 1943. Despite the absence of an equivalent naval rank the Germans had decided to send them there following an *O.K.W.* decision that all newly-captured Warrant Officers should go to officers' camps.

'Marlag was run as a ship,' commented Captain Norwood and this applied to both compounds. Twice a day all rooms were swept out and every Saturday morning all furniture was removed and everything scrubbed down. This standard of cleanliness, in true naval fashion, kept down infestations of lice and bed bugs though the latter still appeared despite vigorous activity with mops and brooms.

Cleanliness went hand-in-hand with health in the camp which was the responsibility of the German MO, *Chefarzt* Trautmann, and a Senior British MO, Major Harvey, who got the Marlag sick quarters enlarged to a general hospital for all prisoners at Westertimke. There were sick bays in each compound for the less severely ill, though a shortage of drugs was sometimes a problem.

At Milag there was also a dental unit run by Captain Green whose equipment was confined to a few instruments and very limited amounts of local anaesthetic. When this ran out he could not await further supplies and so developed a technique for extracting loose and abscessed teeth quickly and, he swore, virtually painlessly. His patients did not always approach his chair with equal confidence.

Each week batches of officers and men were taken about half a mile from the camp to a bath-house for the luxury of a warm shower. It was from here that Lieutenant James made his escape, the only successful break among many attempts from Marlag Nord. Other ones were foiled through ill-luck and the special attention which the Germans paid to the camp's security.

The prisoners were normally called out on *appell*, in ranks of three, twice a day and confined to their huts after dark when Alsatian dogs roamed the compounds. But however formidable the obstacles, with unlimited time on his hands the determined prisoner would always find a way round them. Inanimate barriers could be overcome in various ways – human and animal ones were a different matter.

Guard dogs posed a challenge for some prisoners that they could not resist. Sometimes this proved their undoing; at Stalag VIIA, numbers of POWs were bitten so severely when dogs were used to disperse them that the British Government issued a protest in February, 1942. At Stalag Luft III, new prisoners were given a convincing demonstration of what dogs could do. A heavily-padded German guard set off across fields beyond the wire cheered on by the watching kriegies. Two Alsatians were then sent after him. Pulling him to the ground, they savaged him until called off by their handlers. 'It was a solemn thought,' wrote Sergeant Thrower, 'that one of us might be the next victim, and without any padding to save us.'

Yet despite the very real chance of an attack prisoners took extraordinary and, at times, downright crazy risks in baiting them.

One night in Marlag 'M' a friendly guard was invited in for coffee and Canadian biscuits: 'His dog was a black Alsatian, a fierce-looking brute, but well-trained,' recounted Able Seaman Clark. 'He settled down to eat his biscuit and we asked the guard "Does he do any tricks?" "Oh yes. Put half a dozen four-legged stools in a line." He spoke to his hound, and the dog crawled over one stool and under the next and so on. One fellow said he would not hurt you if you did meet him. So the German laughed, saying, "You walk towards him" – the German spoke to the dog and the next minute he was snarling at the fellow. He certainly put the wind up us.'

This unpredictability fascinated some prisoners. In the same compound, Petty Officer Macey witnessed a bizarre and dangerous bet take place:

'A P.O. Telegraphist in our compound reckoned he could scare the living daylights out of one of these dogs and get it to eat chocolate from his hand. Bets flew high and fast on this. However, one day, when a search had been instigated for radios, the dogs and their handlers were also sent in. The P.O. decided this was the time to prove his claim, had a few tots to give himself dutch courage, armed himself with some chocolate and sallied forth like a knight in shining armour to do battle with his adversary!

He found himself a dog and handler and proceeded to put his theories to the test. Down on all fours he went and crawled his way to the dog, ferociously snarling and growling very realistically until he reached it. The dog was obviously very nonplussed, its hackles rose and it too snarled and growled, but instead of straining at the leash to get at the P.O., it kept backing away. The handler was at his wit's end and no matter what he did, the dog still backed away.

The P.O. manfully crawled on until he reached the dog and then changed his tactics to one of friendliness and produced the chocolate. The dog gradually responded to this treatment and the outstretched hand containing the chocolate and eventually his tail started to wag and he took the chocolate from the Kriegie's hand and allowed himself to be fondled and patted. The bet was won and we never saw that particular dog again!'

Nevertheless, the general reaction to guard dogs was one of fear followed by swift flight. Only the Russians had an answer – at least, according to a story recounted scores of times by Allied prisoners.

It matters little where the incident took place because the camps where it was supposed to have happened are legion. One dark night a dog handler slipped his animal off its leash and sent it racing into the Russian compound after some disturbance. The dog failed to return. In the light of early morning a skin was seen hanging on the wire accompanied by a roughly-scribbled note: 'Thank you for the extra food', it read. 'May we please have more of the same?'

The human element in preventing escapes from Marlag Nord was the presence of security staff. At Marlag Nord they were highly organized. The prisoners' greatest opponent there was the Assistant Defence Officer, *Leutnant* Güssefeld, 'whose presence in the camp,' read a note of protest from the British Government in July, 1944, 'is clearly incompatible with the correct treatment of prisoners of war'.

A journalist in the United States before the war, Güssefeld could be spotted prowling about the camp at all hours. Together with the other security officer, *Leutnant* Schoof, they made a formidable team. Güssefeld's sharp intelligence ensured that only the best-laid plans had any chance of success though his usually excellent English could sometimes break down under the strain of events. One widely-quoted saying passed into naval folklore at Marlag; unable to discover anything after an extensive search of both the barracks and prisoners he is said to have shrieked at a group of grinning officers, 'So! you think I know fucking nothing. Well, let me tell you, I know fuck all!'

One item which he never put out of action was the secret radio. The German security team at the camp enjoyed some success hunting it down but as one set was confiscated another was being smuggled into camp. It was kept in the canteen, inside a beer barrel which had been cut in half and fixed so that the barrel could easily be opened. There were several 'Klim' tins fitted together so that if any curious German turned the tap, weak beer flowed out. News was regularly taken down and read out in the usual way.

When representatives of the three compounds met every few days at the central stores for supplies it was a relatively simple matter for the RN men to barter for wireless parts and, on occasion, complete sets. Those merchant seamen who were out on working parties had easy access to such items.

As time went on searches became less intense. In the last six months at Marlag 'O', Lieutenant Cambell, who ran the illicit news agency, openly carried around a large radio set in a box with two or three records on top and a gramophone in the other hand. 'I worked on the principle that the more open you were, the less chance you had of being caught,' he wrote, 'I never lost it and indeed carried it across Germany . . . at the end.'

Apart from one or two bitterly-disliked *Abwehr* intelligence specialists like Güssefeld, relationships between POWs and guards were relatively civilized. Captain Wilson struck up a mutually sympathetic relationship with the Kommandant, *Kapitän zur See* Schuur (four-ringed naval captain), who took over from Spiehs while they were at Sandbostel. Very short and stout, he was promptly nicknamed 'Grumpy' (from one of Walt Disney's seven dwarves) or, more subtly, '*Das Taschenschlachtschiff*' (the 'pocket battleship'). To the Senior Ratings he was 'Poop Doc Pappy'.

The bond between the two men, based on mutual respect, was evident when Wilson learned that he was about to be replaced in March, 1944: 'He gave me a most friendly farewell and thanked me for

1. Rustic entrance to Oflag XXIB, Schubin.

2. The prisoner's view – inner gates of Stalag VIIIB.
On the right are four RAF POWs just released
from the bunker which is behind the hut.

3. A delegate of the Protecting Power, Herr Narville,
talks to an RAF Sergeant at Stalag Luft III in 1942.
Group Captain Massey, the SBO, in centre with muffler,
looks on anxiously.

4. Prisoners at an open-air boxing match at Stalag Luft III.

5. Bringing up one barrack block's daily portion of soup
at Stalag IIIA, Luckenwalde. Blankets airing on the barbed wire.

6. Daily rations at Stalag VIIIB. The *year* of baking was stamped into loaves.
Seated at table is 'Tex', a Canadian. Behind him, two army prisoners
in RAF guise who exchanged identities.

7. Small market stall at Stalag VIIIB with prisoners
hoping to raise the price of a few cigarettes.
Note pipe out of window made from tin cans
received in POW parcels and connected to highly
efficient cooker built by prisoners inside block.

8. 'Ukraine Joe' Kissel, feared by POWs at Stalag VIIIB,
about to get on his bicycle. This photograph, like all
the others in his collection, was taken by W. A. Lawrence
using a primitive secret camera hidden in an empty
Red Cross parcel box carried under his arm.
There was no viewfinder and the tilt on this picture
is caused by Lawrence's nervousness.

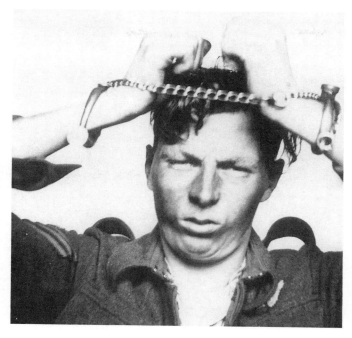

9. Jack Diamond forced to wear handcuffs
at Stalag VIIIB during the chaining period, 1942–3.

10. Daily chores – Army POWs collecting refuse
from Block 10, Stalag VIIIB.

11. Grim-faced American POWs arrive at Stalag Luft III.

12. A prisoner cranks the wheel of a 'blower'
at Stalag VIIA, April, 1945.

13. British prisoners march away
from Oflag IX A/Z, Rotenburg, April, 1945.

14. A Swedish Red Cross official accompanies prisoners
from Rotenburg atop his car piled high with luggage.
He photographed the march from Oflag IX A/Z.

15. Oflag IX A/Z's Medical Officer dealing with an injury to a fellow POW while on the march.

16. A group of elderly German guards assemble on the march from Rotenburg shortly before becoming POWs themselves.

17. Henken and *Fregattenkapitän* Rogge, seeking a ceasefire around Marlag und Milag Nord, are led blindfold to the British lines by two gleeful British soldiers.

18. Liberation! Prisoners from Oflag IX A/Z meet American troops, April, 1945.

19. Release from Oflag 79.
Troops of the United States 9th Army arrive in April, 1945.

20. Two British ex-POWs give instructions to the Red Cross driver
of a 'White Angel' lorry about parcel deliveries to
outlying *Arbeitskommandos* on 29 April, 1945.

21. British officers interrogating former guards while a Russian ex-POW
in rags listens at Stalag XIB on 14 April, 1945.

22. French ex-prisoners lead their former guards into captivity
near Fallingbostel on 17 April, 1945.

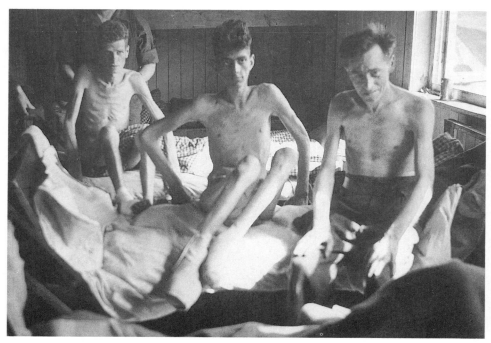

23. The stark results of malnutrition amongst prisoners
liberated at Stalag IIB on 20 April, 1945.

24. A cheerful group of British ex-POWs cross the aerodrome at Lübeck
on their way home in Lancasters of 635 Squadron, 11 May, 1945.

my help. Schuur is a very hot-tempered, obstinate little man, and completely ruthless to friends or foes in achieving his aims. He has, however, the saving grace of a sense of humour, and has done his best to provide us with decent quarters and internal amenities. We have had many disputes, but our personal relations have always been friendly. On the whole I am, at the moment, sorry that he has gone, though the rest of the camp thinks that they have got rid of an ogre!'

Schuur's replacement was *Fregattenkapitän* Schmidt and Wilson found him equally friendly. In April, 1945, there came a final change when *Korvettenkapitän* (naval commander) Rogge took over as Kommandant. A regular *Kriegsmarine* officer who had retired from the active list, he had been a prisoner of the British at Dartington Hall for eighteen months during the First World War.

It may have been the memory of that imprisonment, and certainly his own innate sense of honour, that endeared Rogge to many prisoners. While acting as lager officer he had conveniently ignored or 'forgotten' harsh orders from higher authority. One of them which he failed to implement afflicted prisoners in many camps.

Following the discovery by German intelligence of messages written as morale-boosters on the back of some tinned-food labels by packers at home, the order was sent to all prisoners that POWs should continue to receive their Red Cross supplies but not the containers.

Thereafter, tinned food was tipped out and the resultant mess of powdered coffee, herrings in tomato sauce, sardines, powdered and condensed milk, biscuits, jam, salmon, margarine and cheese handed to the prisoners. Rogge managed to ignore this order until absolutely forced to do so and, even then, caused food to be kept in separate piles. As for the puncturing of tins with bayonets before handing them out in order to prevent their use by prisoners as air-pumps in escape tunnels, this did not occur at Marlag Nord though the practice was widespread elsewhere.

Successive Kommandants at Marlag und Milag Nord were of a spiritedly independent frame of mind which led them to question *O.K.W.* Orders – never an easy thing to do – and to allow discussion over what might and might not be done in compounds.

In May, 1943, for example, Wilson saw Schuur to tell him that he would allow no RN officers to go to Katyn. In that dark Polish forest 1,700 graves had been uncovered and the Germans were desperately anxious to put before the Western Allies evidence of this alleged Russian massacre of Polish officers and intellectuals. Schuur took the matter no further but simply referred it back to *O.K.W.* Eventually, word was received by the SBO that, while the *Wehrmacht* 'would very much like us to go, there would be no compulsion'.

Similarly, when William Joyce visited Dulag Nord on 27 March,

1944, some RN officers were forced to see him, though they gave him a rough reception. However, when the Kommandant told Wilson that two members of the British Free Corps were at the camp and were to visit compounds on orders from Berlin, Wilson protested vigorously: 'I did not wish traitors to come into the camp. The Kommandant said he understood my point of view and would arrange for them to go to the Vorlager only.' The matter was not pressed and most prisoners had no idea that two members of that ill-fated organization were at Marlag Nord.

The men whom *Fregattenkapitän* Schmidt banned from Marlag Nord were part of a dissolute and rather pathetic bunch of prisoners. How they came to be in their unenviable position involved events beyond their reckoning, compromised their honour and led them to abandon their colleagues in prison camps.

As the war turned against Germany her Nazi leaders began to portray her role as that of a bulwark of the West against the Soviet hordes. 'I . . . consider it my duty to offer my services in the common European struggle against Bolshevism,' read the opening lines on the application form signed by volunteers for the British Free Corps.

This same appeal was made to the Allies but it came rather late in the day after the demand for unconditional surrender of the Axis Powers at Casablanca in January, 1943. Nevertheless, the Germans began a recruitment drive for men to fight against the Russians and some prisoners were seduced by it.

There were not many of them – only some thirty or so – who were drawn from their allegiance to the British crown but there were enough sincere fascists and rather more 'rogues and madmen' to form the nucleus of what became known as the British Free Corps.

The formation of this body owed more to the corrupting tongues of William Joyce and John Amery, another notorious traitor, than to any genuine commitment to fascism and to the defeat of Bolshevism among the prisoners whom they recruited. After working with internees, Joyce turned his malevolent attention to the men at Milag Nord and then fixed upon prisoners from the Royal Navy.

At first the Germans were satisfied with a few British prisoners who were brought to the microphone, some of them temporarily unbalanced by the shock of battle and capture, but serious recruiting steps were taken from 1942 onwards. Special 'holiday' camps were established in the following year with decent conditions to where promising candidates could be sent. One for officers was known as Special Detachment 999, set up in a suburban Berlin villa at Zehlendorf, and the other for NCOs and other ranks was attached to Stalag IIID and established in the suburb of Steglitz.

The Germans were careful to approach men whom they thought likely to respond to this free vacation, perhaps men who had been especially hard-worked or in poor health. Gentle propaganda was carefully introduced at the special camps to persuade them to broadcast on the Propaganda Ministry's radio station beaming its English services to Britain and into prison camps throughout the Reich.

The sudden transition to a decent standard of living coupled with a return to the primitive conditions of regular camp life, together with the promise of more good things if the POW would only make a few more broadcasts, worked better on men who were temperamentally suited to this kind of treatment rather than threats.

There is little point in raking over the sordid details of the gullible, weak and plain mad who broke their allegiance. But the British Free Corps, which grew from the twenty or so members of the League of St George established in December, 1943, enjoyed Hitler's express approval, though John Amery lost all interest in the venture as it moved from a propaganda to a fighting role.

In June, 1944, there suddenly appeared in Allied camps a recruiting leaflet written by a member of the RAMC taken prisoner in France four years earlier. Formerly a member of the British Union of Fascists, he transferred to the *Waffen SS* and was serving with them when he was drafted to the BFC. This leaflet caused some hilarity and considerable offence among POWs. It read:

> As a result of repeated applications from British subjects from all parts of the world wishing to take part in the common European struggle against Bolshevism authorisation has recently been given for the creation of a British volunteer unit.
>
> The British Free Corps publishes herewith the following short statement of the aims and principles of the unit.
>
> 1) The British Free Corps is a thoroughly British volunteer unit, conceived and created by British subjects from all parts of the Empire who have taken up arms and pledged their lives in the common European struggle against Soviet Russia.
>
> 2) The British Free Corps condemns the war with Germany and the sacrifice of British blood in the interests of Jewry and International Finance, and regards this conflict as a fundamental betrayal of the British people and British Imperial interests.
>
> 3) The British Free Corps desires the establishment of peace in Europe, the development of close friendly relations between England and Germany, and the encouragement of mutual understandings and collaboration between the two great Germanic peoples.

4) The British Free Corps will neither make war against
Britain or the British Crown, nor support any action or policy
detrimental to the interests of the British people.

Published by the British Free Corps

This anti-Semitic and anti-Soviet appeal cut no ice at all with the vast
mass of POWs though many of them brought home a copy as a
reminder of their captivity. In some camps a most practical use for the
leaflets was devised. They were collected into neat bundles, skewered
through with string, and hung in lavatories.

The BFC was administered by those gentle guardians, the SS. As
for the German authorities they had few illusions that they could
recruit enough renegades to form a fighting unit. They simply put
these volunteers into uniforms, complete with silver-edged black cuff
bearing the legend 'British Free Corps' in gothic characters and Union
Jack shield and, as Rebecca West stated, 'let them go rotten with
idleness and debauchery'.

Quite what else to do with them remained a problem. Some visited
a number of camps including Thorn, Posen, Marienburg and Lamsdorf and they made an extensive tour of the Austrian Stalags early in
1944. At Marlag und Milag Nord they were aided by Güssefeld and
Schoof, who circulated leaflets in compounds and tried, unsuccessfully, to arrange interviews with the prisoners.

When the Allies landed in France, all BFC volunteers were recalled
to their headquarters at Hildesheim. They never returned to the camps
because the Germans decided that the invasion had so raised prisoners'
morale that it was no longer worthwhile trying to recruit them.

Early in 1945 the Corps was sent from Dresden, where they had
been on show, to Berlin. 'We had nothing to do there,' one of them
said, 'and we all used to get around town all day visiting hotels, cafes,
etc.' At the end of the war they were brought back to England, some
to escape scot-free and others to be tried by court-martial where they
received sentences varying from six months' to life imprisonment. In
the civil courts, Joyce and Amery were sentenced to death for their
treachery.

The Germans also made somewhat half-hearted attempts to win
over Irish POWs from their allegiance to the Allies. In mid-1940 the
Irish Republican Army Chief of Staff, Sean Russell, visited camps
hoping to recruit about 200 prisoners for an 'Irish Guard'. For a while
the Germans failed to respond to this idea but shortly after Russell's
death three men took up his cause.

Jupp Hoven, who had spent some time in Ireland before the war on
intelligence work for the *Abwehr* and German Foreign Office, Helmut

Clissman, formerly a student at Trinity College, Dublin, and a German I.R.A. associate of Russell's, Frank Ryan, began to organize a new Irish Brigade with the active help of the Reich authorities. Hoven spent much time screening supposedly potential recruits but many Irishmen affected false sympathy for the venture simply to enjoy the better living accommodation they had heard about.

Prisoners who passed Hoven's scrutiny were taken to Luckenwalde camp, twenty-five miles south of Berlin. But this first attempt proved a fiasco. Three of the nine officers arriving there carried with them MI9 codes which they used to send home detailed information. A number of others were clearly not subversive material and only one man (who was actually a journalist) was sent on to the special camp set up six miles from Friesack, where he joined other members of the Irish Brigade.

The camp near Friesack was divided into 'dams', where men of different nationalities were screened before being trained in sabotage. The Irish inmates suffered from primitive conditions and were clothed in rags. Many were 'Liverpool Irish', having worked in England before joining up for war service. Very few were defectors in the real sense and would, no doubt, have made poor material had they been used on clandestine operations. As it turned out, the Germans had few illusions either. On two occasions the *Abwehr* planned to send Irishmen from Friesack on secret radio and sabotage work in London and Glasgow but Berlin cancelled both operations.

By November, 1943, they had been dispersed to other POW camps and Lieutenant-Colonel John McGrath, the Irish Commandant, was in Dachau after leading the Germans a wild goose chase. He 'played up the Gestapo wonderfully', wrote Captain Payne-Best who knew of him in concentration camps. Not everyone possessed the same integrity, however. In a letter of 14 April, 1945, which was smuggled to Payne-Best while he was in Dachau, McGrath put the finger on Colonel R.S.S.——— who was 'the biggest Rotter I have ever heard of', and at Friesack 'talked and talked' to the Germans, giving them all the information about Allied covert operations he possessed.

There were few such successes for the Germans. They tried again to indoctrinate Irish POWs by concentrating about 1,000 of them at Luckenwalde in the late summer of 1944 and subjecting them to anti-British propaganda. Once more they were persuaded to give up their efforts by an absolute resistance to IRA appeals for recruits and threats against BFC members patrolling outside the wire. All the prisoners were returned to their permanent camps by January, 1945. Their place was taken by South African POWs from whom the BFC attempted to draw recruits, again without much success.

Well removed from these tawdry events, other POWs enjoyed

spells at holiday camps which reintroduced them to a way of life they had all but forgotten. There appeared to be no reason other than to demonstrate that German imprisonment was not universally miserable and as proof to the Allies of the Germans' concern for the welfare of their prisoners.

In August, 1943, word reached the War Office that British prisoners were being sent from all over the Reich to special camps around Berlin where they spent three to six weeks of comparative luxury which included sightseeing tours, entertainments and good food.

No direct propaganda was reported by the prisoners fortunate enough to be selected. The camps closed down later in the year but the same conditions were enjoyed by officers who went to a castle in Bavaria, which Captain Wilson learnt of in March, 1944: 'I am assured that it will not be used for propaganda and will be kept on the same lines as at IIID in Berlin. Officers will remain for about five weeks after which they will return to their original camp. All who go will be volunteers.'

Officers who returned in June reported that it was 'a great success' and though Wilson originally refused to go himself he eventually travelled to Schloss Steinburg at Major-General Fortune's direct request. While there he saw Westhoff, who 'gave a good impression', attended a performance by a quartet from the Bavarian Symphony Opera Company and enjoyed parole walks in pleasant countryside. Unfortunately, before he returned to Marlag there came orders from higher authority which restricted these jaunts, forbade drinking at the local Gasthaus and banned visits to places of entertainment. The prisoners were told that these measures were to avoid entanglements with the SS and prevent them contacting Allied parachutists and agents. Most felt the former was much more likely than the latter.

Another officer from Marlag 'O' who went to Bavaria treasured the few weeks there which 'stand out clearly in the long four years in the featureless camps at Westertimke.' The Schloss itself – actually a comfortable country house in pleasant surroundings – seemed 'quite beautiful to us,' remarked Lieutenant-Commander Mercer, 'after the barbed wire enclosure in the bleak countryside we had grown accustomed to'.

The castle was guarded in an unobtrusive manner but RAF prisoners were excluded because of their current unpopularity with the civilian population. To the senior officers who went out on walks, however, the local people seemed perfectly friendly. How strange all this was occurred to most of the prisoners while they were there: the atmosphere was 'dreamlike', thought Mercer; 'It was probably the most intense period of the war. Germany was being battered from the air, suffering enormous casualties on the East Front and expecting invasion at any time on the West Front; yet here we were in delightful surroundings in an oasis of peace.'

Whatever the German aim in sending officers to this holiday camp, those who were fortunate enough to go found the time there passed all too quickly. Meanwhile, life back at Westertimke followed the usual well-worn grooves of POW life. Prisoners paced around the perimeter – five times round Marlag 'O' equalled two miles – kept their barracks shipshape, attended *appell* and took part in sport, entertainment and educational activities.

'One of the first lessons of captivity is the value of books, and a new realization of how dependent most of us have become on their ministrations,' wrote the Reverend David Read soon after returning from Germany. Despite the creeping paralysis of mind which afflicted most POWs when nothing in the world seemed really worth any kind of effort, much solid reading and examination work was completed at Marlag Nord.

At the end of hostilities, Certificates were handed to POWs as 'a record of educational studies pursued by the holder whilst a Prisoner of War'. Among the many prisoners who had made good use of his captivity was Leading Telegraphist Laurie. His listed a whole range of courses successfully completed, including Parts A and B for London University Matriculation, the City and Guilds of London Institute and the Admiralty Higher Education Test.

Examinations were crucial to the credibility of studies behind barbed wire. While men pursued subjects far removed from their normal civilian occupations simply as a means of passing the time, others wanted some professionally organized examinations which they could sit. 'The most striking phenomenon in officer prisoner-of-war camps in Germany', wrote Captain Harrison, 'was the *demand* for education. It was so widespread as to be universal, and it was also both tenacious and urgent.' The same story was reported from Stalags.

Even on small work detachments library books, musical instruments and organized talks were often available but there were exceptions as at an *Arbeitskommando* where Ordinary Seaman Gant found that 'Only on Sundays was there any sort of get together and even then there was little activity apart from cards, chess, letter writing and so on. No type of educational facilities whatsoever were available and no religious instruction.'

In order to cope with the demand for education facilities elsewhere the Educational Books Section of the Red Cross and St John War Organization's POW Department began sending books to individual prisoners in Germany early in 1940 and set up camp libraries. As the years went by the demand for fiction dropped and that for history, biography and the classics increased.

Difficulties in purchasing books from publishers subject to war regulations had to be overcome and two sets of Censors satisfied. Virtually all publications containing navigational and meteorological charts, tide tables, sailing books and similar items were prohibited by the British Censor from transmission abroad. Every volume had to pass through the Educational Book Section where each mark and map was removed before dispatch. No second-hand book could be sent by a prisoner's relatives.

Additionally, books by Jewish authors and those describing escapes were forbidden by the German authorities and volumes dealing with such ticklish questions as totalitarianism, freedom, democracy and liberty were sometimes returned by them. On the other hand, there were ways of evading censorship and, as one camp librarian wrote, 'the only banned work we never succeeded in obtaining was the most curious of all – the English translation of *Mein Kampf.*' Curiously enough, 'Penguin' paperbacks carrying accounts of POW escapes in World War One were allowed into camps, though later on they were banned because an advertisement on the back page showed a British Tommy with fixed bayonet chasing a cartoon figure of Hitler.

From early in 1942 prisoners were invited to sit for the examinations of over one hundred professional bodies but there were constant difficulties with supplies for the Oxford administrators when everything from paper to microscopes and drawing instruments had to be sent out to camps. A different problem arose for Captain Wilson at Marlag Nord in March, 1944: 'Güssefeld informed me that the papers for the R. Socy. Arts exam in Swahili could not be sent as he was unable to find an interpreter to censor [them].'

Despite many difficulties the examination scheme was a considerable success. By the end of the war in Europe nearly 17,000 applications for examinations had been made in eighty-two camps. Over 10,000 candidates had sat examinations and over seventy-five per cent passed outright. In addition, these were only a small part of studies undertaken by thousands of prisoners; 'their time has not been wasted,' recorded the Education Books Section's Report in 1945; 'they have laboured well and truly.'

Music, acting and sport were the other main activities at Marlag Nord with which prisoners filled their days. The theatre proved immensely popular with officers and, from its inception, a full range of entertainments was put on: 'In the main they were very well done,' thought Lieutenant Cambell, 'and undoubtedly influenced morale and furthermore introduced large numbers of people to shows that they would not have bothered to see at home.'

There was also keen interest in Marlag 'M'. A full programme of amateur theatricals, pantomimes and opera was staged by hard work and clever improvization. Musical instruments arrived from the World Alliance of YMCAs and a first-class orchestra was recruited and trained by a Royal Marine bandmaster who had been captured at Dieppe. Theatrical makeup was a problem, overcome by using talcum powder, margarine and dyes extracted from crêpe paper, while items of dress were loaned by Censor girls who came to see the shows.

Full-size scenery flats were constructed from Red Cross boxes and painted by men who, observed one of those involved, 'discovered their artistic talents while in captivity'. Shows were dressed in the proper manner, using 'liberated' sheets from guards' beds. These were dyed and made up by camp tailors. Later on, when the Germans became suspicious about their vanishing bed linen, a means was discovered of fire-proofing crêpe paper. The stage was equipped with a full set of curtains and tabs – blankets stitched together and embroidered – and the front curtains electrically controlled by a motor removed from the Kommandant's vacuum cleaner.

'It was one of the minor banes of show business in captivity,' wrote one POW, 'that the senior German officers from miles around invited themselves to the opening night of each production. It did, however, lend a certain zest to realize that the officer who had that morning conducted an investigation into the loss of 40 light bulbs, some sheets and blankets, and a vacuum cleaner, could now espy the missing property merely by looking at the stage.'

At permanent camps, some means had to be discovered of distributing limited means among the many competing demands of POWs. In Marlag 'O' communal messing from June, 1943, reduced the problem of equalizing food supplies though attempts at the same time to introduce this scheme in the Senior Ratings' compound failed.

Under Article 23 of the Geneva Convention officers were entitled to receive from the Detaining Power 'the same pay as officers of corresponding rank in the armed forces of that Power' so long as this did not exceed what they would normally have received before capture.

Officers were entitled to sums ranging from about four pounds sixteen shillings per month for a Second Lieutenant rising to eight pounds for a Lieutenant-Colonel. Other Ranks who were not at work received nothing at all apart from some monies transferred into their home accounts. In some camps, including Marlag Nord, officers contributed to funds which assisted them but many men were unable to purchase even the few goods which some canteens stocked such as toothpowder and combs.

Among many natural grievances one thing which particularly incensed naval volunteers and HO ('hostilities only') men was that merchant seamen who had joined the Royal Navy either for the duration of the war or for the whole period of emergency received twice as much as Ordinary Seamen into their accounts because they had what was known as 'danger money' on top of their normal pay.

The pay of officers in captivity was also a bitter source of discontent. In the vast majority of cases they could buy very little or nothing with their *Lagergeld*. Moreover, they were subject to communal fines; whenever the Germans discovered an escape tunnel a large sum was invariably withheld, ostensibly for the purpose of filling it in and repairing damage to Reich property.

Additionally, many POWs received no *Lagergeld* and had no explanation for its non-issue. This happened, for example, at Marlag Nord in October, 1944, when the camp money was withdrawn. In return, credits were supposedly made to officers' deposit accounts by the Germans and senior ratings received *Rentenmark* currency. Neither was advantageous nor satisfactory.

One other matter also affected the payment of POWs and that was rank. As well as 'Stalag promotions' there was much confusion because little information about acting or substantive rank reached camp leaders before the end of 1944. This delay was due to bureaucratic confusion. 'The question of officers' promotions whilst POWs seems to be a little difficult for the German Govt to understand. Indeed, it is not easy for ourselves to understand at times!' wrote one exasperated War Office official in June, 1941.

In Germany Captain Wilson discovered the other end of the same problem with regard to another officer at Marlag 'O'; 'There is some doubt as to our relative seniority, as I do not know whether I retain my confirmed rank during imprisonment.'

Officers and men retained their acting rank on capture and generally reverted to their substantive rank on liberation but there was no steady ladder of promotion inside a POW camp. This meant that regulars' careers remained at a standstill.

In the absence of money as a unit of currency cigarettes became the regulating media of exchange for goods and services. Most trading was for food against cigarettes or other foodstuffs but the cigarette rose above other natural commodities in camps to assume the functions of hard currency. Neither *Reichmarks* nor *Lagergeld* had any kind of circulation except for the payment of gambling debts since they possessed no real purchasing power at the canteen or among individuals.

The subjects of trade and exchange were the contents of Red Cross and next-of-kin parcels. A supply of fifty cigarettes or two ounces of tobacco per week for every British POW was arranged by the Red Cross and St John War Organization – though many did not receive their regular ration. Relatives and friends were able to send special minimum content parcels containing at least four ounces of tobacco or cigarettes through firms in Britain holding special export permits and many former employers also provided gifts.

The availability of cigarettes in permanent POW camps led to a high level of commercial organization with 'Exchange and Mart' noticeboards, where sales and wants were advertised, and shops organized as public utilities. These were controlled by the SBO's representative on a non-profit basis where prisoners left their surplus clothing, toilet requisites and food until they were sold at a fixed price in cigarettes.

In some camps, especially the larger Stalags, cigarette 'barons' flourished who sometimes cornered the market in certain goods and, working on a strict profit basis, amassed a considerable cigarette currency. Price-rings and agreements between traders were not unknown, though, as one officer noted, 'public opinion was hostile and the professionals were usually of a retiring disposition'.

Certain kinds of cigarettes were more popular than others and so those used for trading were rarely brands like Churchman's No. 1 but of an inferior quality such as the truly awful 'Drava' Polish issue. Buyers also had to beware of hand-rolled, 'clipped' or 'sweated' cigarettes, which had been rolled between the fingers so that some tobacco fell out which was used to manufacture more 'currency'. Thin ones might be rejected or others demanded to make up correct amounts but machine-made cigarettes were always acceptable, both to smoke and for what they could purchase.

When supplies were really low heavy smokers turned in desperation to various substitutes including the bark of trees, stripped, shredded and rolled with the aid of makeshift cigarette papers torn from paybooks, old newspapers and even leaves from pocket bibles. The main drawback in using cigarettes as currency was rapid inflation and deflation as stocks arrived from the Red Cross and gradually dwindled away, thereby reducing the volume of trade and increasing bartering which never quite died out.

The whole system was upset due to the disruption of supplies caused by Allied advances in Europe during the latter half of 1944. At Marlag 'M', however, despite large influxes of RAF and American POWs, prices were still generally recognized for trading purposes as late as the first day of 1945, though they had climbed sharply from the previous year. Purchases were debited to men's accounts accumulating at home and high figures were often reached for certain items in strong demand.

Since the Mark had no value, prices tended to be even higher among merchant seaman, as Able Seaman Walker observed: 'Today, 24 February 1945, a man in Milag purchased 100 cigarettes for 1,000

Marks – or 10 Mks, or 13/4d per cigarette.' The price of a packet of twenty cigarettes of reasonable brand at home was 2/4d to the public and only 1/6d to servicemen through the NAAFI. Such high prices reflected quite unmistakably the shortage of supplies at Westertimke.

By no means everyone was happy with this trading and some forms of it were widely condemned, including barter with the Germans for individual gain. Red Cross toilet articles, in short supply, were excluded from trade by law and public opinion. But there was also a widespread feeling that everything had its 'just price' in cigarettes. This varied from camp to camp, was impossible to quantify, yet was known among prisoners to exist. And the only people who suffered adverse public reaction from their fellow POWs in times of cigarette shortages were the non-smokers (who nevertheless received their ration of tobacco and cigarettes from the Red Cross), light smokers and middlemen. On the other hand, they were the prisoners who were least affected by such shortages.

What would be done on returning home – the meals to be eaten, the beer that would be drunk – provided inspiration for countless hours of gossip: 'How much weight one has lost is discussed at length . . . long tirades of all the benefits of camp life which are not our lot to enjoy during captivity,' noted the Reverend John Naylor on Boxing Day, 1944, 'but already most of us realize full well that we shall not for even one occasion tackle the meals we dream and talk about.'

Many prisoners were worried about what would happen after the war: 'Wrote to L——, told her I didn't think things would be the same after this lot,' was Gunner Lenthall's view in September, 1942. The problem of employment bothered men like Private Perry: 'What news we do get hold of is not very pleasing, but I still have a lot of faith in the old country. . . . I might have a hard job of finding work after this packet.' Gunner Folkard was also concerned about this: 'It's one of the things that's worrying me, if I can get a job or not after this, as they will be few and far between I'm afraid.'

Several verses which went the rounds at Milag Nord reflected a determination to resist the evils of pre-war society:

'When the world's at Peace again
And the dark clouds roll away
We'll go marching down the lane
Singing "NIX ARBEIT" today;

When we get home to our goal
And we're all back on the dole
To the means test man we'll say
There's "NIX ARBEIT" today.'

Unlike people at home who grew used to a new sense of security in the industries going full blast for the war effort, prisoners' fears of mass unemployment did not recede; they were still locked into the crippling experience of the 1930s' means test, 'dole' queue and closed factory gates.

To such prisoners the Beveridge Report was of more than passing interest. It pointed the way forward to a world in which the British citizen, under a scheme of social insurance, would be covered from the cradle to the grave. 'We had a very interesting lecture on the Beveridge Plan,' recorded Sergeant Prosser in November, 1943, and Lieutenant Roberts heard of the Report but found it 'difficult to get hold of'.

Gunner Robinson, like other prisoners, dreamed of doing something about such matters when he returned home: 'The last war brought many changes. The working class wanted equality and [in] some degree was listened to. But the thing that is wrong with England, and you don't find it so much in my part of the world, is the middle class and worse still the people who think they are but are hopelessly not . . . their cry being "What's the use, one party is as bad as another". It is obvious you must fight if you want better conditions. I firmly believe that soon a 40 hour week will be in England, bigger pay, smaller families and a general uplift in the mode of living all round. On reading back I think I must be going nuts but I do want to have a try at politics or trade unions when I get back.'

On the other side, some men from comfortable homes began to realize for the first time something about their underprivileged fellow-prisoners: 'It was as if I was learning about a foreign nation, ill-educated, ill-fed, ill-housed and ill-led,' confessed Sergeant Edgar. 'I began to undergo a quiet, slow conversion.'

Some men decided they ought to try their luck elsewhere. Imprisonment with men from other Commonwealth countries broadened their perspectives and suggested fresh alternatives, as in the case of Sergeant Eeles who wrote of 'two choices' confronting him in February, 1945:

One, to go back to my old job, eventually marry and settle down and altogether lead a normal, quiet, comfortable life.

The other is to emigrate. Since being a POW, I've seen a lot of faults with England. Some of the Dominions seem very prosperous, is it possible to make headway at all? It has its difficulties, it would mean leaving home for one thing. By rights, I should show a certain consideration for those at home. I shall never know what anxiety they were through when I was reported missing. I shall make that up to them somehow.

The amount of time available to discuss such matters was very limited on *Arbeitskommandos*. Beyond desultory conversation there was rarely much organized debate because discussion groups after a hard day's work were not very successful. When all the prisoners could think of was food the session often degenerated into argument. An 'old sweat' whom Private Ayling came across at Stalag IVC seems to have beaten the problem, however: 'One of those . . . used to argue that when asleep he wasn't in the camp, and when awake there was no wife to nag him, and in short, it was a grand life.'

There were many POWs for whom, even in their most tongue-in-cheek moments, life was not so grand. Allied military pressure on the Reich was bringing growing danger from the air and severe disruption of internal communications had worsened the already difficult food situation. Attitudes toward the Allied invasion on D-Day, therefore, varied greatly among POWs, from the exultant tone of Trooper Spencer's comment: – 'Rain! Came home early, [to an *Arbeitskommando* attached to Stalag VIIIB] but oh boy! the long awaited Second Front. Great jubilation among the boys! Band and drums for 2 solid hours' – to that of Major Booth: 'The great invasion, so long awaited, now that it has happened, has come almost as an anticlimax, and there has not been nearly so much excitement over it as might have been expected.'

Although liberation was in the air there were some men for whom it had already become a reality. Sometime in 1943 Private Wiseman saw a group of sick and wounded on their way to English shores: 'I had no doubt in my mind that . . . the Germans were feeling the effects of the war terribly,' he wrote. 'We knew that certain prisoners were being repatriated. As they waved us goodbye from a train on an elevated railway line nearby, it hit us hard, very hard. We were under armed guards, they were free.'

Another group of repatriated prisoners lined up before the Kommandant at Marlag Nord on 14 January, 1945: 'They are leaving just after midnight – what a life – and us here with only two parcels issues left – roll on the end,' wrote Able Seaman Walker. What no one could foretell was just when 'the end' would come.

PART THREE

LIBERATION

'England is a fairy tale! No such place exists. I was conceived in a POW camp by POW parents; born in a POW camp; nurtured on turnip skilly and wooden bread; educated — but I'm going crackers.'

Sergeant Nell in his diary, 7 January, 1945.

WOUNDED AND SICK

IN THE AUTUMN of 1943 a first exchange of prisoners took place between Britain and Germany. Men who were left behind were understandably bitter: 'Do you think I shall complete three years here? There is no hope of fit men being repatriated,' wrote Marine Blockley from Marlag Nord, 'you will be having a lot home soon, one leg, one arm, crippled, blind, deaf – I'd rather not be one of those but stay here 'till the end of the war.'

Under Article 68 of the Geneva Convention, nations at war were required to repatriate men who were seriously ill or badly wounded and non-combatants such as medical staff, chaplains and various civilians marooned abroad by the outbreak of hostilities. But to the great frustration of everyone concerned it was only after prolonged negotiations between the British and German Governments, through the Protecting Power, that an exchange of sick and wounded was agreed upon for October, 1941.

A Medical Commission of two Swiss doctors and one German visited prison camps and examined over 1,700 Commonwealth and British prisoners of whom 1,153 were subsequently recommended for repatriation. They were duly collected from camps throughout the Reich and put on trains for Rouen from where they were to be taken to England.

Among that first party was Corporal Hope. There had been 'some rumours about repatriation again' and much speculation as to who would be on the list. After learning that he was to be one of the protected personnel travelling with the sick and wounded he went down with nephritis so it was certain that he would be sent home. 'This is the beginning of freedom,' he wrote after bidding a hurried farewell to friends at Stalag VIIIB.

At Rouen he joined the main body of repatriates housed in a straggling collection of 'Nissen'-type huts on the racecourse where, 'the camp atmosphere seems free and relaxed until, gradually, as the weeks go by, passed also with some sports and hardly any German presence, there begins to steal upon our minds a wondering, then doubt and suspicion. The time is approaching – thoughts of Christmas and where shall we be when it comes?'

Some RAF prisoners became alarmed at the ominous wait and took off; 'We couldn't help feeling they would!', commented Hope. After their recapture the Germans soon put a stop to any more of their efforts by threatening to shoot any civilians found harbouring escapees.

Unfortunately for this first batch of intended repatriates there was to be no happy Christmas by their own firesides. Much publicity had been given to their homecoming in the British Press and expectations were high. To Germany's Foreign Minister, Joachim von Ribbentrop, this seemed a good time to wring concessions out of the British Government. But London remained firm.

On the day before they were due to leave, the repatriates, including Corporal Hope, were rounded up and returned to Stalag XXIA at Shildberg in Poland or to Lamsdorf. 'So! Camp life and hospital duties start again in earnest. A change of town and site is as good as a rest!' The sense of dejection and disappointment was, however, profoundly felt.

Immediately after this near-débâcle the German Government again raised the question of an exchange of prisoners. Uncertain how to respond British officials dragged their feet. 'Any suggestions of delay or indifference in Whitehall . . . are only too readily believed by the prisoners' relatives,' warned Duncan Sandys at the War Office. However, it was not until May, 1943, after several successful exchanges between Britain and Italy, that certain conditions were at last dropped by Whitehall so that 'AVANT PROJET' – as the Swiss, heavily involved in the delicate negotiations, termed the scheme – became a distinct possibility. Nothing about this was known outside No. 1 Report Committee in the War Office's POW Directorate since all publicity was, on the Committee's orders, 'rigorously suppressed' throughout the Commonwealth until final agreement with Germany could be reached.

This sensible course of action had an unexpected result. So well was censorship enforced about the prisoners involved that even relatives had little idea what was happening until one day they suddenly discovered a missing husband, brother or son at their front door.

Lists of prisoners passed for repatriation had been received in advance and the War Office wrote to relatives; but it was at this point where special arrangements were to have been made for men to communicate directly with their next-of-kin that the arrangements broke down: 'There was a certain amount of criticism because the repatriated prisoners of war arrived at their homes from hospitals and dispersal centres unannounced,' noted the Chairman of the British Red Cross Society.

One of the more fortunate who was able to contact home as soon as he reached Leith on 25 October, 1943, was Lance-Corporal McKechnie: 'Arrived safely in England. Going hospital for medical examination. Writing,' read his telegram. McKechnie had been among the prisoners sent to Oflag 64/Z at Montwy in Poland where British repatriates were accommodated in readiness for their journey home. Here the prisoners were issued with luxurious items like knives, forks and spoons, decent beds and bed-linen, though most of them were under no misapprehension that 'this was for propaganda purposes'.

They left Montwy on 16 October by railway carriage in place of the usual cattle trucks. 'High spirits on the part of the repatriates were perhaps revealed,' wrote Hope, 'not so much in excited conversation or in singing . . . but in silent contemplation, a numbed disbelief that, after all, "is this really it?"' Features of everyday life normally taken for granted, such as women and children glimpsed at railway stations, were re-awakened in their minds and was part of the process of re-adaptation which had to begin as soon as they knew they were finally on their way home.

From the island of Rügen the repatriates were taken by boat through the Kattegat to Gothenburg, where over 4,000 of them were transferred to ships; the sick and their medical helpers travelled on the Swedish vessel *Drottningholm*, the mentally ill and protected personnel on the Red Cross's *Atlantis* and *Empress of Russia*.

Escorted by U-boats through the Skagerrak into the North Sea, they were royally treated, though many, including Hope on board the *Drottningholm*, were somewhat overcome: 'The atmosphere of aristocracy to be seen and felt in the first class suites, etc, is most certainly, at least for an ex-prisoner of war, perhaps at first slightly more disturbing than gratifying. The best of everything is at our disposal and this morning I felt rather like a retired veteran, I must say, sleepy, waited upon and sensing that first feeling of over-complacency which we all have at times in civilian life. At the moment possibly it is just all too much journey but most enjoyable because of its ultimate momentous climax.'

It was not until the ship slid under the massive spans of the Firth of Forth bridge that dreams of family and home became a reality:

We already had our embarkation cards, tickets hanging from our great-coat lapels, when Sir Ronald Adam, Army General, came on board to chat and ask questions! Then we were overwhelmed by the crowds! Early morning saw us move in further shorewards, ready for disembarkation by tender. The gang planks leading to the landing stage seemed unusually long and at stages all the way along it, were ladies in uniform representing most official bodies as well as officials of the

Services, nurses, W.V.S., Red Cross personnel, Salvation Army, all of them laden with parcels from which they showered packets of chocolates, cigarettes, fruit, sandwiches, books, newspapers, magazines which our arms would hardly contain . . .

We could hardly notice the 'red carpets' but I saw the huge banner 'Welcome Home' together with the bunting and the myriad Union Jacks and allied flags and heard somehow the band as we set foot on land once more and on British soil at that!

Other men who came ashore at Leith, suffering in mind or body, were not able to appreciate their welcome in the same way. Stretchered ashore or, in one particularly sad group, a number of war-blinded led gently down the gangway, they were taken to reception and rehabilitation centres. Lance-Corporal McKechnie went off to RAF Richmond and Lance-Corporal Rich, who had slogged into captivity on the long trek in 1940, entrained for Netley Hospital, Southampton, with a lung full of tuberculosis contracted at an *Arbeitskommando*.

For all of them the dismal life of a *Kriegsgefangener* was over. No more *appells*, fear, inadequate food, boredom, barbed wire, overcrowding and all the rest of camp life. But for many their first taste of freedom was soured by civic pomposity, lengthy speeches and exposure to newspaper reporters determined to scoop their stories.

At an RAMC Depot near Aldershot a study was made of the repatriates and their comments were recorded. They constituted a sharp reminder of the unsatisfactory way in which the exchange was concluded. As one soldier remarked: 'Being treated like a hero for a few days and then returning to the depot left men with the opinion that they were really being hard done by . . . I suggest that the newspapers made far more of our repatriation than it merited. We didn't expect newspaper reporters, cameras, and civic receptions and our heads were turned by them.'

A widely-held view from another soldier underlined these criticisms: 'The prisoner does not want speeches by people who have no personal interest in him. I was irritated by the propaganda efforts on board ship in Leith which delayed our landing. The newsreel people tried to make us appear what we are not. . . . What a prisoner wants is to get home; anything else is boredom.'

Others repatriates offered more damaging criticisms which deeply concerned the War Office authorities; a common theme was that of military incompetence. One man commented that 'just to get back home' was all a POW dreamed of and added, 'We have had our suffering, now we want to rest and forget it all. We have done our bit for our country and been let down.' Another Rifleman was even more direct: 'In most cases I think you will find that the returned POW has lost his respect for his superior officers. He has been in tight corners with them and has seen the way they have acted, – some were fine – but that was a minority.'

Their insensitive handling also brought out a deep hostility towards desk-bound officials felt by many ex-prisoners. One soldier who had volunteered to remain behind in France in 1940 'because I felt it was my duty', returned home to find the War Office quibbling about his allowances and trying to pay the lowest possible sum. 'This makes a man a little bitter,' he added, with considerable self-restraint.

While there was much food for thought in the untidy conclusion to this first exchange between Britain and Germany, the War Office turned down an offer from the Red Cross to mount a series of lectures throughout the United Kingdom on returned ex-POWs and their care. Meanwhile, repatriates like the Sergeant Major who had been a leading light in his Stalag but found he could not cross Shaftesbury Avenue unaccompanied were left to fend for themselves.

Among the bleakly humorous captions from prisoners' letters said to have been sent by insensitive next-of-kin was one which read: 'The first lot of "repats" arrived home terribly maimed. I hope you are amongst the next lot.'

That there would be another exchange was clear after the success of the first one and the lessons learnt then made later exchanges somewhat less confusing and exhausting for the men involved.

Shortly before the repatriation of 943 British and Commonwealth ex-POWs in the American ship *Gripsholm*, which docked at Liverpool on Whit Sunday, 1944, Red Cross bureaux were set up at hospitals and at dispersal centres where arrangements could be made to notify their relatives when men were on their way home and to organize the travel arrangements.

These practical plans went hand in hand with a strong over-reaction by the military authorities when a secret cipher telegram reached the War Office with news that embarkation on the *Gripsholm* had been very loosely controlled at Barcelona, incomplete and inaccurate nominal rolls compiled and unauthorized persons had possibly acquired British battledress. As a consequence, strict precautions to identify Service and civil personnel on disembarkation were put into effect. The dock area at Belfast was cordoned off by two hundred military police, special passes were issued and reporters were not allowed into the restricted area, nor were they able to approach individual ex-POWs for direct interviews.

Such measures did not stop the Press trying 'every underhand method to evade the restrictions ordered by the War Office', reported the GOC, Northern Ireland, while British and American reporters were furious at what they termed the 'drastic restriction' they encountered. Even a BBC van was unable to get close enough to record Churchill's speech of welcome.

Tight security and strict censorship of all stories, films and photographs, which had to be submitted to the Ministry of Information before publication, ensured a smooth passage for the repatriates and also kept the men from Stalag Luft III, who were thought to be carrying valuable information, incommunicado until they could be contacted at Liverpool by a special interrogator from the security services. Other men went on to the London District Assembly Centre and then to hospital and dispersal centres for home leave.

The journey from German camps was not, however, without at least one tragedy. While on a special train to Marseilles, Pilot Officer C——, suffering from a mental disorder, slipped away from his Red Cross attendants at Lyon railway station and jumped on to the tracks. After a rapid search, the train had to continue without him. What finally became of him remains a mystery.

The difficulties of moving trainloads of POWs across south-west France while avoiding Allied air strikes and the activities of the Maquis, together with the start of operation 'ANVIL' (Allied landings in the south of France in August, 1944) which cut off routes to and from the Iberian peninsula, meant that once again the Swedish port of Gothenburg would be used, instead of Lisbon or Marseilles, for the third exchange.

In a complicated exercise the *Gripsholm* sailed from the United States with German POWs in August, 1944, to Gothenburg, where she was met by the *Drottningholm* and the British vessel, *Arundel Castle*. A series of precautions taken to avoid mistaken attacks included full night-time illumination. Both the *Arundel Castle*, which had her breech blocks removed to disable her guns, and the *Drottningholm* carried the word 'PROTECTED' prominently on their hulls, together with their national colours. Sailing to a strictly agreed route they were met at a pre-arranged rendezvous by a German minesweeper and took on board over 1,800 sick and wounded troops and protected personnel and 552 civilian internees.

When they reached Gothenburg they were received by Count Folke Bernadotte who acted as an intermediary between the British and Germans. A nephew of the King of Sweden, he was elected Vice-President of the Swedish Red Cross in the spring of 1943 and played a vital part in the exchange of prisoners. It was his signature which accepted responsibility, on behalf of the ICRC, for both groups at the actual point of exchange.

One of the British repatriates was Lance-Corporal Sollars who travelled from Stalag IVB on a stretcher suffering from spinal tuberculosis. He found it hard to believe that the Swedes were neutral, so great was their welcome, with officials standing at attention as their train passed through stations *en route* to Gothenburg. 'Suddenly one realized one was a man once more, and not merely a cipher behind barbed wire,' he told a reporter.

At Gothenburg, girls from the British colony distributed copies of *PoW-WoW* – standing for 'Prisoner of War – Warmest of Welcomes' – a news-sheet put together specially for British repatriates. Unknown to the Germans, two prisoners from Lamsdorf, who had kindly helped the disabled to stack their luggage on leaving camp, had craftily carried on their good work and managed to accompany the party right across Germany. Once on board ship they gave themselves up to the captain. One of the few who knew of their presence, Able Seaman Garbutt, presumed that they were interned in Sweden until the war was over. 'A very good and daring escape,' he thought.

While they were in Gothenburg, the German orderlies seemed keen to assure Allied POWs that they were anti-Nazi and returning German prisoners receiving a homecoming which explained why. At Sassnitz, on the German border, an over-zealous local *Gauleiter* harangued them for three-quarters of an hour on the military and political situation inside Germany.

Rather different was the welcome to England. It began in Sweden with a personal letter from Sir Victor Mallet, the British Minister in Stockholm: 'You are returning home at a moment when the enemy you have so stoutly fought is broken and on the run,' read part of his message. This was repeated in newspaper reports after the *Arundel Castle* steamed into Liverpool, followed by the *Gripsholm* and *Drottningholm*, to a massive reception from officials and relatives, accompanied by a shrill chorus of Merseyside ferries and overhead salute from a Spitfire dipping low. 'The repatriates were in great spirits,' reported the *Liverpool Daily Post*, 'they know that victory is not far off, and had themselves seen the steadily drooping morale of their German guards and the German people.'

As for the ex-POWs themselves, they were glad to be out of things and at home – or, at least, very close to it, as Lance-Corporal Sollars explained from his hospital bed: 'Everything here is all that one could wish. How long I shall stay I do not know, but it is sufficient to be on English soil at present and I am not worrying.'

The planning for a further exchange of prisoners was beset with enormous difficulties. SHAEF (Supreme Headquarters Allied Expeditionary Force, Europe) could not guarantee the safety of the special hospital trains needed to take prisoners through southern Germany to Switzerland and on to Marseilles. RAF Bomber Command, too, threw a spanner in the works at the last moment by demanding absolutely precise timings of movements of trains to avoid strafing them.

Despite these problems, early in the New Year POWs began to assemble from various camps. At Eichstätt, Captain Mansell recorded, 'A big thrill today when it was suddenly announced that 15 *Grands Blessés* officers and 4 orderlies are to leave for home tomorrow after lunch. I'm quite convinced in my own mind that everything possible is being done to repatriate old prisoners, but I'm equally convinced that one of the chief stumbling blocks is lack of transport in Germany. I wonder what it feels like to be told that you are starting on your return journey tomorrow. It must take quite a time for the realization of it to sink in and, once it does, there must be a fearful dread that something will turn up in the meanwhile to stop it. That must be frightful.'

Fortunately, nothing did turn up and by February all the difficulties had finally been resolved. The *Arundel Castle* and *Letitia* picked up 1,940 British, Commonwealth and American repatriates who were brought to Liverpool. Among them were some of the 1,400 airborne 'Red Devils', wounded and left at Arnhem, whom the British Government particularly wished to see home.

Various plans were begun for a fifth exchange at the suggestion of the United States' War Department but a shortage of hospital ships, fully occupied in transporting a backlog of Allied casualties from Italy to Britain and America, and delay in receiving any reply from the German Legation at Berne, overtook these negotiations. General Eisenhower also reported from SHAEF on 18 April that, because of the fluid tactical situation, it would be difficult to guarantee repatriates from air attack, whether they were travelling by road or rail, and that Allied advances in the next few weeks would be likely to uncover many of the camps where the sick and wounded were located whom the Germans might consider eligible for exchange.

There was a commonly held rumour in prison camps that plans were afoot to repatriate long-term prisoners. 'The last news I've heard so far,' wrote Private Little in August, 1944, 'is that after we have been prisoner for five years we go to a neutral country to work until the war is over.' A similar scheme came to the notice of Wing Commander McCarthy-Jones early in 1945:

Lots of stories about re-pat of old kriegies going around the camp. Hope they are true, they are usually without foundation. I have done 17 months myself and it seems like a lifetime so hope some of the older kriegies from 3 to over 5 years do get a break.

Am pretty brassed off these days as the war seems endless and instead of us doing all the attacking the G[erman]s seem to have initiative and except in Hungary the R[ussian]s are doing very little. Can't believe I shall ever see home again somehow but know it's a foolish thought. In most optimistic moments put end of war about next September.

This proposal had surfaced so many times that experienced POWs such as Lieutenant Roberts were wearily cynical of it. 'I'm afraid that our reception of Red X announcements regarding repatriation – especially of old kriegies – during and after the end of the war is not what may be called polite. We've heard them so many times in this last four and a half years. We're all resigned to its being a long time, whatever we'd like it to be.'

Yet there was provision made under the Geneva Convention to do just this and a proposal, in January, 1945, did come up to the Chiefs of Staff and War Cabinet in London. It was, however, abandoned upon the rapid disintegration of German military resistance in the west.

The sense of inactivity for prisoners still in captivity was heightened by the sight of repatriates on their way home. 'They left a gap. We all lost friends,' commented Second Lieutenant Baxter and frustrations increased as the war dragged on.

To men still behind barbed wire the dogged German resistance seemed bitterly perverse. 'The war must end soon,' considered Sergeant Nell in August, 1944, 'The Russians will soon be in Germany and so far they have had nothing to stop them. Unless Germany admits the Russians and turns Communist the war must end in the next few weeks. At their present rate of advance the Russians will be here in about two weeks. If that happens and the Germans don't evacuate us the Russians will "swipe" us. But will they repatriate us? I am rather afraid that Churchill would object to the Russians taking over Germany, in which case Britain and Germany may go to war with Russia. I daren't think of this happening.'

These same questions were in the mind of every prisoner. With the Reich visibly crumbling, how much longer would their imprisonment last and who would win the race to liberate them? And over all hung another dark cloud – could they hold on until conquering armies reached them or would they perish from malnutrition, in Allied air attacks, or at the hands of the *SS*? Whatever happened, for many it was going to be an unconscionably near-run thing.

8

WIR KOMMEN!

IN THE EARLY days of the Allied bombing offensive prisoners rejoiced when they saw high above them formations of aircraft dragging condensation trails in their wake, winging their way to deal death and destruction somewhere in the Reich.

Gradually, however, war came to the camps themselves. 'First priority on arriving at work sites in the mornings – where is [the] nearest air raid shelter? – we run on hearing overhead alarm, nothing improved our performance like the sight of those B17s passing over,' recalled Trooper Jameson. 'My God how we ran.'

Signaller Warsop was one of many POWs forced to clear up railway débris after a very heavy raid on Halle on 31 March, 1945. They hated this task because their secret radio repeatedly carried BBC reports warning German and foreign workers to keep away from transport routes, considered prime targets by the RAF. Their work was constantly disrupted by air raid alarms when they were allowed to return to their own shelter. It was rumoured among them that Halle had been declared an open city but they were not sure if the RAF knew this as well. 'It was quite possible that they would do the opening themselves,' commented Warsop, 'wide open too.'

Air raid precautions varied widely. In some camps the men were shut in their barracks during raids and told to keep away from the windows. There were a number of tragic incidents when prisoners were shot for disobeying or misunderstanding these orders. 'Have been air-raid alarms,' wrote Major Booth in March, 1944. 'POWs have to remain indoors during these. Two officers shot dead by guards when caught outside – second shot while trying to bring first back to barracks.'

While at Stalag Luft VII Sergeant Tomblin recorded another need-less death: 'We were under the flight [path] from Italy to Russia and had been warned to stay indoors whenever the Camp air raid warning sounded. On this particular day we were poised to fetch our soup from the cookhouse, just as the air raid sirens sounded. Sgt S—— thought he could make it and raced across the Parade ground, only to be shot by a sentry in one of the towers. The whole Camp volunteered to attend his funeral outside the Camp, but only about a dozen men were allowed to attend under heavy guard.'

On *Arbeitskommandos* POWs were often kept working through the heaviest attacks: 'We are not allowed to enter Air Raid Shelters wherein there are civilians,' complained Trooper Sabin in October, 1943. 'These shelters are solely for Germans. All other races are excluded and must take pot luck.' When the banshee wail of alarms sounded over other areas, prisoners hurried off to civilian shelters or, when things became really bad, made for woods or open spaces outside the target zone. What prisoners did not know was that monthly information on camp locations in Germany and a detailed map from MI9 was provided for Bomber Command. But the imprecision of area bombing still made the chances of being hit uncomfortably high.

The sheer intensity of raids was an ever-present fear for prisoners at Oflag 79, situated as it was in a frighteningly exposed position between factories and an airfield. Arriving there with 2,000 other officers in May, 1944, Lieutenant H.C. M—— recorded on average forty-one alarms every month until February, 1945, when the sirens were sounding continually.

Tragedy was never far away when the sky was filled with the thunder of engines and in August, 1944, heavy explosives, anti-personnel bombs and 'countless' incendiaries straddled the camp. Three officers were killed and thirty-seven wounded. Every building was damaged, the cook house destroyed, many essential services put out of action and the compound cratered.

Prisoners like Second Lieutenant Robson who were not in the exact target area had a grandstand view of the storm of fire and steel visited upon the Reich. A devastating night attack virtually obliterated Heilbronn on 4 December, 1944:

I went to look and the sky was like the inside of a huge circus tent with flames breaking into light and giving off clouds of white smoke.

Within half an hour, Heilbronn, hitherto relatively untouched, was a flaming town with, as we heard later, 15,000 casualties. We estimated there were some 200 planes. They came circling over, wave upon wave, black shadows gliding across the floodlit ceiling, releasing their hissing bombs and slowly veering away. The flames were replenished from time to time and the countryside for miles around was flooded with yellow light. Windows could be heard tinkling to the ground all over the camp. I was in the slit trenches. A plane screamed to earth in the east.

Fighters could be distinguished by the lights that occasionally showed – enemy fighters. A vast cloud of smoke rolled over the camp from Heilbronn. Pieces of AA shell whistled to earth too close to be pleasant. A smoke flare. . . [landed] just outside the compound wire, making a hole 18 inches deep.

The whole raid was most awe-inspiring. The fierce efficiency of the raiders, the uncanny light of the flares, the tremendous effect, seen in the vivid glow and smoke, of the messengers of destruction.

In the inferno of blazing ruins, a demand for reprisals began to grow. And there were people in their midst on whom the Germans could visit their hatred and revenge.

Reichsmarschall Hermann Göring, never slow in such matters, had already suggested to Hitler, in August, 1943, that camps for captured aircrew should be sited in residential quarters of German cities to prevent Allied bombing. Discussions were far advanced with the city of Frankfurt but no new camps were built; by the time agreement in principle had been reached the German economy was on its last legs.

Late in May, 1944, Joseph Goebbels, the twisted genius behind the Reich's Propaganda Ministry, published two articles in the *Völkischer Beobachter* and *Das Reich*, suggesting that low-flying pilots should be killed like 'mad dogs' if they were shot down. Numerous letters were received afterwards from an infuriated public demanding that captured aircrew be shot, hanged, or tied to trees near vital industrial targets to witness what their comrades were doing. But in ruined cities and destroyed towns a sorely-tried populace sometimes took matters into its own hands.

Appalling incidents occurred when Allied airmen were lynched by enraged civilians. At Essen *Hauptmann* Erich Hayer virtually invited local people to attack three newly-captured British aircrew who were marched through the city, thrown over the parapet of a bridge and kicked to death. Likewise, *Oberfeldwebel* Karl Amberger shot five unarmed Allied POWs who bailed out over Dreierwalde aerodrome in March, 1945, killing four of them, including two RAF aircrew.

Hayer and Amberger paid for these atrocities after the war with their own lives but there were similar incidents elsewhere which went unpunished. Several injured RAF and American aircrew were seen by Bombardier Stonard at Hallendorf in the heavily-bombed Brunswick-Hanover-Magdeburg triangle. After bailing out they had been savagely beaten by civilians before the authorities could get to them. One prisoner claimed to be the only survivor after being shot down over Halle – the rest had been hanged from lamp posts before the police could intervene.

Two aircrew seen by Sergeant Caton at Stalag IVB had rope burns across their necks where they had been strung up by an incensed mob, while Sergeant Simister came across a Flight Lieutenant at Stalag VIIA who was the 'only survivor of [his] crew – strung up last – cut down first – marks on throat. Civilians did it and Gestapo cut him down.' Some aircrew wore an army battledress while flying over German territory in case they were shot down, in the hope that they would be taken for POWs on the loose rather than airmen.

Efforts to whip up feeling against Allied aircrew by the Germans included taking a party of them to Munich in October, 1943, to show them bomb-damaged residential areas.

One of the survivors of the Munich raid, Sergeant McLean, had visions of being put on public show and was 'really very worried' at the sight of numerous armed guards:

> A speech was read out, in English, to the effect that after the destruction of the beautiful, unarmed city of Munich, Reichsmarschall Göring had declared that we were to be shewn the results of our 'terrorism', ending with the phrase, 'Unlike your Mr. Churchill, the Führer does not often quote the Bible, but there is one saying that he has been known to use, and that is, an eye for an eye, and a tooth for a tooth, and when the time comes, as come it will, you will be made to pay for your crimes in full.'
>
> After putting the wind up us with this, it was an anti-climax to be put in a coach, where we had one prisoner between two officers. Nine were artillery officers, who spoke perfect English and pointed out the brewery, football ground, maternity hospital etc that had been damaged, and asked us what we could possibly be trying to destroy. It dawned on me then that they were trying to find out how much we knew about their rockets. . . . We got out at the Opera House and the ring of police around the square brought back my apprehension, but, on entering it was obviously not peopled. I remember being cheered by a bust of Shakespeare which was on a landing and, when we reached the circle, we could see that a bomb had gone straight through the middle of the roof.

In an effort to make the British pay for their raids on the city, the Germans forced prisoners from nearby *Arbeitskommandos* to clear up afterwards. The prisoners loathed repairing bomb damage at the main railway station because it was a favourite bombing target. There were no air raid shelters for prisoners, like Private Sudworth, who were forced to crouch during attacks in the entrance to the railway employees' shelter. 'We dreaded the first sound of the siren's wail . . . and it was a gruesome occupation, picking over the débris of a raid. Parts of human bodies and limbs were scattered about, and all had to be collected together, put into sacks and loaded onto lorries.'

Few Germans witnessed the shooting or manhandling of POWs during the climacteric death throes of the Reich, but feelings ran high on both sides. Private Collett, in Munich during the raids, witnessed black looks, raised fists, and the occasional attempted assault on Allied prisoners. However, one of his jobs was to dig grave after grave for the victims and he saw lines of civilians carrying their dead children to the city's morgue.

Many POWs reacted to the bombing of German cities with grim satisfaction. When Munich's railway goods yard went up in dust and flames, Gunner Palmer was sent in to help clear the damage: 'We saw . . . everything was molten with the heat, molten glass was hanging from the girders. We even laughed as we worked that day as the bombing boosted our morale and the thought that we were getting our own back on the blighters for our misfortune. The civilians disapproved though and let us know with a few shouts. . . . What we called them was nobodies' business. It was British Army language!!'

Despite these scenes of death and destruction, Private Freeman, engaged in tearing down bomb-damaged houses, found both German guards and employers 'very, very fair' and the tramway employees with whom Private Sudworth worked in clearing débris, filling in craters and repairing damaged tracks, were decent enough and made allowances for the prisoners' lack of food.

It was the triple attack of Operation *Thunderclap*, incinerating over 100,000 people in the beautiful, unarmed, city of Dresden, which broke this mutual tolerance.

Among a group of British prisoners labouring in a cement works six miles west of the city was Gunner Martin. When the air raid warning sounded on the evening of 13 February, 1945, there was nothing to suggest that the alarm was any different from many others which were constantly heard. But from a shelter he witnessed the city's immolation and saw the second attack three hours later. A huge glow spread over the sky above raging fires: 'It had come at last to Dresden'.

Before the firestorm, Martin and his fellow prisoners had been on reasonable terms with the local civilians. The day after the raid the French were indifferent, while the Russians went about with wide grins on their faces; the German reaction to them all was one of pure loathing. Nine days later they were sent into Dresden to help clear up bomb rubble and were amazed at the still-smouldering ruins and the sheer extent of the devastation. One of the jobs, a 'terrible business', was to clear a graveyard hit by bombs where disinterred corpses lay sprawled across piles of earth and shattered gravestones. All the while the Kommandant, hitherto a decent and humane man, gave the prisoners such a tongue-lashing that they thought he might have become unhinged.

Among another group of British POWs who witnessed a daylight attack on Dresden – probably by Flying Fortresses and Liberators comprising the third prong of Operation *Thunderclap* on Ash Wednesday – was Private Sudworth. He was some miles away when he felt the ground tremble beneath his feet. 'We knew something terrible had happened to Dresden as the guards took us well out of the way and made it plain to us it would not be too healthy for us to go near the place so soon after the bombing.'

If rage and hatred were German reactions after the destruction of Dresden, what was the attitude of British prisoners in return? 'Inwardly I felt rather glad Dresden had got it at last,' was Gunner Martin's immediate thought, 'as many Germans were so cocksure it would not be. I couldn't feel sorry for them as they needed the war to be brought to their doors to make them realize its horrors.'

Other prisoners, like Fusilier Hester, were, however, torn between a desire to see the war brought home to the German people and the appalling reality of the city's destruction. 'I couldn't help thinking of the women and children trapped in Dresden when the bombers struck. You can tell how near we were by the fact that we could see the bombers coming out of their run. All this was against a blood-red sky from the tremendous fires that were started. It was really terrible.' Yet this compassion was felt at a time when POWs were literally begging for bread, dragging themselves through bitter winter weather on forced marches and dying in their hundreds.

While on the move from an *Arbeitskommando* at Freiburg, Signalman Hoare was shaken by the same sense of divided emotions: 'Recently . . . I had been shocked by the utter devastation of Dresden which we had gone through – or more appropriately over, as there was nothing but rubble. I felt guilty.' But this had to be set against seeing 'emaciated, virtual walking corpses who had got away from various camps. It was a great shock.' Hitherto considering the Germans as equals, the spectre of concentration camp victims posed for him an unsolvable dilemma.

'Our combined air forces have made a special effort and have considerably churned up the German landscape. Whole residential areas have been blotted out. This seems inhuman but all war is inhuman so what does it matter?' asked Private Nell in October, 1944. 'And at this stage of the war – and the year – the bombing of residential areas is almost as important as bombing industrial areas. The German people must be struck very forcibly with the fact that a cold and homeless winter awaits them unless hostilities cease.'

But the German people could do no other than stumble on, dazed and exhausted, until the Nazi leaders called a halt by their unconditional surrender. In the meantime Private Nell could hear the RAF pounding Leipzig some twenty miles away as he lay in his bunk on the night of 24 March, 1944, and thought of 'the children and old people, terrified and being maimed, and killed and rendered homeless. . . . Why does this man-made hell have to continue? It is so silly – and at the same time so bloody and cruel.'

In witnessing it at first hand, some prisoners managed a rare degree of detachment about the nature of war in those last months of the Reich. Sergeant Eeles was one who seemed in reflective mood when thinking of the 'present conflict':

> German bombing of English cities made me realize what total war was. Paying that back two years later cost me five of the best pals I have ever had, and for myself a term of imprisonment in the hands of the Germans.
>
> Surely, some day someone will see the futility of war. All things can be settled amicably, if both parties concerned will be prepared to give way a little to each other.
>
> However, can human nature ever reach fully that stage of thought? My scanty knowledge says no. I sincerely hope I am wrong.

Waves of Flying Fortresses above Oflag IXA in July, 1943, on their way to bomb Kassel caused great excitement. 'It is quite impossible to describe our feelings,' recorded Major Casdagli. 'How we cheered!' By September, 1944, his comments from Oflag XIVB had taken on a more sombre tone: 'Many heavy air raids these days – we had a ringside seat for the Limburg bombing. . . . Five waves went over: pretty horrible really to watch in cold blood.' Regular fleets of anything between 700 and 1,000 Flying Fortresses and Liberators with fighter escorts could now be seen regularly in the skies over Hadamar.

The cost to the Allies in trying to pound Germany to destruction was all too evident among prisoners who observed the horrific loss of young aircrew. In a camp near Leipzig Corporal Rowley was half-deafened by incessant German anti-aircraft fire within 300 yards of the wire. Hit by flak, an American bomber spun out of control and crashed near the camp. With several others Rowley was detailed to go to the scene, accompanied by two German guards and a horse-drawn cart:

> We dug parts of four bodies out of the smashed up aircraft, a fifth body – that of the captain – was lying about 50 yards from the plane. This body was unharmed except for what I thought was a bullet mark in the forehead; he was stripped naked. I formed the opinion that he had come down by parachute and had been killed and stripped by the Germans.
>
> We were not allowed any coffins; we dug the grave on the outskirts of the village cemetery at Rendon. . . . A short time later a British bomber was shot down in the town of Zeitz and I recovered the body of one of the crew from the river.

This grim harvest of death was reaped all over the Reich. At Marlag Nord Able Seaman Walker recorded one such loss during a raid on the last day of December, 1944: 'Large numbers of Allied aircraft flew over and I saw them return later, presumably after attacking Hanover and Hamburg. Four hit and down in flames. One American bailed out, parachute failed to open. Fell just outside wire at noon, but his watch had stopped at 11.20 a.m. Surmised that he must have died in 'plane and fell out when [it] broke up in air.'

Some men survived. 'Injured [para]chutist in camp – shot through arm by cannon-shell so ordered to bale out,' recorded Sergeant Simister in May, 1944. Such casualties soon arrived behind the wire because the Germans no longer had the transport or human resources to interrogate them all at Dulag Luft, though the camp there operated up until the last few days of the war.

Men of the United States Army Air Forces shot down in the combined offensive over Europe began to gather in increasing numbers from 1942 onwards in prison camps. Their arrival often generated considerable hostility from other POWs: 'A few decent Yanks – mostly dirty and no good as fighters as far as we could gather,' noted Sergeant Simister. 'Yanks moan at Jerry – prisoners in U.S.A. treated like lords. Sleep in shifts – day and night. Yanks have one groundsheet issued – no blankets. Filthy habits (speaking generally very bad opinion of them here now).'

When the Americans were moved out of his hut, Simister and his colleagues watched as they were searched for missing blankets, eating utensils, cigarettes and other pilfered goods.

A more substantial charge against the newcomers was the damage they caused to painfully-constructed trading systems. With the arrival of the Americans at Stalag Luft IV in September, 1944, 'Our carefully nurtured trading scheme with the Germans almost broke down,' complained Flying Officer East. 'The Americans wanted individual trading and their efforts caused the price of a loaf of bread to rise from 5 cigarettes to 80 cigarettes. Eventually they saw the wisdom of the English method but by then it was too late.'

Many criticisms of American POWs were due to the excessive overcrowding which they unwittingly caused and the sharing of scarce rations with them. There was also the question of American troops in the United Kingdom.

Dark rumours about them circulated among British prisoners like Private Perry, who considered that one of his relatives ought to have no problem in finding a man, 'especially under the existing conditions that must now prevail in England, with so many Colonial and American troops around. I met a fellow who was in Weymouth this time last year,' he added, 'and he certainly enlightened me somewhat as to conditions, etc, there.'

It was at Stalag Luft VI that Flight-Sergeant Younger observed that prisoners, who wished to move freely between the two British compounds, were keen to keep the Americans firmly bottled up.

Many of them, 'disapproving of American boisterousness, were glad the Americans had their own compound and wished it further away.'

While the unfortunate Americans could not be blamed for problems which were not of their own making and were victims of their own reputation, British prisoners coupled their genuinely-held grievances about them with a general gripe about all Allied POWs.

Australians, for example, were none too welcome to Stalag IVB since they 'always had plenty of cigarette parcels and personal parcels', wrote Sergeant Caton. 'They sat in a group apart at evening "eating" time, enjoying comparative luxury which they never dreamed of sharing.' At Stalag VIIIB there was a tremendous set-to between a Glaswegian razor gang and some Canadians. Arming themselves with anything available, the Canadians had a 'battle royal' with the Scots. 'The Germans didn't step in either,' said Trooper Forbes Moreton. 'There was nobody killed but that was the end of the gang.'

The French and British at Stalag IVB detested each other and fought over cookhouse jobs. When the Australians arrived they were 'prepared for a little of the usual strained relationship which arose between the French and British troops . . . but not for the bitter, caustic reception which greeted our arrival.' The only welcome they got, wrote Ian Sabey, 'was the demand if we had any watches or fountain pens to swap for food.'

The Germans were happy to encourage ill-feeling between the two sides; from the early days of captivity their policy had been to drive a wedge between the Allies. This was not difficult when the French blamed the British for running away at Dunkirk and carrying on a futile war which prevented them returning home. On the other hand, while there were often bitter disagreements, heavy-footed German efforts usually resulted in the prisoners turning on them and at a personal level there were often mutually sympathetic ties, as, for example, between 'Dixie' Deans and Paules, the American Man of Confidence at Stalag Luft VI.

As POWs were forced out of their camps in the early months of 1945 they struggled through scenes of desolation in which the spirit of defiance, still alive among civilians, earned their grudging admiration. '*Deutschland muss leben und wenn wir sterben mussen*' (Germany must live, even if we die) proclaimed the message on bombed-out buildings and '*Nie wieder ein 1918! Sieg!*' (Never again 1918! Victory!)

Part of the psychological warfare against civilians during the bomber offensive was to drop millions of leaflets over the Reich. The C-in-C Bomber Command, Air Marshal Sir Arthur Harris, never had any faith in this work. 'My personal view is that the only thing achieved was largely to supply the Continent's requirements of toilet paper for the five long years of war.' What he detested above all was the loss of valuable aircrew on questionable 'nickelling' raids.

At Königstein in southern Austria, Signalman Hoare found branches in a nearby forest festooned with 'window' (strips of silver foil dropped by aircraft to confuse enemy radar detectors) and 'here and there copies of the beautifully-produced miniature newspaper telling the Germans the truth about the war'. But the cleverest propaganda was that dropped from Russian aircraft – blood-red sheets of paper which bore the simple but terrifying message: *Wir kommen! Wir kommen! Wir kommen!* 'I fancy I know which wrought most havoc in the German mind,' he added.

Whatever their effect on civilians, the Germans made strenuous efforts to keep leaflets away from POWs: 'Air raid warning, heard 'planes and guns, lasted about 90 minutes, leaflets fell outside camp about one hour afterwards,' noted Flight-Sergeant Bulmer at Stalag Luft III in October, 1944. 'Gerry in a panic running round in circles to prevent Russian prisoners collecting them.'

On the night of 23/24 April, 1945, 80,000 Allied troops stormed a passage over the Rhine on a twenty-five mile front between Rheinsberg and Rees with Wesel at its centre. At the same time thousands of leaflets bearing a 'Solemn Warning' from Churchill, Stalin and Truman came floating down from the skies over the shrinking strip of territory still held by the Germans where some 3,500,000 Allied prisoners were trapped and over 140 camps were still to be liberated.

The all too real possibility that POWs would be used as bargaining pawns or might become victims of last-minute mass executions by the SS when the Allies began their final assault into the heart of Germany haunted the minds of military planners on both sides of the Atlantic. There was also fearful speculation among prisoners themselves.

Tension about the ill-treatment of Allied prisoners was heightened by the arrival of officers, specially briefed by SBOs, who were among those repatriated in September, 1944. They reported on the poor morale of German guards and the menacing attitude of the SS. Attempts at fraternization by civilians and guards had been curtailed through fear of the Gestapo and some prisoners had heard hints that they were to be used as hostages or executed.

All this, together with a grim recital of the murder of Allied POWs captured in France since D-Day and warnings from Berne early in March, 1945, deeply alarmed officials in London and Washington. Unconfirmed rumours, circulating in Berlin, whispered of a German intention to massacre the inhabitants of POW camps in danger of being overrun by advancing Allied forces. It was said that Hitler had threatened to take reprisals on Allied POWs after the destruction of Dresden and had only been restrained by Himmler.

On 5 March, 1945, Anthony Eden wrote to the Prime Minister urging every effort 'to forestall a disaster', including an approach to Truman and Stalin seeking their agreement in issuing a joint warning over the treatment of POWs to Germany. After much diplomatic activity between the Allies on the exact wording, which tested Churchill's patience to the full – 'Do please get it out,' he instructed Lord Halifax on 22 April – the joint declaration duly showered down over the Reich and was read out on British radio and printed in the Press.

In January, 1945, Major Miles Reid, newly-repatriated from Oflag IVC, was summoned to an audience with the King. A little while later he was taken to see Major-General Jepp at the War Office. The subject of both interviews was the fate of the *Prominente* at Colditz.

Sometime in 1942 the Germans began to collect at Oflag IVC a group of prisoners whom they believed to be particularly important and applied to them the term *Prominente*. 'It conveyed, as a distinction, not that we were considered individually especially dangerous . . . but that we were "prominent" on account of personal connections,' wrote Lieutenant Alexander, nephew of the GOC Middle East, Field-Marshal Alexander.

He joined Giles Romilly, Winston Churchill's nephew, who was sent to cover the Norwegian campaign by the *Daily Express* without proper papers and was captured at Narvik. Others soon arrived: Captain The Earl of Hopetoun, elder son of the Marquess of Linlithgow, Viceroy of India since 1936; Captain The Earl Haig, only son of Field-Marshal Haig; Lieutenant Viscount Lascelles, nephew of King George VI; and Captain The Master of Elphinstone, nephew of the Queen.

Three more prisoners were added late in the war; Lieutenant Max de Hamel whom the Germans thought mistakenly to be distantly related to Churchill; General Bor-Komorowski, C-in-C of the Polish Home Army and defender of Warsaw and, finally, Lieutenant John Winant, son of the US Ambassador in London, who had been imprisoned in Bavaria since 1943 when his Flying Fortress was shot down.

'The King thought it rather sinister that the Germans should have collected in one Oflag all these young men who are near relatives of prominent people in this country,' reported his Private Secretary to 10 Downing Street. 'I certainly agree with the sinister aspect of these movements of well-connected prisoners,' replied Churchill, who added in an unusually impotent side, 'There is nothing we can do.'

Only forty-eight hours before Oflag IVC was liberated by American troops, they were moved out on the first stage of a journey towards the Austrian redoubt of Obersalzburg where, it was widely supposed, the Nazi leaders and fanatical *SS* men would make a last stand.

In camps and *Arbeitskommandos* Allied prisoners were caught up in Germany's agony. Rations sank to a new low, supplies of precious Red Cross parcels were badly disrupted by Germany's growing internal dislocation, guards were nervous and unsure and men were forced out on terrible marches in the bitterest of winters. At Oflag XIIB an officer collapsed and died from heart failure and others constantly blacked out from lack of food and cold: 'Things look pretty bad as regards food but we shall get used to it,' reported Major Casdagli with unquenchable optimism.

Paradoxically, their major difficulties began with Allied successes in eastern Europe. As Soviet armour rolled onwards the Germans began to withdraw camps westward into the Reich. In July, 1944, prisoners in Stalag Luft VI at Heydekrug – the most far-flung prison camp in East Prussia – were hurriedly transferred by train and boat to two other camps, Stalag Luft IV at Gross Tychow in Pomerania or to Stalag 357 at Thorn.

There had been many rumours that they would be moved away from the rapidly advancing Russians but a general notice to evacuate the camp was followed by news that the Americans would leave within hours. 'Fantastic and bulky haversacks, kit bags, cases and valises appeared by magic and waterbottles made from "Klim" tins and coffee pots were everywhere to be seen,' recorded Sergeant Green. Throughout the compounds towering stacks of kit were being crammed into incinerators and smoke billowing from bonfires of reserves of food, sports kit, books and personal items hung in a heavy pall.

Behind them prisoners left nothing but scorched earth to the enemy. Carefully planted gardens were kicked to pieces. From everywhere streamed toilet paper, festooning the barbed wire and fluttering from telegraph poles – 'the ultimate expression of contempt,' thought Flight-Sergeant Younger.

As a proper curtain-down on life at Heydekrug and after another huge meal, the camp's theatre gave its last performance. Then the Americans were on their way to the railway station, showering kit by the roadside as they staggered under enormously heavy loads. Among prisoners like Sergeant Green who were left behind there was much excitement; the general opinion seemed to be:

'Take everything you can and eat the rest.' Alternatively, 'The best thing to do is to save food,' said Jock, placing half a tin of Spam between two biscuits and demolishing it. 'The Jerries have had it but won't admit it.'

    – A Goon wanders in – 'How long before we move?' we ask. A shrug
of the shoulders is the answer – complete indifference.
    'Better be quick. Joe will be here.'
    'Nix nix – nix Rusky.'
    'You don't think so eh?'
    'Ja – Christmas!'
    General condemnation of German optimism.
    'Who ever heard of a German *Wi*ctory – ridiculous; – no "V" in their
alphabet!'
    'I heard Rusky guns this morning.'
    'We'll be cut off – surrounded, we hope.'
    'They are within 150 kilometres.'
    'I saw one in the reserved seats of the theatre.'
    'The Poles have built a figure surmounting a "V" and laurel wreaths.'
    'I hear H.[eydekrug] has fallen already to the Ruskies, or the Yanks,
I'm not sure which.'

And so the half-serious, half-hilarious bantering went on until they
too left in a 'struggling, sweating stream of men, heaving and
plunging across dry and sandy pathways' to the waiting train.

    An orgy of destruction had been seen in Italy as British prisoners
were rounded up in their camps and transported to the Reich. But this
time there was a significant difference. Civilians at the local railway
station stared enviously at the 5,000 POWs leaving Heydekrug, their
anxious, drawn faces betraying their awareness of the Russian advance
and fear at the coming occupation.

    On their journey to Thorn or Gross Tychow, the prisoners saw
long lines of transport ferrying the scrapings of German manpower to
the Eastern Front and, travelling in the opposite direction, the results
of that mighty conflict – smashed men and machines. There were few,
however, who were excited by such sights: 'Well, my four years as a
POW are up tomorrow,' wrote Flight-Sergeant Steele, who had
been transferred to Stalag 357, 'what a war this has been for me,
just four years of wasted life, and quite a lot of cold, hunger and
depression.'

    The 3,000 RAF prisoners taken to Stalag 357, which moved *en masse*
to Oerbke, near Fallingbostel, had an easier journey than 2,000 of their
colleagues sent to Stalag Luft IV. In conditions reminiscent of the
stinking, dark holds of Italian ships the latter were crammed into a
small tramp steamer which took four days to sail from Liban to
Swinemünde.

    They eventually reached Kiefheide railway station, three miles from
Stalag Luft IV, where a demented German security officer, spittle
flying from his mouth, screamed at them about their bombing of
civilians. Then the *Luftgangster* and *Terrorflieger* were hustled along to

their new camp. They ran the gauntlet of young Hitler thugs who had whetted their appetite for blood on American prisoners the previous day. Many men who fell exhausted by the wayside were clubbed, stabbed or bitten by dogs.

Despite the harshness of this journey the evacuation of Stalag Luft VI was achieved fairly quickly and in decent weather. However, the movement of prisoners in the early months of 1945 was to be a very different matter.

Men were forced out in appalling weather conditions. From mid-December, 1944, until the end of January, 1945, temperatures on the European mainland regularly dropped to minus fourteen degrees centigrade and below while day-time temperatures rarely rose above freezing. Biting winds whipped deepening snow into massive drifts which covered much of Germany, Poland and Czechoslovakia.

The prisoners who left their camps were totally unfit for any kind of travel. They were suffering badly from malnutrition and had the desperate weariness of men weakened by prison life and extreme cold. Above them the Allies ruled supreme and anything moving by day, down to a single horse and cart, was liable to sudden and devastating attack.

But, despite such problems, the German High Command decided to withdraw their prisoners from the path of the Russians' swift advance from the Vistula in January, 1945. The dislocation and destruction of the Reich's internal communications by Allied bombing meant that most of them were to be moved out on foot and so it was that Stalags XXA and XXB, apart from their sick and wounded, were virtually emptied before being overrun. Their inmates started out in long columns with whatever possessions they could carry, accompanied by armed guards.

The Germans who went out on the road with their prisoners had only the haziest notion as to their likely destination because no proper plans were ever made for the mass-movement of POWs and, in the event, the rapidly-deteriorating military situation inside Germany would have made them useless.

This did not prevent prisoners on *Arbeitskommandos* throughout the border area of eastern Poland and Upper Silesia being forced to move. Some were brought hastily into their main Stalags before joining the general evacuation, while others in small work detachments waited in larger *Arbeitskommandos* and still others were collected at *Kontrol* centres.

Originally the German authorities planned to march them in orderly columns westwards towards Stalag 344 at Lamsdorf or Stalag VIIIA at Görlitz. So quickly did the Russians break through the desperate German rearguard action, however, that many columns splintered into wandering groups struggling into the Czech Protectorate of Bohemia and Moravia or, like the men from Posen and Marienburg (Stalags XXA and XXB), westwards towards Brandenburg and Brunswick.

To many men this trek seemed as bad as anything they had previously gone through: 'There is a lot of "for" and "against" with this and the 1940 march,' thought Private Woodley on his way from Danzig westwards to Dummerstock early in 1945. 'We cannot yet decide which one is the worst.'

In worsening chaos the prisoners struggled on blindly through atrocious weather, many of them suffering from dysentery and everyone from terrible hunger. After they had passed the snow was stained with their blood and excrement. Their boots and clothing were saturated. They slept in barns, factories and, when all else failed, in open fields. Mixed up with many of the columns were thousands upon thousands of civilians fleeing from Danzig and East Prussia, packed into open cattle trucks and jamming the roads with their lorries, cars and horse-drawn carts.

Many doubted if they could survive the dreadful journey: 'All you saw and heard was the fellow in front of you and the crunch of his boots in the deep snow and for mile after mile your mind became completely blank,' wrote Gunner Joyce. 'This went on for days on end, where all your actions became automatic.'

As the days went by bitter hunger reduced even the hardest prisoners to ravenous packs desperate for anything to eat. If they left the column, however, there was nowhere to go and no hope of receiving the lifegiving Red Cross supplies. All around them the stench of death arose from towns and cities.

Yet even at this late stage of the war brutal guards could still kill with terrifying casualness. Private Corderoy was sent sprawling by a vicious blow and a rifle barrel shoved in his face kept him moving as he knelt by a prisoner who had dropped in his tracks 'without a sound'. When he looked back two guards had rolled his mate's body into a ditch. 'When he was face down one guard stood on the back of his head in the snow. If he wasn't dead already he would suffocate and freeze . . . in a few minutes. . . . I seemed to forget it the moment it was all over.'

Another common sight was that of Red Cross parcels and stores looted and left strewn about as German discipline collapsed in the face of imminent defeat.

To remove their prisoners from the Russian advance, the Germans planned to transfer inmates of Stalag 344 at Lamsdorf to Stalag VIIIA at Görlitz so that prisoners evacuated from Stalag VIIIB at Teschen and from various *Arbeitskommandos* situated in Upper Silesia could be taken there.

The Russians outpaced this withdrawal but were too late to prevent another mass of POWs starting out from Stalag VIIIB, late in January, 1945; instead of marching northwards towards Lamsdorf they now swung westwards and struggled across the mountain ranges of eastern Sudetenland to Königgrätz where they entrained for Stalag XIIID at Nuremberg. Other groups from the camp and its associated *Arbeits-kommandos* marched towards Karlsbad where some remained on working parties while the rest went onwards south-west into Bavaria.

The prisoners tramping into Czechoslovakia were heartened by the marvellous help they received from the civilian population. Suffering themselves under the harshest of occupations the Czechs did every-thing they could to help Allied POWs, often taking very considerable personal risks. 'People in Slovakia very amenable towards us and dislike Jerry,' recorded Lance-Corporal Groom. The same welcome was witnessed by Ordinary Seaman Gant who left Stalag 344 to the sound of Russian gunfire. After a tough journey with Russian, French and English POWs, concentration camp Jews and German refugees, he reached the Czech border on 4 February: 'Entered Czecho-Slovakia; thank God, people here cannot be too highly spoken of. They are trying to give us bread, cigarettes, and are risking their lives to do so. Boys scrambling in the streets for bread thrown from windows. One of the boys shot through head for rushing to a civvy for bread.'

Moving south-west from the vicinity of Prague, limping on septic feet, bodies racked by malnutrition and their tattered clothing alive with lice, this group eventually marched some 400 miles, passing over 200 towns and cities on the way. They ended up on working parties near Amberg, due east of Nuremberg which had been heavily bombed.

From Lamsdorf, all but 2,500 POWs were on the march in columns a thousand strong towards Stalag VIIIA, 150 miles away at Görlitz. They set out on 22 January, 1945. Sleeping in barns, brickworks, a boiler house and sugar factory, 600 out of 1,000 RAF prisoners who left the camp struggled to Görlitz on 3 February through icy winds and deep snow. Elation at being outside the wire soon gave way to a 'really dull slog' in temperatures which fell to minus thirty-five degrees centigrade. No soup or hot drinks of any kind were provided and on five days there was nothing at all to eat.

Food was equally scarce on the subsequent 500 mile march to Stalag IXA at Ziegenhain between 10 February and 12 March. The prisoners' staple diet was now thin soup, raw potatoes and a scrap of bread with an occasional brew of coffee or tea except on some days when supplies ran out completely. 'Believe me, it's wicked,' recorded Sergeant Margerison sheltering in a ditch, 'where I am writing this amongst quite a bit of flak from a nearby air raid.'

By the time they reached Stalag IXA most of them could hardly walk. 'I estimate my weight now to be approximately seven stones,' noted Sergeant Fermor. 'I can nearly put my hand round my thighs and every bone is sticking out all over me.'

Some men never made it as far as Ziegenhain; nine were shot for stealing food and many dropped out suffering from frostbite, dysentery and hunger oedema. Sergeant Bruce, becoming progressively weaker from dysentery, spent most of the time during rests in nearby ditches emptying his bowels. During one of these enforced stops he was handed a death warrant by someone who stole his precious bread supply.

Following him in the column was Sergeant Peachey who came across Bruce lying helplessly in the trampled snow. Believing his mate to be dying, he gave him his own bread ration. 'Now that's something you could never repay,' remarked Bruce, 'It's something I'll never forget.'

Yet POWs, like Sergeant Margerison, who reached a permanent billet recovered their spirits remarkably quickly after receiving rations of barley, potatoes and mint soup at Stalag IXA. 'We have moved from the sound of the Russian guns to within earshot of ours. It is a glorious morning, makes you feel happy and glad to be alive. I have been listening to the larks for two mornings – they are beautiful. I am feeling pretty weak but hope to recover in time, for the news is splendid.'

Sergeant Bruce in the meantime was in a bad way and hazy about what was happening. Without medical attention, his weight down to about six stone, he lay in a filthy hovel which passed for a Russian hospital. Eventually, he was moved out again and landed up in another POW hospital where the living skeletons were liberated by American troops.

The very fact that they were still alive and in one piece after their terrible march seemed remarkable but while they were enduring it prisoners thought only about putting one foot in front of the other and where the next scraps of food were coming from. Sometimes men were so near the end of their tether they could not manage to do both: 'A plate of soup today, just enough to keep us from starving,' recorded Ordinary Seaman Gant on 24 April, 'Marched from 6 p.m. until 7 a.m., 13 hrs. Boys lay down in road and refused to march, ended up in barn.' The next day all their German guards disappeared, leaving them without food and 'in a terrible state'.

While this batch of prisoners was on the march the ICRC had tried desperately to get supplies of food to them and to other columns on the move. The problems of air attack, clogged roads and the highly uncertain direction of travel by prisoners made this a difficult task. While some received food parcels, other POWs had to rely entirely on what they could beg, barter or steal from civilians. Able Seaman W—, stumbling along in a pair of boots taken from a dead concentration camp victim lying by the roadside, saw one POW triumphantly wrestle scraps of food from a dog in the farmyard where they lay overnight. When men were reduced to eating half-frozen raw mangels, turnips, swedes and sugarbeet, such scavenging was a common sight.

A second batch of 2,000 POWs left Stalag 344 on 21 February, 1945, and was taken by rail westwards to Stalag XIIIC at Hammelburg and then aimlessly on foot southwards. The sick among them were sent on a punishing journey from Stalag XIIIC to Stalag XVIIB at Krems in Austria by cattle truck.

Those who remained at Lamsdorf were moved out by the Germans on 2 March and put on trains at the Annahof railway station in the usual cattle trucks. They were taken to Stalag XVIIA at Kaiserstein-brück, about twenty-five kilometres from Vienna. After a short stay some were again on the move and ended up in a forest clearing near Braunau, where they met men who had come from Stalag 398 at Pupping. Building for themselves a shelter of branches and leaves to keep out the rain and sleet they lay in soaking wet clothes and with little food. Their guards had no idea what to do with them.

From Stalag VIIIA at Görlitz, columns of POWs were forced to leave on 15 February, 1945, taking a line due west and slightly north of Dresden. On this desperately hard march the veteran British prisoners watched as morale collapsed among newly-captured Americans. Soon the Yanks had stopped washing or shaving and became early victims of malnutrition. They simply gave up, dropping out by the wayside or dying in their tracks.

Other POW camps near their line of march were already overcrowded and the survivors were forced ever onwards, in freezing rain, until they reached Stalag XIC, a large, cold and dusty brick factory at Duderstadt near Göttingen. Here they were grossly overcrowded in filthy conditions with one warm meal each day. Some order was at last restored by medical staff after the removal of those who were less seriously ill by train to Stalag 357, at Fallingbostel, during the last week of March, 1945.

On its way to Duderstadt was also the mass of prisoners from Stalag VIIIC at Sagan. Among them were men who were quite obviously unfit to move any distance in winter conditions and yet the majority eventually slogged on through great difficulties, dragging many of the seriously ill in open horse-drawn carts, to reach their destination on foot – a journey of some 300 miles.

Another batch went to Stalag IXB at Bad Orb, which was even further away. Again, they had to walk every step: 'Arrived . . . with poisoned leg and [in] very bad condition,' recorded Private Whelan on 8 February. During thirty-four days on the road he received only ten loaves of bread, five hard biscuits, three tins of meat, one sausage, a half kilogram of cheese and four issues of soup.

Such a poor ration supply affected even those prisoners who had toughened up while out on *Arbeitskommandos* instead of spending months and years behind barbed wire like Whelan. They all too often fell prey to the relentless effects of cold and wet weather. And many RAF aircrew, hitherto relatively secure in their own camps, were soon to be added to the toll of victims.

On 27 January POWs from Stalag Luft III at Sagan, and from the small camp nearby at Belaria, (sometimes known as Stalag Luft IV but never independent of Stalag Luft III and not to be confused with the regular camp at Kiefheide), were out on the road heading for Spremberg in ankle-deep snow and freezing winds. They had been given an hour's notice of the move: 'Got all set with packed kit bags much too heavy, and almost wept to see food, cigs, clothes and drinks we had to leave,' commented Wing Commander McCarthy-Jones.

The move came as no surprise. A Russian armoured spearhead was smashing its way through German defences only forty miles away. 'Everyone wondering if we'll be moved and hoping we won't,' he had written earlier. 'Although I feel an inner excitement I still can't believe we'll still be here if and when the R[ussians] arrive and am therefore outwardly calm.'

Starting in pitch darkness, prisoners from the six compounds were issued with one Red Cross parcel, from which they could carry only essential items, and set off in halting columns – the most westerly compounds first with East and Belaria compounds bringing up the rear. Many men dragged sledges, improvised from stools, chairs, cupboards or torn-up sheets on which were piled their few possessions.

Accompanying the columns were their guards, many of them elderly and in poor physical shape. Most were on two hours' notice of posting and expecting at any time to be called to the Russian Front which made them edgy and nervous: 'The farther I went and the more I saw on the trip,' wrote Pilot Officer Harvey, 'made any sympathy I had for them rapidly disappear. I realized I was back to [a] 1940 position and hated them all together with their lack of human feeling which has brought me back to thinking that either the whole race needs re-educating to a decent way of living or scrub them as a nation.'

On the first night the prisoners bedded down on the stone floor of a draughty barn: 'Awful night, with cramp and coughing,' reported McCarthy-Jones. 'The place sounded like a consumption ward.' By the following day miles and miles of columns of men were on the move. 'There were times when I felt so battered and beaten by life that I just wanted to crawl into a hole and lie there exhausted,' wrote George Harsh, USAAF. 'My life appeared to be one long black joke perpetrated by the gods, and this march was the culminating piece of black humour.'

Local people were, however, very friendly and helped where they could by providing hot water. But even at this stage 'rackets' were operating strongly and the 'market' for bread, onions and other foodstuffs was ruined by prisoners willing to hand over fantastic amounts of coffee and cigarettes. To add to their problems a sudden thaw made sledges useless and discarded items of kit and tins of food soon littered the wayside.

At Spremberg 500 NCOs were crammed into cattle trucks and issued with three-fifths of a loaf each and one Red Cross parcel. After three days' and two nights' travelling north-west they arrived on 4 February at the nearest station to Marlag und Milag Nord. 'Conditions on the train were bad, with regard to crowding and ventilation,' reported Sergeant Eeles. 'We were seldom let out and during the whole journey we had less than half a pint of water for the trip.'

In 'tired, miserable, irritable columns', 1,980 RAF officers later marched to Spremberg suffering from the rain and cold. In the railway trucks there was an 'awful squash, 40 men per truck, no straw and a lot of kit which was suspended from ceiling and no room for us all to lie down. The only light was a small marg.[arine] lamp someone made.' Staggering from their trucks at Marlag Nord, McCarthy-Jones and the others spent over five hours standing in mud, slush, rain and bitter cold outside the camp as each man was searched before entering: 'it is funny to think back on it how eager we all appeared to get behind wire again,' he commented.

All these RAF POWs were crammed into Marlag 'M', 'nearly dead beat', recorded Captain Wilson. 'About 20 of the officers were sick from exhaustion and frostbite, and one guard died.' To make room for this mass of new arrivals about 700 naval ratings and all the British internees were hurriedly transferred to Milag Nord while 250 Petty Officers were sent to Marlag 'O'.

On their first night in camp, the newly-arrived prisoners spent uncomfortable hours in soaking wet greatcoats and blankets on a concrete floor covered only with wood-wool. Once they had dried out, however, their spirits began to rise, though many officers, used to the ways of Stalag Luft III, detested Marlag 'M' at first: 'This isn't much of a camp,' thought McCarthy-Jones, 'and is pretty short of everything. No coal, very little wood, broken stoves and electric light fittings. . . . Realize how everything is comparative. Wish we were back in the comfort of Sagan which would have given anything to leave two weeks ago.'

On the second day their patience under these miserable conditions finally ran out when they refused *en masse* to turn out for *appell* though part of the problem lay with the naval Man of Confidence who thought the newly-arrived officers should look after themselves. 'I intend that his views shall be overridden,' remarked Captain Wilson. Yet it was fortunate that there was not more trouble between the prisoners because conditions had been getting worse there for some time.

At the turn of the year Able Seaman Walker had been suffering from the many shortages in camp: 'Boys today used an old stool for fuel as we haven't any. It's bitterly cold and we are feeling the effects of that plus the little food we are getting.' By late February severe cuts in their meagre rations had led to an outbreak of stealing between POWs who were kept penned in their huts while British fighters shot up the neighbourhood. On alternate nights prisoners were forced to sit in darkness as the Germans strove desperately to conserve precious energy supplies; there was no fuel at all beyond what could be collected from around the camp and 'blowers' were the only means of heating water.

The arrival of Red Cross parcels and more organized living accommodation made matters easier for a while until on 8 March came news of a further move (carried out on 9 April). Many men were dismayed by this including Sergeant Eeles who had soon felt at home in Marlag 'M':

> No ferrets or dogs
> No Red line routes
> Allowed out during air raids (This is wizard)
> Rations in some cases better, others worse
> Plenty of tools for digging, sawing etc.
> Plenty of wood parties
> Rackets galore, until B—— was shot and others shot at!

McCarthy-Jones had also established himself there: 'How I hated this place and wanted to . . . [leave] on first arrival but now having got settled in with good stocks of R.C. parcels should hate to move again.'

Thinking about the 'awful' journey from Sagan, he could still see its sights and sounds: 'Very dull country on march and very disheartening to see thousands of us in column. Awful stops for counting (which was useless) and rests in bitter winds – The feeling that no one knew where we were or cared what happened to us. The lack of any discipline on march. Stragglers made their own way to where we were going. . . . Feeling very bucked we made it and marvelling that so few fell by the way.'

Not everyone who had been at Sagan went through this ordeal. Other groups left Spremberg by train for Stalag VIIA at Moosburg in Bavaria, Stalag XIIIC at Hammelburg or Stalag IIIA at Luckenwalde.

Two more RAF camps were moved westwards under very difficult circumstances. On 17 January prisoners in Stalag Luft VII at Bankau on the Polish-German border were told they were to be ready to move at one hour's notice. This camp had only been set up in Silesia in the summer of 1944 and some prisoners arrived there almost as it was evacuated.

The prisoners left two days later in atrocious weather on what was to become a trek of over 250 kilometres. 'Up 3.30 a.m., bitterly cold morning, heard gunfire most of night, little sleep,' recorded Flight-Sergeant Bulmer. 'Left camp at 5 a.m., coldest wind ever experienced. Started in direction of Krugberg, walked all day until 4 p.m., treacherous under-foot, snowstorms most of the time, ten minutes break every 5 kilometres. About 11.0 a.m. managed to get hold of discarded suitcase which I used as a sledge for kit. Bottom wore through about 2.30 p.m., had to carry kit again. Slept night in barn in Winterfeld having walked 29 kilo[metre]s.'

Even for men like Sergeant Wagner who had been sitting down to bacon and eggs in an English mess only a month earlier, the march was extremely arduous. 'Feet very bad with blisters, as tied boots on with wire. Appalling heavy going. Very slow halting freezing march.'

The prisoners were forced along for anything up to thirty kilometres a day and were poorly fed, mostly medically unfit and billeted in badly-organized temporary quarters. Many collapsed by the wayside and had to be left behind despite *Oberfeldwebel* Frank's threat to shoot five men for every one who dropped out of the column. Fleeing civilians were also mixed up in the general exodus: 'Marching all night to cross the Oder before bridges blown,' recorded Sergeant Webster on 20 January. 'Intense cold – 6 refugee children died on route – many falling out of ranks exhausted – frostbite gets a grip,' and, later on the march, 'Numbers thinned by sickness – fellows lying in snow by roadside – unable to help them.'

By 5 February those prisoners still on their feet had reached Goldberg where they were packed fifty-five to a cattle truck and arrived four days later, ravenous, thirsty and cold, at Stalag IIIA. Here, overcrowding was so severe that up to 400 men were crammed into each room and German rations, as always, were totally insufficient. Nevertheless, it was at least some relief for newly-arrived prisoners to be off the road as Sergeant Wagner discovered when he entered the camp feeling 'very weak'. 'Body very thin, Got a billet . . . not too bad a position, on floor on wood straw, underneath a window. Warm and light anyhow and room to stretch out. Porridge and potatoes from Germans and a cup of good pork soup from our own field kitchen.'

At about the same time that this group of prisoners were nearing their journey's end at Luckenwalde, some 800 RAF men were moved out from Stalag Luft IV, at Kiefheide, and marched west across the Stettin estuary to Neu Brandenburg. So poor was the general health of these prisoners, however, that they could make no further progress. After waiting two weeks in barns they were put in cattle trucks and reached Stalag 357 at Fallingbostel early in March, 1945.

By this time there were roughly 240,000 British, American and Commonwealth POWs on the move. Great columns of prisoners were herded somewhat aimlessly along a northern route towards Bremen, Hamburg and Lübeck. Another 60,000 were drifting westwards through central Germany around Berlin, Dresden and Leipzig, while a further 80,000 struggled south, across northern Czechoslovakia, some going on towards the Sudeten border area, into Bavaria and southern Würtemberg.

Reception centres for prisoners who had been uprooted were hurriedly established but conditions in them deteriorated sharply. At Stalag IIIE, for instance, 237 RAF officers were packed into a hut thirty feet wide and eighty feet long: 'The place was indescribably depressing,' thought Flying Officer East who had travelled there from Belaria. Disputes arose between the POWs over Red Cross parcels and the arrival of many Americans led to a further reduction in German rations. Before long the SBO told all men in the RAF compound that they were to consider themselves once again under full discipline and act as if they were on a RAF station. 'This was done,' explained Flying Officer East, 'partly as a morale-boosting exercise and partly to impress the Germans who were becoming very despondent.'

After an influx of men into Stalag 357 even the tables, seats and palliasses disappeared. Amongst this chaos, Bombardier Mordue recorded the last feverish wait for liberation:

I think it not out of place to mention here that at 10.0 a.m. I was sitting on my bed very, very hungry, and then the news came in of the arrival of food parcels. What a Godsend! a little good food at last; 2 o'clock the same day we hear of the sweeping advance of our troops; how many more days now? Only a POW can realize what hunger is, what a cigarette is, what kindness is, a decent bed, decent food have been so far away from me, intimate friends and affectionate ones. How long will it be before I have the pleasure of seeing them, listening to the music of their conversation. You, who are reading this now, could never understand the agitation of my mind at this time, 30th March 1945.

At Stalag XIIIC the problem of overcrowding was critical but the German authorities no longer seemed able to do anything whatsoever about it. Conditions were also bad in other places which received extra prisoners, including Stalags XIA at Altengrabow and XIIID at Nuremberg.

Prisoners who were forced to await liberation from them, and from hundreds of *Arbeitskommandos*, found it difficult to contain their impatience, fearful that their food stocks might run out completely before Allied troops could reach them. Signalman Trewin, still labouring at a colliery in the Sudetenland, wondered how many more shifts he would be forced to work:

We are eagerly – anxiously – awaiting the next move of Patton's forces – Which way will he come is the question. Patience, patience, patience and in the end it boils down to plain impatience and short tempers. Still, a smoke saves the situation and even if it stinks like garbage it soothes the savage breast. We're having a most phenomenal Spring . . . the country looks charming (if German)!! England would seem so much more delectable were we in her – perhaps we soon shall be – who knows? That's the trouble! we don't. We've heard guns . . . from just over the hills and then all has gone quiet and we are left more doubting than ever – as in Italy – so near and yet so far. Hey ho! we shall see in due course. Just patience – always patience, through silly rumours, false news – and suchlike. Meanwhile another small and yet universal whisper goes around 'When will those little white wagons come – or will they at all?'

Every prisoner knew now that their liberators could not be far away but the chance of a delivery of Red Cross parcels kept most of them from trying to escape and orders had been transmitted to camp leaders about this from London. Nevertheless, there were many who remembered the Italian fiasco and were determined not to be caught again. They were ready to break out from their camps just as soon as they could.

A new spate of forced marches was touched off by the Allied crossings of the Rhine at Remagen, and on the wider front centred on Wesel, in March, 1945.

Now the prisoners faced north and east as they began to trudge away from the sound of British and American artillery. One of the first to move was Oflag XIIB at Hadamar, on 21 March, when officers were taken by lorry to Lollar transit camp. The special train waiting to take them to Brunswick was, however, bombed in the station and they were forced to remain in limbo awaiting liberation by advancing US troops.

Oflag IX A/Z at Rotenburg was evacuated on 29 March. The prisoners had heard on the grapevine of the terrible marches away from camps in the east before the Russians arrived and wanted to stay put. However, the exodus was a fairly humane affair. They were allowed to organize themselves. Most carried a great deal of food, elderly and disabled prisoners led the march and even two women from the censor's office joined the column. The camp guards were generally old men and caused little trouble but the real danger came from *SS* troops, Hitler *Jugend* and *Volkssturm* wandering about the ruined countryside: 'A shot in the head would be a poor finish to four or five years' captivity, and we all wanted to get home,' remarked Second Lieutenant Baxter. Consequently, the prisoners stayed close together.

On the march from Rotenburg each company carried bed linen which they laid out as a warning sign to Allied aircraft. At one stage they saw officers from Oflag IX A/H also tramping towards the Harz mountains though no contact was allowed between the two columns.

The prisoners from Spangenberg had left early on the morning of 30 March. They had been ready to move for some time, after previous false alarms, and most were heavily laden with various goods after giving much thought as to what they ought to carry. 'The question of relative values comes strongly to the fore here,' wrote Captain Sewell. 'People were offering articles which normally are of considerable value – but no takers.'

As the camp was emptied in two batches, stores of food were thrown to local villagers; there was the crash of glass as one tin sailed airily through a window. The pace was sedate and the weather good. Camping in barns under primitive conditions, the prisoners observed a profound change in their captors: 'All our guards were the original Spangenberg "postens" who marched with us. They were very decent indeed, no shouting – "fall in gentlemen, please" etc. A march under conditions of German retreat,' considered Sewell, 'is certainly a very different matter to those earlier marches – all shouting, all prodding – of the days when the Germans thought they were winning.'

After celebrating Easter Day in the open on a makeshift altar, using a farm gate and roughly-constructed cross, the prisoners moved on past streams of German military vehicles, many towing others through lack of petrol. All around them Allied aircraft bombed and strafed villages and towns.

By 4 April they had reached the village of Lengenfeld-Amstein near Kassel where British and German representatives went off to contact US troops. 'Several odd German soldiers are hanging about here apparently ready to give themselves up – a most extraordinary situation,' remarked Sewell.

Other POWs on the move included men from Oflag VA who entrained from Weinsburg on 31 March and travelled through areas systematically devastated by bombing on their way to Stalag VIIA at Moosburg. There, officers found the buildings and latrines overflowing, light fittings smashed and mattresses badly soiled. 'I had seen some pretty good "lows" in my POW career but this was an "all time low",' observed Second Lieutenant Robson. 'The situation seems to be quite out of control,' he concluded.

Prisoners from Stalag XIIIC at Hammelburg were marched out of their camp on 27 March and ended up over 200 hundred miles away to the south-east near Moosburg, on 22 April. Two thousand of them had already been transported from Stalag 344 and their further wanderings were particularly tough. In the same way, at Duderstadt some of the men who formerly came from Stalag VIIIC at Sagan found themselves again on the road drifting northwards towards Brunswick and Magdeburg.

Some camps, like Stalag XIB at Fallingbostel and Stalag Luft I at Barth, were not evacuated. The Germans attempted, unsuccessfully, to force prisoners out of Stalag IIIA on 12 April shortly before groups of haggard prisoners limped into the camp from Lamsdorf after three months on the road.

The inmates of Stalag 357 were not so lucky. To the sound of Allied gunfire and the noise of German demolition charges they were forced out on foot on 6 April, led by the indomitable Warrant Officer Deans. 'They are moving very slowly and the Germans seem to be rather half-hearted about it,' recorded Sergeant Nell, 'but the fact is that they *are* moving.'

Two days later the remaining prisoners left but, 'living like gypsies', were forced to return when they nearly walked into the Allied front line after crossing the Hanover-Hamburg autobahn. Their German guards were now very lenient; '*they* are virtually prisoners,' remarked Nell on 11 April. When the British returned they had to sleep in the open because thousands of other prisoners had moved in and gone on the rampage, destroying everything. But the thunder of artillery could be heard day and night and everyone knew that liberation was close at hand.

The fate of the other prisoners who had left was far less settled. After two days on the road struggling north-east towards Lübeck they 'saw flares, gunfire and heard bombs all round us'. By 9 April Sergeant Owen was 'on his knees after marching to Witzendorf – "Allez Out" the Goons are bleating and out we are going to the woods for looting cattle fodder and Lupin seeds. What a life. I'm packing this [diary] in now,' he added, 'it's too much of a fag to keep it up; better to spend the time sleeping and looting.'

Shuffling slowly along open roads, exhausted and in rags, their limbs weak and stick-thin from lack of food, the prisoners tried to spruce up as they passed through a succession of hamlets north of Boizenburg on the Elbe. From one column to another rode 'Dixie' Deans on an ancient and fragile bicycle, anxiously watching over the 12,000 starving kriegies.

Three days after crossing the Elbe, on 16 April, the prisoners were outside Gresse in Mecklenburg. Here Deans, after a hair-raising journey to Lübeck and back, had arranged for them to receive Red Cross parcels brought up in massive white-painted lorries, dubbed 'White Angels' by the ravenous men. At once parcels were opened and the prisoners fanned out along the road, eagerly wolfing down such food as they could, stowing tins in their packs and littering the verges with packing paper and empty cans.

Then the Typhoons, wheeling overhead, found them. Thundering down from open skies, seven fighters poured rockets and anti-personnel bombs into the stricken POWs. Some men tried in vain to warn them off, others threw themselves headlong to the ground or into ditches. An eighth, its pilot perhaps realizing the appalling mistake, climbed away on full throttle and in seconds they had dwindled to small dots on the horizon.

At the roadside was a scene of bloody carnage. Over thirty prisoners died where they had fallen while others were rushed, seriously wounded, to Boizenburg hospital. Several of them succumbed later to their injuries. Among them was Flight-Sergeant Steele.

'It was known to our authorities that thousands of POWs were on the march in that district,' wrote Deans to Steele's father in August, 1945, 'and one can only believe that the flight commander who made that attack, in doing so, made a terrible mistake. As a fellow prisoner,' he added, 'and a good friend of many of the casualties, and being one who was subjected to bombing on this and other occasions by our own aircraft, I was deeply shocked at this "incident" as the authorities call it.' As for the dead, they were buried in Boizenburg cemetery and later some of them were reinterred elsewhere. Flight-Sergeant Steele now rests in a plot in the British Military Cemetery off the Heerstrasse, West Berlin.

With Allied fighters ranging far and wide over what was left of the Reich, tragedy was unlikely to be confined to this single incident. Thus it was that RAF and naval prisoners were again badly shot up by Allied aircraft while moving by road from Marlag Nord, north-east towards Lübeck.

On 9 April the Kommandant informed Captain Wilson that he had received direct orders from Berlin to evacuate the camp. The prisoners, led by Captain Barker, moved out under protest the next day. They left behind the sick and some 400 RN POWs who were in hiding at Milag Nord or in the woods outside the camp.

All officers and men officially remaining were shifted to Milag Nord on 11 April and Marlag 'O' was subsequently occupied by 1,000 Americans and a sprinkling of British POWs. Marlag 'M' was then filled with Poles, French and Rumanians who had marched from Sandbostel and arrived in a very sorry state.

Those prisoners who left the camp went under intense aerial activity which made any movement by day extremely dangerous. Nevertheless, they pushed on towards the promise of comfortable barracks. On the second morning of their march they awoke cold, damp and stiff from a night spent in open fields. Commander Scurfield, immaculately dressed, washed and shaved, moved among them stopping to chat with Lieutenant Cambell about the danger of attack from the air. 'If they did front gun us I can't make up my mind what to do,' he said laughingly. 'If I turn sideways on I'm a smaller target, but if my legs are hit both of them are damaged; or if I face the aircraft I'm a larger target but perhaps only one leg would be hit.'

That afternoon, just beyond the village of Zeven, a pair of P.47 Thunderbolts swooped on the resting columns of men. With a complete disregard for his own safety, Commander Scurfield leapt aboard a car waving frenziedly to alert the attackers. Men ran to him as he was seen to be hit and fall while the aircraft circled again for another pass. There was nothing that could be done to save him. Cannon fire had shattered both his legs. The dead and wounded were removed to hospital where Scurfield, after an emergency amputation of his left leg at the roadside, died later of his injuries.

After this tragedy it was agreed that the prisoners would make no attempt to escape and the Germans allowed them in return to proceed in a prolonged line at their own pace. On 16 April they crossed the Elbe to the west bank at Blankenese and then the column split in two. Some men pushed on to Lübeck without their guards and the main group ended up on a massive estate at Trenthorst.

In the meantime the men at Marlag und Milag Nord waited impatiently for liberation. 'Many RAF and RN Prisoners returned here after breaking away from column which was broken up by . . . strafing,' recorded Stoker Tipple in Milag Nord. 'Casualties known so far – three RN prisoners killed, two injured. Germans search camp with aid of dogs for Navy men but with a few exceptions are unsuccessful. The boys have done their job well – Now known as Underground Navy. Escapes from many places round the camp where wire has been cut.' But the period of waiting was not without its dangers. On 20 April an unguarded light in one of the barracks invited attention from an inquisitive Allied fighter. Bombing and machine gunning as it passed over the camp, the attack sliced one barracks neatly in half, wounded many prisoners, and cost seven their lives.

As the Allied forces closed a ring of steel about Germany, prison camps in northern Bavaria were hurriedly moved south-eastwards towards Moosburg where, in Stalag VIIA, over 9,000 British POWs were among 100,000 men of many nationalities. Before leaving Oflag VIIB at Eichstätt on foot for Moosburg, officers lost all their mattresses, tables and chairs as a German reprisal for what were alleged to be miserable conditions suffered by German prisoners in Egypt. But the Eichstätt men like Lieutenant Roberts were not worried: 'I think we have obtained more amusement out of further improvisation to offset its effects than any supposed hardship which may have been expected to result.'

On 14 April, the prisoners began to leave the camp. Almost as soon as they were on the road in bright morning sunshine USAAF fighters spotted them. Believing the long, ragged lines of slowly-moving figures to be German combat troops, the pilots came winging low over the columns dealing death and destruction as the ranks broke and scattered for cover. 'No attempt at concealment or dispersion had been made as we had not considered the possibility of attack, and casualties were heavy,' noted Lieutenant Shaw.

Carrying their dead and wounded and greatly shaken, they went back to Eichstätt and set off again thirty-six hours later, moving only at night and lying up in villages alongside their route during the day.

They were on the road for ten days and allowed a fair measure of freedom to barter with civilians because the SBO had given parole to the Germans against escaping after the first couple of nights when anyone who wanted to break away from the column had done so. Marching behind several 'White Angel' lorries they reached Moosburg to find the 'most amazing scenes of chaos' and the same filthy conditions and overcrowding encountered by earlier arrivals from Oflag VA and elsewhere.

Some prisoners destined for Moosburg never reached there at all. NCOs from Stalag 383 at Hohenfels, for example, who started out on 13 April drifted slowly *en route* for Stalag VIIA leaving behind their sick and wounded. Others, like Sergeant Allwood, escaped into the forests surrounding the camp. They kept alive by slaughtering a sheep, using a spare razor blade, and cooking it over a fire deep in the forest. 'My father brought me up to poach in the hungry '20s and it came in handy.'

Those men who stayed with the columns found no trouble from the

German guards who were reluctant to move far while Allied fighters ruled the skies. It was the presence of vicious Hungarian *SS* troops which kept them going, though it was obvious no one had any idea of their destination. After twice crossing the Danube following a line generally in the direction of the Czech border and with the sounds of battle coming ever closer, the prisoners split into groups of 200–300 men and billeted in farms along the way.

The Germans also attempted to move POWs out of their Austrian camps before they could be liberated. From outlying *Arbeitskommandos* and scattered farms men were called in to collecting centres and then forced out on the road with their guards.

Late in April all the sick and unfit at Stalag XVIIIA were sent by train to Stalag XVIIIC while their colleagues set out on foot, following a line running roughly north-westwards from Wolfsberg. Much of this journey was in good weather but prisoners who started from *Arbeitskommandos* in the south and east had a more difficult time, slithering through waist-deep snow in howling blizzards away from the sound of Russian gunfire, scrounging food by the wayside and suffering from the cold and wet until sub-zero weather gave way to milder conditions.

Some columns of prisoners were on the road until the very last day of the war. On the loose, too, were many small groups, precariously avoiding *SS* troops or Hitler *Jugend* and living off the land. Inside their prison camps thousands upon thousands of men waited in an agony of suspense for the final battle to release them from captivity.

British paratroopers, specially briefed by MI9, parachuted into Stalag XVIIIA at Wolfsberg on 8 May and liberated the sick and wounded left there. But in other places prisoners had to await the arrival of British, American or Russian tanks. Far to the east, British POWs were already in Soviet hands as their camps were overrun.

'Please God, let everything go well from now on and let time pass quickly. . . . Oh God, I'm in a fever of excitement,' wrote Sergeant Wagner as British officers took over Stalag IIIA at Luckenwalde. In the north of Germany the prisoners at Stalag Luft I also set up their own security system on 1 May as the German guards melted away. The next day a drunken Russian soldier arrived waving a gun and ordered the prison gates to be opened. With the Stars and Stripes, RAF Ensign, and Red Flag fluttering over the camp and former prisoners engaged in an orgy of looting and destruction, the local Burgomaster went quietly home and committed suicide. Liberation came to men in different ways.

9
HOME IS THE HUNTER

I N THE SPRING of 1945 an army of ragged ex-POWs began to converge on routes leading westwards, their transport an extraordinary variety of 'liberated' jeeps, lorries, battered German wagons, horse-drawn carts, bicycles and even fire engines and steam rollers.

When their vehicles ran out of fuel they simply abandoned them. Along the way they lived off the land, foraging for food and using all their cunning developed in the hard school of prison life. 'At this stage of our freedom,' wrote Trooper Stopford, 'it was vitally important to avoid officialdom since otherwise we might be caught up in a vast dragnet of displaced persons and put into a camp.'

This was not how the planners at home had thought things would work out but when Germany's resistance collapsed into bloody confusion long-term arrangements by planners at SHAEF for the liberation and repatriation of POWs had to be hastily revised. Originally staging and transit camps were planned for the orderly transfer of released men to England. Early in 1945 it was decided to set up advance collecting centres situated, in the first instance, at Brussels and Goch (for 21st Army Group), at Namur (12th Army Group), and at Epinal and Sedan (Communications Zone).

In order to get men home as quickly as possible and mindful of the massive disruption to transport on the European mainland, the great bulk of Allied ex-POWs were to be repatriated by air. These would be handled by Combined Air Transport Operations Room (CATOR) and flown straight to England, except for the Americans and a few others who would embark at Le Havre.

As the Allied armies tore the heart out of Germany, camps were overrun in east and west and few prisoners were forced out of them after 18 April when Britain, France and the United States accepted a German offer to leave POWs where they were near all fighting Fronts.

In the north-east, combined forces of the Canadian First Army and Second British Army liberated Oflag 79 on 12 April, Stalag XIB at Fallingbostel on 16 April and Marlag und Milag Nord on 28 April, together with prisoners out on the road. In the central zone the Ninth, First, and Third United States' Armies, and in the south the Seventh Army, caught up with prisoners from Oflag XIIB held at Lollar transit camp as early as 28 March and overran Oflag IX A/H, Oflag IX A/Z, Oflag VA and Stalag XIIIC after their inmates had been moved eastwards. Oflag IVC was liberated on 15 April, Oflag VIIB ten days later and Stalag VIIA on the 29th. But POWs at Stalag XVIIIA had to wait until VE Day (8 May) before Patton's men released them.

The power and scale of Allied military might was now revealed to men who had not seen active service for months or years. An unending column of fast-moving tanks, guns and armoured vehicles advancing toward the Elbe certainly surprised Private Dyson, on his way to Hildesheim aerodrome after liberation by United States' troops: 'Our memories were of 1940 when a poorly equipped, partly amateur army was attempting to halt the advance of the panzers and failing dismally. We could see now the avalanche of sophisticated hardware descending on a Germany . . . powerless to avoid the inevitable catastrophe. It was exciting and very reassuring.'

Some camps were only liberated after the cutting edge of war had sliced through them. At Marlag und Milag Nord Kommandant Schmid told the SBO that *Korvettenkapitän* Rogge and one hundred guards would remain while the rest of the German staff were pulling out. Immediately a RN guard was placed around the inside perimeter and on the gates of all the compounds to prevent anyone making a quick dash for freedom.

A tremendous artillery barrage from the west started on 25 April accompanied by strafing of German emplacements in the woods around the camp by RAF fighters. In the nearby village hung the body of a dead German soldier as a warning to other deserters.

On the following day the German forces pulled back, their tired remnants streaming past the camp. Women and children sought the safety of the perimeter wire while, in a last desperate attempt to spare both prisoners and civilians the full horrors of what was to come, Rogge and another officer, Henken, were persuaded to approach the British under a white flag to ask for a negotiated truce.

As they arrived Squadron Leader Evans saw them led, blindfold, to 32nd Brigade HQ where they were told they would be treated as enemy POWs. 'I must own that this treatment seemed to me pretty drastic at the time. The two Germans protested as violently as they dared, but no one felt inclined to treat Germans as if they had any "rights" whatsoever.'

Back at Marlag Nord, Captain Wilson was 'horrified' when he found out what had happened to them and though Rogge eventually returned to the camp on parole, Henken was sent to a front-line POW assembly camp where his watch and pen were stolen.

The Guards Armoured Division, engaged in a life and death struggle with German forces dug in around Westertimke, were out to destroy the remnants of the northern German armies. But they were hindered by the need to save the lives of Allied prisoners as Stoker Tipple noted: 'The lads have been greatly handicapped, having to get to this place without any heavy stuff for fear of blowing up [the] camp.'

Inside the compounds tension remained high throughout the final days and hours and there was continuous action: 'The gallant Germans have placed tanks and heavy guns all round the camp and have been blasting away all day taking advantage of prisoners. Very bad visibility,' noted Tipple, 'otherwise Typhoons and Spitfires would soon put paid to their tricks. Prisoners making the best shelters they can in ground.' British infantry finally 'crept up under a smokescreen with only small arms and got to work on the German tanks. Blew one up and the rest have fled. . . . Our tanks are coming up now and there is a big battle going on. Shells are whizzing over camp from all directions. Shelling nearly all night. Have been very lucky in this camp, [Milag Nord] only shrapnel and small bullets landing here.'

Before it was light on the morning of 28 April, with British tanks surrounding the perimeter, Lieutenant McGregor of the Scots Guards met Captain Wilson at the main gate of Marlag Nord. The German guards, who had taken no part in the fighting, were led away to captivity. Amid scenes of great jubilation Red and White Ensigns were simultaneously hoisted over the camp with bugle and general salute followed by three cheers for the King. By mid-morning the Press had arrived, though Wilson, absorbed in an enormous amount of paper-work and about to hand over protection of the camp to Lieutenant-Colonel A——, missed the photo sessions.

The following day Squadron Leader Evans saw Lieutenant-Colonel A—— make his first serious mistake. 'To the general disgust of the camp leaders and of the vast majority of the prisoners themselves, the gates of the camp were thrown open and the prisoners allowed to wander round the country . . . hundreds of prisoners looted the countryside for twenty miles around, travelling in every sort of vehicle they could commandeer, cars, motor cycles, horse buggies and push bikes. They returned quite openly to the camp during the day time carrying the loot.'

Captain Wilson was appalled by the 'absolute chaos' which ensued in the surrounding villages when 'the foreign and tough element from Ilag [Milag Nord] started looting and ill-treating the inhabitants and also getting arms and drink.' A riot squad from the Royal Navy had to be formed to deal with any major trouble, though the discipline of the RAF and RN remained excellent. What angered many of them was that the villagers who were now being assaulted and having their homes ripped apart had frequently sent in food to the prisoners.

News about the liberation of Marlag und Milag Nord spread swiftly to men who were still out on forced marches. 'Officially heard that our camp had been liberated, what luck!' commented Able Seaman Walker, adding, 'Himmler offers us peace. Can't last much longer. Jerries are pulling out of here.' At Trenthorst on 1 May news reached the RAF prisoners that Hitler was dead but Wing Commander McCarthy-Jones felt little elation. 'Apart from a few ironic cheers and buzz of conversation it was taken very calmly. I can imagine people at home being far more excited.'

For the men around Lübeck liberation came on 2 May. Soon after midday, British tanks arrived in the temporary compounds amid great excitement. '[I] dashed up the road to see an armoured wireless car drive up the road amidst wild cheers of ex-POWs,' recorded McCarthy-Jones. That evening was also a time for a 'terrific bash' of food and to bask in the extraordinary sense of freedom again: 'Can't really recollect my thoughts,' he revealed. Lübeck itself was captured in the afternoon after a massive display of Allied strafing and bombing.

Some ex-POWs got spectacularly drunk and a guard had to be mounted over German girls in the camp. In addition, old kriegie habits were still well to the fore. At Trenthorst there was a mass 'acquisition' of cars and motor cycles by ex-prisoners who roared around the surrounding countryside.

Not even the Colonel in charge of evacuation was immune from their lightfingered instincts – his jeep went missing. And ex-prisoners also found themselves showered by their well-meaning liberators with watches, cigars, compasses and other gifts looted from German prisoners. 'I . . . hadn't the heart to take anything,' confessed McCarthy-Jones. 'Couldn't watch them search an elderly Luftwaffe officer but any treatment they get isn't really a patch on what our fellows got. I think it's just a feeling of pity as I know just what it's like to be a P.O.W.'

When they were released some men expressed all their pent-up frustrations and anger in looting, rape and general mayhem – the prerogative of the victor down the ages. Germans hiding in the woods around Stalag IVB were hunted down. 'There was no mercy shown [to them] nor to the civilians, by the Stalag boys. Mühlberg area was gutted when we eventually left it. The German people might have some idea of the sensation of hunger by now,' wrote one former prisoner.

Ordinary Seaman Gant was also among men who were intent on 'having a bit of our own back now'. He spent the time after liberation 'bashing up Jerries, driving around in cars, eating, drinking and doing everything we wanted'. There was a darker side still. 'Russian POWs strung up their guards – other things I shall not mention.'

The reaction of ex–POWs sometimes uncannily mirrored what had previously happened to them. So, while he felt sorry for newly-captured Germans being herded into captivity Wing Commander McCarthy-Jones could not resist shouting at them the old remarks 'we had used on us on the march' (from Marlag und Milag Nord). Private Vincent too came across ex–POWs who were ridiculing their former guards. 'As I watched them it suddenly struck me that the expressions on their faces were very much the same as those I had seen on the faces of some of the Germans who had taunted us as we walked through the French villages on our way into Germany.'

Although violence, chaos and death reigned all around them, there were prisoners who remained remarkably calm. 'Rumour has it that the German guards at the jail are leaving,' noted Corporal Williams after a day of furious activity around Stalag IVB. 'I should be excited as this means that tomorrow will be the end but I feel too tired to feel anything.' And at Stalag IIIA Wing Commander Beaumont was concerned 'with the possibility of freedom nearer than it has ever been, the possibility of getting the chop is rather great. But to hell with the war! The only course is relapse into one's normal state of mental rigidity and sunbathe.'

When men began to emerge from their captivity many of them, like Flying Officer Brittain, could not understand the reason why their passage home was so delayed. 'Politicians in England are certainly letting us down. We hear that bases in England can accept no more kriegies right now, so Yanks have preference of evacuation over us, completely. Maybe they don't want us at all.' After being liberated by Patton's men, the nine days' wait at Stalag VIIA seemed intolerable.

A genuine attempt was, however, under way by American and British repatriation teams who were sent out to the main reception camps in April, 1945, to bring home all prisoners, and especially the sick and wounded, at the earliest opportunity.

Careful arrangements had been in hand at the War Office ever since February, 1945. Some of the planning was based upon psychological and medical findings already available from careful observation of repatriates, evaders and escapers. However, the rapid collapse of German resistance nearly caught the authorities on the hop and a hastily issued message, 'POWBULK EFFECTIVE 21 APR. 45', set in motion the machinery of Reception Centres throughout southern England and the Midlands.

Since it was estimated by War Office staff that the numbers of ex–POWs from Germany in need of physical rehabilitation would be 'negligible', most would be allotted to these Centres. Here they were to be kitted out (special emphasis being placed on having correct medal ribbons attached to tunics), pay, ration and travel-warrant cards issued, a preliminary medical examination arranged, relatives notified and, with a minimum of delay, they were to be sent home on six weeks' leave. At Chalfont St Giles, Cosford, Amersham, Beaconsfield, Horsham, Portsmouth and a score of other Centres, voluntary staff and the Services were alerted to meet the incoming planeloads.

Despite the very detailed planning which had taken place, there were few in the reception teams who knew quite what to expect, though it was assumed within the War Office's POW Directorate that all former prisoners who had spent over four years in captivity, and the bulk of those imprisoned for more than three, would need 'mental rehabilitation'. It was calculated that one-fifth who had been captive for less than three years might also need psychiatric help.

Above all the War Office wanted to avoid mistakes made after the last war when one unit was said to have left its train at Victoria, failed to parade outside the station, and had not been seen again. 'It must be repeated that not only first impressions on joining but last impressions on leaving the Army are of great importance in building up friendly or hostile attitudes, not only to the Army itself but to all authority,' wrote Lieutenant-Colonel Wilson. That thousands of repatriated prisoners would be let loose on civilian life, carrying with them a legacy of bitterness, guilt and fragile respect for authority, was something which the authorities were determined at all costs to avoid.

When Churchill met Stalin at the Yalta Conference in February, 1945, camps containing nearly 51,000 British and Commonwealth prisoners had already been liberated by the Russians. Stalags XXA and XXB, Stalag Luft VII, Stalags VIIIB and 344 together with *Bau und Arbeitskommandos* XX at Heydebreck and XXI at Blechhammer had all been overrun, though many prisoners had been marched away to the west before the Russians could reach them.

In the following month Stalag 357 and Oflag 64 were liberated, soon to be followed by the remaining POW camps lying east of the Elbe, including Stalag Lufts III and IV, Stalags IIIA, IIID, IVB, VIIIA, VIIIC and XIA. But many prisoners soon discovered that their initial doubts about the Russians were rapidly confirmed as they passed from one form of captivity to another, adding to London's 'great embarrassment' at having virtually no information from the Soviets about their release.

Even at first sight the liberators were not reassuring. In Stalag IVB Sergeant Simister witnessed their dramatic arrival:

4 Ruskies on horseback ride into camp armed with tommy-guns, pistols and hand-grenades – barebacked riders, like brigands – I believe they are

escaped prisoners who have rearmed and joined their forces. Roll call cancelled.

We are liberated. All nationals hoist flags in camp. Wet and cold day. Lots of the boys go out of camp – in spite of no looting orders they return with food. . . . We hear that all Jerries who *were* here have been caught and killed. Atrocities committed – people murdered.

Then came a period of interminable waiting. 'Getting restless in camp and despondent at lack of organization to evacuate camp,' recorded Guardsman Adams on 4 May; 'Rations very low. Five days without bread. Visit by British Brigadier to tell us what is being done and to be patient for a few more days.' In the RAF compound Sergeant Simister felt the belt-tightening lack of rations: 'It's obvious the Ruskies want to get rid of us.' The next day the ex-POWs were moved out and crossed the Elbe, foraging for food and shelter as they went, suffering from blistered feet and plagued by fleas.

This disorganized Russian approach to POW problems, which left men to manage as best they could, was due to very differing attitudes between the Allied Powers.

Various delays and mishaps in the handling of ex-prisoners by SHAEF were due to the immense problems of dealing with millions of displaced persons and widespread upheaval in Europe. At the same time the military drive towards Germany's utter defeat took precedence over everything. Mistakes that were made in dealing with ex-POWs were recognizably an unfortunate result of the demands of total war. But the Russian experience was different, both in thought and practice.

Where the Western Allies considered the safe return of their men in German hands as of the utmost importance, subject only to the higher demands of winning the war, the Russians had systematically destroyed any communication with their own people taken prisoner. For all practical purposes over five million Russians simply ceased to exist so far as Moscow was concerned.

Despite German efforts to negotiate some kind of agreement with the Soviets over the treatment of prisoners between 1941 and 1942, Stalin remained entirely unmoved. 'There are no Russian prisoners of war. The Russian soldier fights on till death. If he chooses to become a prisoner, he is automatically excluded from the Russian community,' he replied.

The horrifying results of this attitude were witnessed, for example, at Stalag IIIA, when Soviet liberators entered the camp. They shot their own men lying sick who were too ill to join in the final battle for Berlin.

British, American and Commonwealth prisoners in Russian hands soon found that they were regarded as a nuisance by the Soviet authorities though Stalin himself wished them no harm. 'The Russians were not cruel to the British prisoners of war whom they encountered as they advanced westwards, but they did not bother very much about them,' said Lieutenant-General Sir Gifford Martel, Head of the British Military Mission to Moscow in 1943.

One serious worry for the British Government was that its ex-prisoners might be used as bargaining counters with their release dependent upon the repatriation of Russians in the West. The Yalta Agreement on Prisoners of War, signed on 10 February, 1945, was supposed to deal with this problem.

On the basis of this Agreement, Britain and her Allies forcibly repatriated well over 2,000,000 captured Russians to Stalin's firing squads or the murderous régime of forced labour camps. Virtually nothing of this was known to the public, yet the Agreement was to have little effect on the way in which Allied prisoners were treated by the Soviets.

Despite the fact that Russian prisoners – most of whom showed a marked disinclination to return to their homeland – were being shipped back to Odessa during the last months of the war, there were virtually no signs of mutual co-operation by Stalin. 'It is, indeed, surprising that there should be any problem about the movement of allied prisoners in the Russian zone,' remarked *The Times* on 19 May, when an estimated 30,000 of them languished in eastern Germany and another 30,000 in Austria and Czechoslovakia.

In the absence of any hard news from inside Russian-occupied territory the British Government could do little. 'At present all entry into Poland is barred to our representatives,' Churchill wrote to Roosevelt on 16 March. 'An impenetrable veil has been drawn across the scene. This extends even to the liaison officers, British and American, who were to help in bringing out our rescued prisoners of war. . . . There is no doubt in my mind that the Soviets fear very much our seeing what is going on in Poland.'

Some limited contact was, however, achieved through the Red Cross War Organization which was allowed to send a team of welfare workers to Odessa. They joined a section of the Military Mission already established there but contact personnel were not allowed to remain by the Soviet authorities at the staging posts for British ex-POWs formerly established at Lvov and Volkovysk.

At the port of Odessa liberated British prisoners waited to be sent home. They were seen there by Mrs Churchill during her tour of the Soviet Union in April, 1945. In accordance with the letter, if not the spirit, of the Yalta Agreement on Prisoners of War, a number of them were put to work. And once again the Red Cross had to step in and supply food parcels and canteen services.

An unstable mixture of child-like delight coupled with an almost complete disregard for human life gave Allied prisoners good cause to fear their liberators. These two facets of the Russian character were to be much in evidence in the days after camp gates had been opened wide and barbed wire trampled in the mud of prison compounds.

After the first wonder of liberation was over many former prisoners were shocked at the casual brutality of Soviet troops. 'What a state of affairs exists,' recorded Sergeant Nell at Stalag 357. 'The looting that is taking place is simply awful.' Russians and East Europeans 'aren't human in their present state,' he added. 'I don't like the Germans but I don't believe in robbing old people.'

In one village an elderly couple suffered more than this. A Russian girl who had been forced into working for them claimed she had been ill-treated. Private Copland arrived as 'the Russian soldiers took the old couple to a barn and set fire to it. The screams from the old couple were terrible, I could do nothing about it; I just had to stand and watch the Russians [who] were laughing and shouting.' And at Stalag IIIA, Wing Commander Beaumont recorded a tragic end for four French POWs and several women discovered by a Russian patrol: 'Russians shot and killed the Frenchmen for refusing to obey an order. They probably wanted the women for themselves.' In woods around the camp Russian soldiers killed off wounded Germans hiding in the dark undergrowth. 'Nice people!' he commented.

Various stories of barbaric Russian behaviour circulated among Allied prisoners and German civilians alike. Flying Officer Price came across one of the milder ones at Stalag Luft I:

> When relieved by the Russians, they asked us how we were situated; we replied 'Food for ten days – Rest O.K. except that we believe Germans have cleared off with our money. The key of the safe is believed to be in Zingst.'
>
> Reply was: 'Carry on with your food; if you run short we will take it off the Germans. . . . As to the key, we will send three tanks to Zingst and flatten it.'
>
> The Colonel replied: 'That isn't necessary.' 'All right', says the Russian, 'we will send one. More can be sent later if necessary.'
>
> On its arrival at Zingst, the people met them. The key was produced.

Russian soldiers could often be seen with numerous wristwatches strapped to their forearm. Any timepiece appeared to hold insatiable delights for them. Ex-prisoners soon adopted a well-known procedure when asked the time by a Russian – they thrust their hands deeper into their greatcoat pockets and shrugged their shoulders indicating polite regret that they were unable to help. An unguarded glance at a wristwatch and the wearer was soon invited to add it to a prized collection.

The combination of simple and murderous behaviour certainly gave ex-prisoners much pause for thought at Stalag IVB where Sergeant Simister saw 'tank and motorised men chiefly – [who] have one ambition it seems – to ride a bicycle! They "commandeer" them from Jerries and our boys all day long – our boys often pinch them back again!' Then there suddenly re-appeared in the camp one man who had been living in a village close by: 'Russkie broke in – got drunk on cognac, raped one of the women, threatened to kill all so R—— vanished.'

Since most Russian troops resembled nothing so much as travelling arsenals – festooned with burp-gun, carbine, captured machine-pistol or revolver and hung about with bandoliers of ammunition – few ex-prisoners had much inclination to argue with their liberators. Those who did were lucky to escape with their lives. A few, unhappily, did not.

The link-up of Allied ground forces from east and west on the Elbe, near Torgau, on 25 April, 1945, obviated the use of Odessa as a transit camp. Consequently operations there were run-down and ex-POWs were sent on their way overland from their camps.

Impatient to be exchanged *en masse* for Russians, many could not wait and set off towards the American forces. The safest course was to stay put until official handovers took place but this did not commend itself to men who had been behind barbed wire for far too long.

'All the boys [at Stalag IIIA] want to push off west and are doing so in increasing numbers. I would be right with them,' noted Wing Commander Beaumont, 'if I hadn't this damned responsibility.' Only thirty miles away were the Americans and for many the temptation was too great. 'Told officers and pickets to dissuade the men from going through the wire if possible but if told to "b——off", to "b——off" promptly and avoid incident.'

Two hundred men left the RAF compound on the day that the American transport arrived. It was as well they did. The Russians sent the trucks back empty and fired over the heads of men streaming out of camp. Those who stayed were not exchanged for two weeks.

There were also prisoners in Austria who were liberated by the Russians and they too had to wait impatiently for transport to American or British reception camps. Not until 24 May did an exchange begin at Graz, though many took their chance as the Russian armour rolled in and made their own way westwards.

The Allies' plans for bringing home men from Austria involved an overland route south into Italy. Among them was Driver Parslow who ended up in tented accommodation near Salzburg. Before American troops arrived on 8 May the German guards slipped away: 'I don't remember any POW going "mad" about this. It was time to sit and think about home and the past four years.'

By this time some 4,000 ex-POWs were on foot over the Brenner Pass and a fortnight later most British prisoners from Stalag XVIIIA at Wolfsberg and its surrounding *Arbeitskommandos* had been flown from Klagenfurt aerodrome to Bari or Naples.

When sufficient numbers had been collected at Naples they sailed for England on the *Empress of Scotland*, arriving to a splendid reception at Liverpool on Derby Day (9 June, 1945).

Many prisoners had been moved by the Germans to Markt Pongau or even further along the road from Innsbruck to St Anton at Landeck. They were liberated by troops of the American 7th Army which struck at Munich and Salzburg and took the German redoubt at Berchtesgaden. Among those released were the *Prominente* from Colditz.

A combat spearhead of the 1st Army reached the camp on 15 April and discovered 1,300 POWs, packed together on the ground floor of the inner courtyard and in the cellars of that grim fortress.

During sharp fighting in the nearby village, shells crashed into the castle walls and *Kommandantur* building. Though no one inside was killed Wing Commander Bader, standing imprudently close to a window, was knocked clean off his tin legs. It was only at the very last moment, when a French flag was spotted at another window by a keen-eyed GI, that plans to blast the castle with high explosive and fill it with phosphorus were abandoned. 'Ten seconds – between us and oblivion!' commented Lieutenant Wood of the Royal Canadian Engineers.

On receipt of the code word *Heideroslein* from Army Command forty-eight hours earlier, the *Prominente* had been taken by bus to *Festung* Königstein, about thirty kilometres away, despite the strongest protests from Colonel Todd, SBO at Oflag IVC. At this fortress two of the prisoners, Hopetoun and Haig, were left behind because they were too ill to travel further.

The rest of the *Prominente* were taken on through Czechoslovakia, passing frantic last-minute work on road blocks, anti-tank ditches and weapon pits. At the castle of Tittmoning, near the Austro-Bavarian border, they went to ground, their whereabouts concealed by Dutch officer POWs. Giles Romilly got away altogether and made his way successfully to Munich just in time to witness American troops entering the city.

Eventually rediscovered, the remaining *Prominente* were transferred ever further into Austria, past Berchtesgaden to a massive encampment of huts surrounded by barbed wire set in a wide valley at Markt Pongau. Here they were kept strictly isolated from the other prisoners. *SS Obergruppenführer* Berger told them that he had disregarded Hitler's direct orders to have them shot and, consequently, his own life was in danger. To forestall any attempt at abduction he was going to provide a heavily-armed special guard under an *SS* colonel. Thus they set off for the American forces in two lorries draped with enormous Swiss flags accompanied by a Swiss Legation attaché.

Gottlob Berger, however, had one more trick left in his repertoire. At a small village in the mountains, where the prisoners halted on their last night in captivity, an extraordinary scene was played out. In an upstairs room in one of the local houses he appeared among drunken *SS* officers who were surrounded by rare foods and wines. Swaying slightly, as if drunk, mouthing a flood of anti-Bolshevist propaganda, he finally presented the senior POW present, Captain The Master of Elphinstone, with a scarlet leather case. 'Inside,' wrote Elphinstone, 'was an elaborately carved ornamental pistol of ivory, brass, and enamel, with his own signature engraved across the butt.' Every other man received something befitting his role as an officer and a gentleman – a huge cigar, complete in glass container.

After this strange interlude the POWs were driven down the Inn valley and passed cautiously through the American front line. Eventually they reached Innsbruck, 'all gold in the morning sun', observed Michael Alexander, with its good food, war reporters and the strains of the Andrews Sisters over the public address system.

In the central zone, prison camps were liberated one after another. Sometimes, the situation degenerated into farce. On 27 March the Kommandant at Lollar transit camp, where officers from Oflag XIIB were held, made a mistake. Handing over the guard to the prisoners he realized that surrender would have to be made to the rapidly-advancing Allied forces and so recalled his staff. They were disarmed by troops of the American 1st Army the next day: 'it is hard to believe one is actually free,' remarked Major Casdagli. Full military discipline was soon restored. 'One naturally resents it; however, it keeps the brigadiers amused.'

The ex-POWs had thoughts only 'for getting away from these humble huts and stone floors and messy feeding arrangements – and incidentally from the thousands of foreign workers who are crowding in on us.' On the last day of March they were moved to Dulag Luft at Wetzlar – 'all the horrors of prison life, the only difference being no Germans' – and three days later many of them, Casdagli included, touched down in Oxfordshire, 'too excited and dazed to know really what was happening'.

The officers trekking from Spangenberg were liberated by American troops on 4 March. A German major arrived late in the afternoon: 'Gentlemen, you are free. This is the blackest day of my life.'

'We have disarmed the guards,' recorded Captain Sewell. 'I have got some German maps as souvenirs. One can scarcely imagine the thing can really be true.' Taken by lorry to Eschwege aerodrome he had the satisfaction of ordering about several German POWs: 'They worked quite well, and I gave them some bread and a cigarette each on completion of their work.'

On their way home the former prisoners flew directly over Oflag IX A/H. The upper camp in the castle lay in ruins but the lower remained apparently undisturbed. What they did not know was that it was packed with over 4,000 German POWs. At Wing, near Leighton Buzzard, Sewell received a 'grand reception' but the marks of captiv-ity could be observed on the faces of some men: 'Several of the O[ther] R[ank]s . . . looked terribly ill – they must have had a dreadful time.'

At Rheims, Halle, and Brussels, the major reception centres for ex-POWs, a trickle swelled to a torrent by mid-April, 1945. Men arrived by every conceivable means and were greeted by PWX staff and Red Cross representatives.

They were treated to all the delights they had missed for so long while behind barbed wire – white bread, unending mugs of sweet tea, doughnuts, 'Chesterfield' or 'Lucky Strike' cigarettes and candy bars. Each man was also presented with a Red Cross gift bag containing chocolate, cigarettes and personal toiletries together with a card of welcome. Every item of clothing was disinfected and those whose uniform was in tatters received new outfits: 'Oh! where did the fleas go???', asked Guardsman Adams.

Pocketing their newly-issued allowances, some men got exceeding-ly drunk. Many, however, were disappointed that their first genuine alcoholic drink after captivity had remarkably little effect. Others visited local cinemas and re-acquainted themselves with Judy Garland in 'Meet me in St Louis' or sympathized with Lionel Barrymore caught 'Between two Women' – not a problem for most of them.

A genuine favourite with them all was the BBC. 'Heard the Greenwich time pips, also Big Ben over the radio for the first time – brought back memories of Whitehall defences,' commented Guards-man Adams. The news of Roosevelt's death was received in shocked and dismayed silence on 12 April but King George's broadcast to the Empire on 8 May, followed by the growl of Churchill announcing that Germany had been beaten to her knees, was a cause for much celebration among those abroad or already at home like Gunner Jamieson. 'I never realized I would have been in a position to sit at my own fireside and listen to the announcement of the unconditional surrender of Germany.'

By the time that prisoners had been released they were making the headlines themselves. Radio War Correspondents were among the first to enter POW compounds and transmitted eyewitness accounts and interviews to regular programmes such as 'War Report' and 'Radio Newsreel'.

Listeners at home heard of the resilience, bravery and cheerful discipline of British POWs and the appallingly casual way in which some had been killed by the Germans. The famous American War Correspondent, Chester Wilmot, was one of the first on the scene when Stalags XIB and 357 were liberated and recorded the plight of men who had been forcibly marched from Poland: 'I saw them in hospital – drawn, haggard, starved – starved beyond description – limbs like matchsticks, bodies shrunken till their bones stood out like knuckles.'

The lesson to be learned from this was twofold: 'I wish those people who think the Germans should be treated lightly had seen what I saw today. But I saw also something that was inspiring and encouraging. All this German oppression and brutality and starvation hadn't been able to kill the spirit and self-respect of these men of Arnhem, men of Crete, of Dunkirk and Calais, men of Bomber Command and the Eighth Air Force. They'd managed to rise above their sordid environment. . . . They were proud that they had their own camp running when our tanks got there. They felt they had almost liberated themselves.'

Another War Correspondent, Rober Barr, came across hundreds of newly-liberated 'Red Devils' lining the pavements of a small German village on 17 April: 'It was an American officer, I think, who . . . said "Prisoners? Gee, I thought they were troops going into the line." That was no exaggeration – they looked just like it – if you'd seen them today you would have been proud. But what I don't understand is where some of them got the blanco.'

Such accounts, however, while popular with listeners at home only revealed part of the story. There were brutal killings of POWs while they were on forced marches but this was often the work of the *SS* – as in the case of four men taken into woods near Putlitz on 24 April and gunned down – rather than regular *Wehrmacht* troops. The guards who had stood helplessly by were visibly aghast. 'After five years as POWs then a thing like this has to happen,' commented Private Woodley. 'Such an incident will never be forgotten.'

While such cold-blooded murders were painfully etched in the minds of recently-liberated men, and with many of them in very poor health, their systematic ill-treatment assumed almost universal currency among BBC War Correspondents, newspaper reporters and the general public. Yet even in the desperate last days of captivity twenty or so guards were hidden by prisoners from Stalag IVA and handed over to the liberating Americans. 'All had "chits" signed by N.C.O.s requesting lenient treatment for them,' explained Bombardier Stonard, 'as they had treated us fairly and humanely.'

The steady character and good humour of the former prisoner was also something of a myth and recognized as such by some of them: 'The ex-POW is *not* a good type – I hope they, indeed us, will change on returning home,' commented Second Lieutenant Robson, who was put on guard duty to prevent looting at Stalag VIIA shortly after its liberation. The same thought occurred to the Reverend John Naylor while he was at Oflag VA: 'This life in the bag seems to be killing the spontaneous generosity which the great majority of us usually possess. . . . We all seem to suspect one another of sharp practice. . . . It would be fatal if we were to be treated with special care and consideration because we had once been POWs. We should almost certainly come insensibly to trade on it.'

A great deal of ingenuity and hard graft had been involved in order to survive prison life and the habits ingrained from months or years of captivity were not forgotten on liberation: 'Generally speaking, prisoners of war are not fit to be given uncontrolled liberty,' observed Squadron Leader Evans, 'certainly not during the intense excitement which follows the liberation of a camp. Inside barbed wire, to which after several years they have become accustomed, the prisoners act like sane human beings and can be controlled with ease for their own benefit. Once outside, however, liberty goes to their heads and often all sense of responsibility departs.'

Some ex-prisoners tried to grab an early lift home by claiming they had been captured earlier than their mates. Others found it difficult to let go of the free-ranging life of an ex-kriegie. 'Quite a large number of the boys did not seem very particular about going home,' said Signaller Warsop. 'They were having such a great time in the town [Halle].' But there may have been other reasons, as Private Dyson suggested: 'In retrospect I can appreciate that many who were unemployed and living in poverty before the war were in no hurry to return to the dole queue, to housing problems and in many cases to estranged wives and children who had grown up without father.'

At Stalag XIB many men wandered the surrounding countryside, 'moving from village to village, from farm to farm, apparently without a sense of direction or purpose'. Yet Sergeant Wood came to look back nostalgically on those free-wheeling days: 'Whatever a freed prisoner did was on impulse. He acted suddenly and without consideration, seldom working to plan, often letting himself be diverted to a new plan with one part completed.' Eventually, he had to give up this gypsy life and return to Fallingbostel:

Day by day now our world was changing. Administration was moving in. In ourselves too, a change was taking place. The pleasure we had once found in lunching with Hungarian transport soldiers off horses freshly led from carts abandoned along miles of scorching road, the exhilaration of hunting wine and food, even their taste was fading. Somehow, although it was still May, an autumnal melancholy drifted in the mid-day dust that hung above the fields. Evening brought an indefinable sort of sadness in the fading light. And dawn? Well, the growing light promised no more than another day.

Clearly there was no place for us in a country slowly but inexorably returning to a former civilization.

Back at the camp, Wood was soon involved in a plan to 'liberate' fresh transport but, somehow, his heart was no longer in it. Regulated by army rules and fed on rations delivered daily, the ex-POWs were 'drained of enthusiasm and urgency'. At the main gate they met an army captain 'who gently, with great understanding and kindness but with an inflexible authority, issued us with identity cards and movement chits. It was over.'

The final seal on those halcyon days came when they crossed a temporary bridge over the Aller: 'Across the entry to the bridge a "king size" notice exhorted everyone to "get going – keep going." That bridge and that notice left no doubt that we were entering a society demanding obedience in exchange for the food, shelter and security provided. Somehow I knew it was a point of no return and although I suppose I had known all along that the price would be inevitable I recall clearly the feeling of loss, perhaps regret even.'

Compounding this sense of regret for companionship fast slipping away was a compulsive desire for possessions which had been honed to razor sharpness in prison camps. There were 'some amazing tales' of ex-prisoners in no great hurry to reach England before they could pick up saleable souvenirs and slip past the officials awaiting them. Some men even went back across the Channel to secure more illicit goods by hitching a ride on military aircraft to Paris and elsewhere.

A weekend in France was enjoyed by more than a few cunning ex-kriegies and a tale circulated during these mad weeks of liberation about an aircraft returning with motor-cycles strapped beneath its wings. Much sadder, however, were the stories of ex-prisoners who tried to bring girl friends home with them.

The Russians at Odessa and elsewhere invariably turned back Polish, Russian and, in some cases, German women who tried to accompany ex-prisoners to the west, even when they were pregnant or carrying a babe in arms. The American and British authorities were more lenient with them, though their numbers were few.

After spending some time at one of the main collecting centres men were taken to nearby airfields and flown to their reception centres in the United Kingdom. Ex-prisoners frequently discovered that the wait for transport, while they were laden with various bits and pieces and PWX forms including a Certified Disinfected Embarkation Card (for some reason marked 'Secret'), was maddening.

The great airlift began on Easter Tuesday (3 April, 1945) when 400 officers and NCOs from Oflag XIIB landed at Oakley near Oxford. At the height of operations, on 8 May, more than 13,000 ex-prisoners were flown in and the loudspeaker at Westcott base boomed out: 'We have now completed the landing of our 30,000th ex-prisoner of war at this station. Well done, boys and girls! Let 'em all come.' As the Lancasters droned away that evening they flashed the letters 'VE'.

Within a week of the German surrender virtually all Allied ex-POWs had been flown out by Bomber Command and the USAAF. Many different aircraft were pressed into service in an attempt to get them home. Lumbering into the air over Europe Lancasters and that standard workhorse, the twin-engined Dakota, ferried groups of them across the Channel.

The sight of an English shoreline was often rather too much; men sat huddled with their thoughts, choking with emotion, tears of happiness running down their faces. When Sergeant Tomblin flew from Brussels on 15 May, thick cloud spoiled his view, 'but when we were over the Channel I was invited into the cockpit by the RAF crew, and as we approached England from Dunkirk, the clouds cleared and the sun was shining on the White Cliffs of Dover – oh! what a sight for a prisoner of war returning home – it couldn't have been staged better. I must admit a lump came into my throat, and I returned to the fuselage just a little overcome.' But for Flying Officer Brittain the trip from Le Havre to Dunsfold was something of a busman's holiday – he had to navigate.

Unfortunately, no airlift of this size and complexity could have been expected to be free of unforeseen accidents. Ordinary Seaman Coward was about to enter a Dakota when he saw an aircraft lift into the air with its cargo of ex-prisoners and suddenly explode in a huge ball of flame, killing all twenty-five men. 'Nothing shocks me any more,' he remarked. But Captain Christopherson was more fortunate. He survived a crash on takeoff from Brussels and arrived safely at RAF Benson in Oxfordshire.

There were other tragedies, however; tired, over-taxed pilots flew into the sea, into the very cliffs of the English coastline which seemed so welcoming or crashed on landing. Few reports reached the Press and there was silence apart from a very brief paragraph in *The Times*, which recorded the deaths of twenty-five ex-POWs on 9 May in an accident somewhere between France and England.

Ex-prisoners like Sergeant McLean were keenly aware of the narrow dividing line which separated them from tragedy. Soon after being liberated from Stalag IVB he witnessed a double sorrow:

> There were two soldiers in the same unit, who were married to sisters. . . . They had been captured together in the Desert and had spent their captive years with each other, right through the various camps in Italy, and latterly in Germany. They had been in regular contact with their wives, until the very end.
>
> One day, one of these two was sitting on his top bunk shaving when an Me109, being chased by two Mustangs, flew fast and low over the camp. The Americans opened fire, and some of the bullets went through the roof of the hut, killing one of the men. No word of this could be got out at the time, as the war was in its last few days. On the war ending, several of the prisoners, whilst waiting to be taken away, went into the local woods, where they found some Panzerfaust, a type of German bazooka. These they were firing at trees, for sport.
>
> The survivor of the two friends picked one up to fire, and it exploded, killing him.
>
> The pathos in this is that, somewhere in England, two sisters, whose husbands were prisoners of war together, and who had been in regular, limited, communication with their husbands right until postal contact was impossible, were awaiting expectantly for their husbands to arrive, with the other prisoners, and no one would come. Perhaps others knew their identities and could give them the sad news. I don't know, though I often wonder what the sequel was.

There were other men who failed to return from the disturbed ant-heap of Europe. Their non-appearance brought tragedy and heartbreak to those who had awaited their return so anxiously. Nothing was ever heard of Warrant Officer Squirrell, who was thought to be at Stalag IVC when it was liberated by Russian troops, despite widespread correspondence with other relatives, ex-prisoners and even German refugees. 'Most of the British public seem to think . . . that all the prisoners in German hands are home, which is quite untrue,' wrote one correspondent to Squirrell's sister on 7 July, 1945. 'There is too much fuss made in the papers about the Election and Joyce and such matters and it really makes one wonder if the War Office are really doing their utmost to find these men and bring them home.' But the War Office was as much in the dark about the movements of former prisoners in Russian territory as anyone else.

There surfaced in 1975 some suggestions in the *Daily Telegraph* that some British ex-POWs might have been imprisoned by the Soviets after the war. There was, however, never any proof of this and the most likely explanation for Warrant Officer Squirrell's disappearance is that he was killed in skirmishes between Russian and German troops.

Another mystery surrounded the disappearance of Lieutenant Birnie of 2nd SAS Regiment who never re-appeared from his prison camp. Reports eventually received in 1974 were confused but suggested that he was killed in an air raid on Stalag XIIID thirty years earlier though his grave was never located. 'I am afraid Lt. Birnie's death must remain a mystery,' wrote Airey Neave to Birnie's former fiancée in October, 1976. 'He is not the only member of the S.A.S. or similar organization to whom this happened. I myself know many people who disappeared altogether as a result of escape activities and have never been heard of again.'

In equally distressing circumstances, some ex-POWs came home to find an unexpected tragedy awaiting them. Flying Officer Dilley changing trains at King's Cross saw an officer, clutching a bottle of perfume bought in Brussels for his wife, go up to a fellow ex-kriegie: 'You can give this to your wife,' he told him, producing the perfume. 'I've just 'phoned my home and my wife was killed in an air raid.' For Private Bowers, sadness came even as he met his mother for the first time in five years – she was dying of cancer.

Fortunately, most ex-prisoners found their arrival happily fulfilling all their dreams. Travelling from Westcott in Buckinghamshire to his reception centre, Second Lieutenant Baxter and his colleagues savoured that moment:

'The lorry I was in was one of the last. We drove through the landing field's gates and went through country roads on a sunny Spring afternoon. As we turned a corner we saw from the rear of the lorry a country policeman leaning on his bicycle, talking to a countryman.
  "Look, there's a policeman! We're in England now. Give him a cheer!" We cheered.'

Now that the ex-POWs were safely home, their emotions often overflowed. 'I listened to myself giving this information,' said Able Seaman W— at a Reception Centre, 'it seemed so far away now. Everything came back crowding my mind. I wept hiding my face in my hands. The excitement of being out of it and home again was a bit too much.'

Reception Centre staff, the WRACs, WAAFs, WRNS and Red Cross, were very tactful. 'This is Reception Camp no. 90 [just outside Watford]. It's great here, they make you feel like a man again, and not a number,' commented Trooper Spencer, 'The food is great, and there was a show for us in the evening. A great welcome, but the boys are chafing to get home, it seemed like an eternity today. We can hardly realize we are in England again.'

Despite good intentions some well-laid plans went awry. When Captain Sewell arrived at his Reception Centre at Amersham 'it appeared we were not really wanted . . . and they had not sufficient food to give us a meal.' Nothing daunted, he went off and stayed with friends. Sergeant Spencer, returning from Fallingbostel soon after-wards, also found that the sight of RAF blue at Westcott confused those used to dealing with khaki uniforms – 'We six RAF men were not really wanted.' The arrival of 'Bomber' Harris himself soon saw them on their way by Lancaster to Cosford.

At some aerodromes and Reception Centres the authorities got carried away by their own enthusiasm. This was resented by ex-POWs but generally they were smoothly processed. 'Wonderful reception by all and made welcome,' noted Lance-Corporal Groom at Wing in Buckinghamshire; Private Poll walked into 'a great reception' at Westcott which extended all along the route to his Reception Centre – 'people thronged the streets waving and cheering as we went by'.

Such scenes of public approval surprised many men and, on finding how warm their welcome was on returning to England, they were genuinely astonished. 'When we got home,' wrote Captain Wilson, 'I found the house was decorated with streamers and the White Ensign hoisted, a crowd of boys gave me a great welcome . . . I felt really quite shaky now all the troubles are over.'

Prisoners' next-of-kin had received War Office advice not to 'be hurt if he does not come and see you for a bit. Don't give him too much of a party when he does come to see you. . . . Be a good listener. . . . Answer all his questions carefully. . . . Don't pity him. All he wants from friends and relatives is understanding help until he finds his feet.' However, in the outpouring of emotion they some-times forgot this. So for Guardsman Whitehouse the excitement was just altogether too much – 'home to a family and village that wanted to fete and be proud of their P.O.W. and I could not cope, mentally or physically.'

But no matter how festive the bunting and how heartfelt the public speeches, every reunion was wondrously private to those involved. Able Seaman W—, home at last, experienced this moment: 'I peered over the garden wall surrounding my home. My mother was scrub-bing the front door step. A Union Flag hung over the door with "Welcome Home Son." Was this one of those blasted dreams I used to get? Should I awake back in the P.O.W. Camp? What was real in this life? I wanted to shout "Mother", but a hard lump in my throat prevented me so I made my appearance at the end of the wall. I must have stood there for some time before Mother stood up and looking around at me she shaded her eyes with her hand and came running to me sobbing.'

It was somehow fitting that a mother's tears should mark the end of the long night in captivity.

A WASTED WAR?

A HAZE OF contentment and wellbeing filled the six weeks which former prisoners spent on leave. Just to be at home was satisfaction enough and a double ration allowance did nothing to spoil things, though official instructions stressed the need to avoid over-eating and heavy drinking and the necessity of a balanced rehabilitation diet. 'Take as little exercise as possible. . . . Get plenty of sleep and avoid late nights and parties,' was sound advice.

Freed from the monotonous and meagre diet of a prison camp, however, many of them found that they quickly added too many pounds: 'At one stage I had gone down to 8st 4lbs from my normal 12st 4lbs, but with a leave pass in my pocket for 10 weeks' leave I looked forward to doing something about that,' recalled Sergeant Tomblin. 'In fact I blew out like a balloon to 14st in that time, and was remonstrated with by a Military Policeman in London for not having my serge done up – it was too tight!'

Other important matters were put right. There was a rash of marriages by special licence as ex-POWs took the earliest opportunity to wed the girl who had waited through the long months and years of captivity. On the other hand, some had to come to terms with a wife's or fiancée's desertion or infidelity. On both sides new relationships needed to be worked out, as had been foreseen by some prisoners, like Lieutenant Morgan, while they were still in captivity. 'How will they find us at home?' he had asked. 'A little changed perhaps, but then they will have changed too. A little more reflective, better read, a trifle more argumentative and dogmatic, absent-minded, suspicious of authority, resentful of restrictions, unimpressed by fine-sounding phrases, liable to take our places in queues, reluctant to hurry, unable to catch trains – but of one thing I am sure, for a long time, at any rate, we will not be late for meals!'

While they were rarely mentally ill, ex-POWs often suffered from a sense of irritable unrest and a desire to mingle only with those who had known the bleak life of a prison camp.

Returning to Service life or awaiting demobilization made them more depressed still: 'By God, this is a deadly joint – sweet F.A. doing, nowhere to go, nobody I know and a fearful Sergeants' Mess,' recorded Sergeant Wagner at RAF Stamford in August, 1945. Not long after this he had regained his composure: 'Looking back, it hasn't been a bad year. I was a prisoner, lucky to get away with my life. Freed and brought safely to England. A lot of leave. . . . Demobilized from the R.A.F., and ready to start at the University again.'

While awaiting release from Catterick Camp Sergeant H—— complained about the same restlessness and isolation: 'It's pitiful to see the blokes hanging about doing nothing and at the same time not allowed to do [anything]. They'll get so that they've no desire to do anything at all shortly. Thank goodness I'll be out in Feb. for good. But whilst in this kettle of fish find it hard to do anything at all. Unfortunately the course at Darlington Tech was not what I wanted and the mixing of the army course and that didn't help matters at all. However, when I get out and can get cracking I don't expect too much difficulty. I know it's going to mean a hell of a lot of really hard work but I guess a bit of that will do me good after so much inactivity.'

After being away for so long many ex-POWs were strangers in their own homes; they were confused by rationing and much of their general information on home conditions was not up-to-date. They felt easily embarrassed in company, were irritated by the noise of children and often felt they were being watched by, and were suspicious of, their neighbours. This led to such behaviour as going over the garden fence to avoid meeting acquaintances on their way to a pub – which was chosen so that nobody would know them there.

Wives also had their problems. When their husband returned they lost the independent role they had acquired by working in war production or in the social services while he was away. As one researcher commented soon afterwards: 'Not infrequently she occupied a position of authority, and earned more money than her husband had done.' The abrupt loss of this newly-won financial and social independence was a hard cross to bear.

The aim of the twenty Civilian Resettlement Units (CRUs) operating in all parts of the United Kingdom was to provide a controlled community which would act as a bridge between army and civilian life and help to smooth away some of these problems.

When the moment came, however, to decide whether to attend a CRU, ex-POWs were very hesitant because they could not know precisely what they would do there. They were also considerably influenced in that decision by their immediate circumstances and future prospects. In consequence, about a third of all repatriated men subsequently volunteered for them.

Despite the good work of many CRUs the profound emotional disturbance of being captured and the results of camp life made it difficult for many former prisoners to readapt to civilian life or pick up the threads of a military career. All regular soldiers retained for further service passed through special units administered by 45 Division where they were interviewed by reception teams.

For regulars, the time spent in captivity could not easily be made up. Promotion prospects were blighted, as Major Whitcombe discovered: 'I think my chief disappointment when I returned home was the lack of consideration and understanding of those in authority at the time. . . . I find it a little difficult to express my feelings in words. All most of us asked was to be allowed to be able to take up life as far as possible where we left it.' He was retired in 1948 – 'a dissatisfied customer'.

Captain Irwin was another. 'For a Regular Officer, captured in his twenties, who had not wasted his time in Germany, there was a definite future and the possibility for him still to attain high rank. However, I do not consider that those in High Command in 1945–'46 – the most crucial years for the returned P.O.W. – believed this.' In any case, he was 'very uncertain' about his future in the army, finding much of his regimental soldiering a waste of time: 'I desperately wanted to utilize the mind which I had been forced to use to survive mentally in Germany, and the talents, which I had there acquired, to some creative end.'

Stricken by polio soon after repatriation he spent two years in and out of hospitals. 'At no time during this period or after, did the Army or the Government consider it had any responsibility towards getting me really physically fit again, or towards guiding me, or indeed providing me with, not money, but the faculty – the educational faculty – so that I could take my place in civilian life.'

Those who resumed their military careers generally became philosophical about their lost prospects: 'It is possible that I would have been commissioned at a much earlier date and as a result may have reached higher rank,' reflected Staff-Sergeant McGee, 'but, on the other hand, had I escaped from Crete, I might well have been killed in some other theatre of operations.' The fact that they had survived was, of course, some compensation for blighted prospects, though it was only time that enabled them to get this into perspective.

When ex-POWs were discharged with at least six months' war service behind them, they walked away in a wide-lapelled 'demob suit' and were entitled to leave payments, a war gratuity calculated according to rank and special post-war credits. None of them added up to a princely sum though some officers had also managed to save a few pounds in their home accounts.

Ex-prisoners were also able to make use of after-care facilities through the CRU extension scheme. In common with other men released from the Forces they could also visit the Resettlement Advice

Service and they enjoyed certain limited rights if they wished to return to their former jobs in civilian life.

But many of them found that after the emotional disturbance of camp life they did not want to resume their former job; in fact they were unsure what they wanted from civvy street at all. Life in post-war Britain was certainly difficult. It was austere and often far removed from that remembered from the past. The bleak aftermath of war on the Home Front involved queues, rationing, travel difficulties, house-hunting, 'spivs', shortages, and, to cap it all, a succession of grey, wet days in the summer of 1946 which compounded the general drabness. Men like Sergeant Wood were greatly depressed by all this:

> I suppose the most common sensation of a returning prisoner was one of anti-climax. It had been a long time coming and the imagination had created a sort of mirage. Life in England fell far short of this illusion of course. As well, we seemed to have left behind the goose which had laid so many golden eggs. Here there was little hope. Any talents we had acquired whilst away had little value now and it soon became clear few had anything to offer employers themselves trying to adjust to new conditions. We were now in a strange situation, perhaps best summed up in the changed meaning of the word 'liberate'; a word which had so recently meant no more than to acquire but which now meant theft.
>
> The search for old friends too became a melancholy business. People remembered as amusing, maybe even wild, were now either dead or settled for a great deal less than they had done in our memories.
>
> For some time, life in a house caused me a discomfort amounting almost to claustrophobia. I recall too a triviality and lack of purpose in civilian conversation which produced at times a need to escape as strong as any I had experienced in Germany. Yet where would you go? Escape to the past was clearly impossible.
>
> Strangely enough, one felt most comfortable in the company of other 'kriegies', a company so long and often irksome. Only their reactions and behaviour seemed completely logical, predictable and understandable.

Universal shortages – of goods, employment and future prospects – greatly shocked ex-prisoners, not because they expected an easy living but rather through having deluded themselves that only in Germany were there such conditions and that better things awaited them at home. The rough companionship of prison camps was also deeply missed: 'In the early days I almost wished I was back there with all my mates. After five years that life was my normal life and home was new,' recalled Private Maggs.

Sergeant Tuck was also the victim of this sense of loss: 'Finally towards the end of 1945 I returned to civilian life. Oh how strange it seemed at first. It was so lonely. Remember it did not matter who you were, rich or poor, we were all on the same level as P.O.W.s and tried to help each other to survive. Now in civilian life we appeared to be just a number after all.' Thinking he would be unlikely to get a job, he avoided a full medical on his return home despite a troublesome stomach complaint.

Camp life had been by no means free of petty jealousies, intrigues and occasional violence between prisoners, as Captain Burns acknowledged:

> In the long run – and this counts in the years of Stalag life – most men adopt an habitually ingratiating manner towards those in useful positions, and will do far less for other people in general than they did before they were captured. The occasional memory – and the occasional consciousness of their continued existence – of these developments in oneself is one of the most disturbing legacies of P.O.W. life. Perversions, sexual or criminal, were not, I think, widespread, but they were practised fairly openly and without challenge. A curious and revealing circumstance was the existence, for most of my two years in Germany, of a Stalag razor gang which intimidated British W.O.s in charge of certain camp affairs, who engaged in one or two quite bloody exploits, among minor bullying and rough-housing, without, so far as I know, any counter move being made by the thousands of us who knew of them. This is, perhaps, the extreme case to which was applied a governing principle of social relationships in prison camp – the right of the private individual to make himself a public nuisance.

Now they were home and could no longer rely on this principle to guide their actions. However, prison life for many had not been 'absurdly grim' and ex-prisoners like Lieutenant Morgan knew that only the highlights and sunnier parts would be recalled. 'Thus we will remember the comradeship, the freedom of mind, the leisure, the absence of economic worries, the entertainments, the rare moments of community spirit; we will forget the wet days, the wet weeks, the days when it was an effort to do anything and our bunks seemed the only escape.'

Some men learned a great deal from their hardships. 'I experienced a comradeship strengthened in adversity, which has helped me today in my understanding of my fellow men,' claimed Fusilier Hughes. Others however, including Private Howarth, bore the scars of their captivity more deeply. 'The effect of being a POW was to prevent me for many years from learning how to enjoy the company of ordinary folks. I presume my outlook on life was governed by the fact that we could not trust many people around us.'

There were former prisoners who suffered also from terrible night-mares, recurring over many years. They involved sadistic punishments and an overwhelming feeling of claustrophobia. This condition struck at unexpected times, when sitting in a darkened cinema or travelling on a crowded train, for example, and could bring on terrifying attacks of sweating, breathlessness and blind panic. Many years later Captain Christopherson discovered this when a routine camp visit turned suddenly into a frightening ordeal. Surrounded by wire, with only one entrance and exit, all the old experiences in captivity came flooding back – yet visits to more open places had no effect.

There was little official help for men whose deep emotional disturbance of captivity surfaced much later to disrupt their lives. As a War Office spokesman explained after the CRUs were disbanded in June, 1946: 'The majority of chaps were back at work. The last thing they wanted was to be reminded they were old P.O.W.s. There weren't sufficient of them to fill the centres. They became in the same position as invalid soldiers and were put under the Ministry of Pensions.'

Yet the Returned British POW's Association, started in August, 1945, by a small band of dedicated people, dealt in its first year with 19,017 ex-prisoners (including those from Far Eastern captivity) seeking support or advice, arranged for the medical treatment of 534 cases and found jobs for 479 men.

The British Legion, Red Cross and the Soldiers', Sailors' and Airmen's Help Society also provided valuable aid to former prisoners but the Association was the only body after June, 1946, working specifically on their behalf. Even so, it was desperately short of funds and could not run to any kind of organization outside London though as late as 1950 some 6,000 parcels were sent to ex-POWs who had fallen on hard times.

When it collapsed, men who had been POWs were left with no national supporting organization catering specifically for their needs, either on a voluntary or official basis. The few regional or local organizations, like the Midland Ex-Captives Club, also folded up in the early 1950s.

Some ex-prisoners, however, like Private Daniels, kept in touch: 'From eating, cooking and sharing together, [we] established real friendships which were strong enough to outlast the severe test of Prisoner of War life.'

It was from such experiences that Sergeant Dexter became a founding member of 'The Stalkers' Club' at Zedlach: 'At our last Christmas in this Camp – 1944 – we said that if we were free by Christmas '45 we would all meet in London to celebrate.' Their numbers are now thinned by illness and death but the few who remain still recall the days when they 'stalked' food and other necessities.

That ex-POWs would gradually lose contact with their former comrades after the war as they rebuilt their careers and lives was not unexpected. But for men like Staff Quartermaster Sergeant Crisford the legacy of his days at Stalag 383 was a maximum disability pension. Never recovering from his savage treatment there, he died only five years after being repatriated.

Among many ex-prisoners who carried with them souvenirs from their prison days was Private Maggs, with a lungful of tuberculosis and Private Taylor who suffered from recurring blackouts which caused him to make several attempts on his own life. The severe physical and emotional ill-effects of camp life had profound long-term effects on Private Clarke: 'I was always active mentally and physically but as time went on I find I have become one of the handicapped . . . I am depressed, disillusioned'; and on Private Copland whose claustrophobia made him believe that he was becoming insane. Too frightened to tell anyone of his troubles it was not until he was happily married that his health improved, though he was never able to work again and was 'disgusted at the way the British looked after their own people'.

The way in which men like Private Andrews were treated was certainly little short of scandalous. While a prisoner he received no mail or parcels and was discharged from the army in 1947 suffering from psycho-neurosis. His reward for many privations was one payment of forty pounds eight shillings, and six pence per week which stopped after two years. This mean-spirited compensation helped towards the breakdown of his marriage and divorce.

For every ex-prisoner who suffered severe mental or physical disability there were others, of course, who managed to shrug off the effects of their captivity. But some thirty or more years after they left behind the squalor of POW camps there began to appear in men coming up to retirement symptoms of ill-health which many of them swear could only have been sown by the time they spent in them.

This apparent link between wartime captivity and ill-health later in life has only rarely been accepted by the British authorities. With the onset of late middle age, scores of ex-POWs have discovered the difficulty of substantiating their claims: 'Somehow I have been fighting for my pension ever since,' said Able Seaman Garbutt after treatment for a mental breakdown in 1944 when he was repatriated, 'but I failed to get any satisfaction even when I had to retire from my work due to a similar breakdown.'

Demonstrating symptoms of malnutrition or psychological stress had not been too difficult – Sergeant Watson, for example, underwent a serious internal operation for a condition which seemed positively linked to the reduced diet of Stalag 383 – but proving beyond doubt that they arise from POW hardships is another matter, as he found out when his claim for a pension was refused.

While it might be thought that former prisoners would suffer from higher mortality rates or more psychological and physical disorders than the general population, it is impossible to assess accurately the long-term effects of internment or war-related deprivation. There has been no full study of this, though some attention has been paid to the particular difficulties of prisoners who suffered a merciless imprisonment by the Japanese.

Most other countries gave former prisoners the benefit of the doubt in cases where mental or physical ill-health probably originated during the years of captivity. But despite many efforts on their behalf by the Royal British Legion, the British Members' Council of the World Veterans' Federation and other ex-servicemen's associations, White-hall remains unimpressed by the case for Britain's ex-POWs who are still unable to claim pensions which many would undoubtedly maintain – rightly so – were their due. After all, had they not lost an important part of their young lives in captivity?

'Regarding the POW period,' wrote Lance-Corporal Clark, 'I unofficially deduct 4 years from my age as I reason I did not exist as a human being for that time, so it does not count.' Less than one hundred pounds seemed to Gunner Woolley pathetically inadequate compensation for three years' imprisonment: 'I felt that the paltry amount . . . was not a fair return for a soldier who had been away from home in the thick of the fighting for the best part of the whole of the war years. This was a grievance which many servicemen felt and still do.'

No money could compensate men for that lost time, nor could it erase the vivid mental scars carried by such former captives as Sergeant Hawkes who was at Stalag IVB: 'Memories come back when I am alone. I can still see Russians being poleaxed with pickaxe handles when they lined the route from the canteen waiting for the cart coming with potato peelings to eat. The noise of their bones breaking will be with me for ever.' As a sign, however, that the Government valued their wartime service and as a late recompense for their suffering, some payment would be a just recognition.

There is a continuing resentment, too, at the shabby financial treatment of some officers. In 1945, those who protested about the withholding of monies due to them by the Ministry of Defence were warned that they risked prosecution under the Official Secrets Act if they made their grievances public in the next thirty years.

At the heart of the matter lay the issue of *Lagergeld*. The British authorities acted strictly in accordance with the Geneva Convention by deducting about one-third of an officer's pay as soon as he was captured, on the understanding that the Germans would be reimbursed at the end of the war for the *Lagergeld* they issued. A fine Treasury toothcomb also taxed gross incomes; officers had to pay back money for the issue (or, as it often turned out, non-issue) of worthless camp money whose only use was in endless games of bridge.

When these officers came home they were, according to the Ministry of Defence, reminded of the need to claim back refunds of pay, including that stopped in lieu of *Lagergeld*. There is evidence to suggest that such arrangements did operate and the Ministry claims that 'refunds were substantial and widespread'. But numbers of outraged ex-POWs claim that this was never done. Most of them were not in a fit state to check bank balances, fill in forms and apply for rebates at that time.

Even had ex-POWs not made individual claims, many officers' camps kept precise accounts which were brought home and sent on to the War Office. Most of these records were unaccountably destroyed some time before all the money owing, somewhere between three and four million pounds, was paid over to the Exchequer in 1950–51.

The absence of records and the difficulty of substantiating individual claims so many years after the events in question were arguments used by Whitehall consistently to avoid tackling the problem. In the face of repeated obstruction by officials and bland denials of claims, many ex-POWs gave up in disgust the task of getting back what was due to them: 'In the end I wrote it off as an act of robbery by the Treasury,' said Captain Dick Howe, formerly Escaping Officer at Oflag IVC. 'You can't fight a government department. It's like a plastic bag – no recoil.'

The individual sums involved were not large. In any settlement of this matter somewhere between 1,000 to 3,000 former prisoners could expect sums ranging from about five hundred pounds up to three thousand pounds (not allowing for any element of interest in the intervening period!) and with a more sympathetic interpretation from Whitehall, the widows of those who have died would also receive similar amounts.

But even more important than this long-withheld pay is the fact that the West German Federal Republic, Commonwealth countries, France and the United States all gave POWs their back pay when they returned home. Yet despite a national campaign which petitioned the British Government in 1950 demanding a clause in the peace treaties guaranteeing them similar compensation to that awarded by the United States' Congress to former American prisoners, the British never received comparable treatment.

'I do sincerely feel that much more could have been done for those in similar circumstances as myself, with some form of compensation from the German Government,' wrote Gunner Joyce, 'for all those years of hard and forced labour for which we received little . . . Nothing has so far been done.' Their wives and families could also have made good use of the pay withheld from them and many men are still resentful at what they see as the obstinate meanness of Whitehall.

An added imposition on officers was that their pay was stopped for loss of kit when they were captured. This was applied in blanket fashion by officials at home – though quite how this could be justified when a man was lucky to survive in nothing more than what he stood up in was never made clear.

The payment of cash to most ex-POWs is, however, no longer central to this issue, for, as Flight-Lieutenant Grant remarked, 'at this stage it is not the money but the principle' that matters. Since successive governments have maintained that 'there is no case to re-open decisions taken by the wartime and post-war Governments so many years ago' there is nothing to suggest any change of attitude, despite the claims of officers whose case appears, morally at the very least, to be beyond dispute. There is also a further sobering thought: in a few years time, there will be few of the original claimants left alive to receive the justice which they richly deserve.

Some moments, some events, remain frozen into total recall in the mind, their vividness reminding the former prisoner with great clarity of what it was like to have been in captivity. In looking back the mind is, however, selective, as ex-prisoners readily admit: 'One always tends to remember the better things,' observed Sergeant Upton, 'the sharing of cigarettes and food, the taste of a piece of chocolate or biscuit from those who had them. The friends one made and still keeps. P.O.W. life was bloody, but not all bad.'

In recalling the days behind barbed wire Corporal Walker considered that 'the passing of time may not obliterate all the memories but . . . does help to rub away the nasty and rough edges.' 'Well, I try to forget the endless days and weeks of hopelessness,' said Private Hawkins, 'the fear, hunger, privations and try to remember the amusing moments, the friendship.'

The passing of time has somewhat dimmed the positive horror with which they regarded the scrap of cheese-rind left uneaten on a plate but ex-POWs, like Guardsman Whitehouse, still rarely dispose of anything 'even though I know full well there is no further need for it'.

For many years after being released from captivity, Trooper Moore had a habit of licking a forefinger and dabbing it on any crumbs left after a meal. Now, in his later years, he is horrified by the world's millions of hungry who will suffer as he has. Corporal Robertson, too, hates waste, 'especially of food, and a dislike of over-indulgence', adding 'I have no ill-feeling for the Germans. I now realize that they also were afraid.'

When they were first liberated, ex-prisoners often had a different attitude from that of the British public towards the defeated enemy, as Squadron Leader Evans discovered: 'It is worthy of note that P.O.W.s by no means always have unfriendly feelings towards all Germans. This attitude people in England, who have had no personal experience of Germans, find difficult to understand; it is easy to lump all the German nation together as devils and hold each individual responsible for every atrocity, so difficult to draw a line between the good and the bad.'

Many years later this sympathetic attitude toward their former captors is still widely shared by ex-POWs. 'I have great friends in Germany – I *do not* blame them completely for anything. . . . Certainly I found them a brave and honourable foe,' wrote Sapper Fennell, despite the nightmares that trouble him even now. Likewise, Sergeant Tuck bears no malice toward the Germans, 'although of course there were some whom I regarded as monsters and will never forgive'.

Many ex-POWs now recognize that their former enemies were caught up in the brutality of war and seek a reconciliation. Men like Sapper Kirk have gone back to the scenes of their former captivity and forged new friendships in those places. Visiting the very dam which he laboured to build at Eisenkappel, south-east of Klangenfurt, brought back many memories: 'It was a strange feeling as I stood on the bridge looking over the great expanse of calm water.'

A return to Ergolding in Bavaria where he was liberated was very important to Private Ward. On meeting the family who helped him on the desperate march to freedom there were tears and shared memories: 'Now it had come to pass, perhaps of not much importance but, to me, these experiences had used part of my younger life, and it is just one man's time of being a soldier and P.O.W.'

Ex-prisoners who lived and worked on small *Arbeitskommandos* in Austria have renewed links there more often than others who were locked away in permanent camps. Driver Hall, for example, still corresponds regularly with people on the farm near Pisselsdorf to which he was sent in 1943 where he was fairly treated.

But for men who laboured under brutal conditions or suffered the degradation and misery of camp life a burning hatred of the Germans sometimes remains. 'Even today I cannot regard the Germans as I do other people. I find I cannot forgive or forget their savage treatment of us. Even now,' remarked Rifleman Porter, 'when I see a German car, or motorcycle, I feel I could easily kick it to pieces. I am also offended that no compensation has ever been offered from our own, or the German, governments.'

In Private Hayden's experience, the dreadful journey into captivity in 1940 branded the nation for ever in his mind: 'I know there are thousands who like me can never forgive the Germans, not so much for what they did but for how they tried so hard but failed, to degrade and break us.' Sergeant Bruce is just as direct in this matter: 'I don't like the Germans and I never will.'

'Knowing what it was like to have nothing at all makes a man grateful for what he has got,' wrote one former prisoner and this is a lesson which many have never forgotten. Indeed some, like Sergeant Geary, have come to see their POW days almost as beneficial: 'In retrospect, I feel that the experience on the whole was well worth-while, for one saw the best and worst sides of all with whom we shared our lives through this period. I feel that I was afforded a unique opportunity of observing human nature under many varied circumstances and this in itself is an education.'

Despite ill-health, Trooper Moore is like many others in believing his time in captivity to have given him greater understanding of his fellow men but added one final thought: 'I swore to myself that I would never ever put myself in a position where I had to exercise willpower to such an extent. I don't know that it's been possible to keep that vow, although I don't think I've ever been called upon to exert willpower to the extent that I had to during the various hell marches and as I had to get through each day in the forced labour camp.' That so many young men had to grow up rapidly in such a hard and difficult school of life might also have been an advantage: 'I went in a boy and came out a man,' said Second Lieutenant Varley.

To set alongside this forced development was a blunting of high ambition. Captain Nicholls remained puzzled by an apparent contradiction between the two.

This three years incarceration at a very formative time had deep impressions on me as I am sure it must have done with most of the fellow prisoners. . . . During those 3 years I must have rubbed shoulders with about 3,000 fellow prisoners, all officers and it is reasonable to think that they represented possibly the top ten percent in talent and intelligence of that generation. They were almost all between 20 and 30 years old. But I haven't heard of a single one of them really making a mark in the world. I don't think any of them turned out to be great actors, writers or politicians and yet I would have expected some to achieve such ends. I have sometimes thought this may be due to the fact that we all had these years to do a bit of philosophising and we adopted a different set of values in which being important or influential didn't rank very high.

Some ex-POWs, such as Fred Mulley, formerly an inmate of Stalag 383, Tony Barber at Oflag XXIB, Angus Maude, Airey Neave and Peter Walker, achieved Cabinet rank, while others, like Robert Kee, the distinguished writer and broadcaster, took their talents elsewhere. But for large numbers of former prisoners a desire for public acclaim, worldly goods or the desire to serve others to which they were committed while in captivity seemed to be burned out by the time they returned to civilian life. Perhaps it was like those gargantuan meals which prisoners promised themselves when they got home; they were hardly ever eaten.

All the carefully-laid plans and high hopes rarely came to anything. 'Also I must admit it, for good or ill it shaped my endeavours – in a sense killed ambition, and in consequence I've missed out on the material assets in this very materialistic age,' commented Marine Mine. 'Very strange thing comparisons,' he added, 'it either creates a desperation to reach higher or a gladness that there's been worse.'

Lieutenant Kingsford's experiences 'made one realise one's luck if well fed, clothed, etc; and so probably limited one's future ambition,' and many ex-prisoners, like Lance-Corporal Merryweather, knew after surviving prison camps 'that worldly goods mean nothing, as against health and self-preservation'.

After many years when it was not fashionable to talk of their experiences, unless as a member of the very small and select band of escapers who made a successful run home, former prisoners began to meet and reminisce about the war years. Various associations were formed to bring them together, notably the RAF Ex-POW Association and the IVB Ex-POW Association.

Successful annual concerts in Croydon began in June, 1976, when anything up to 3,500 men met again to swap stories, renew old friendships and belt out some of the favourite songs that helped keep up their spirits in the darkest days of captivity. Ex-prisoners and their families have also been back to many former camp sites including Thorn, Blechhammer and Lamsdorf. Central to such visits has been a solemn Service of Remembrance at the British Cemetery where the dead from Lamsdorf now rest.

For many, the old flame of comradeship, sprung from adversity and strengthened by hardship, has never died; indeed, the passing of time has strengthened it. When Corporal Bell visited one of the mass get-togethers in London he encountered mixed emotions: 'It was sadly gay. . . sad because of the grey heads and lined faces, sad with hallowed memories of those who never made it, memories of crosses and tears and gay with that rake-hell air of bravado that sustained us for so long.'

Others have preferred not to disturb the ashes of their youthful past:

'Since the war I have not seen any of my comrades, in a way I am glad of this,' said Private Handley, 'because to me they seem ageless, and I only have to close my eyes in order to see their young, eager faces before me. Funny thing,' he added, 'they always seem to be laughing.'

There is probably no better epitaph to the unquenchable spirit of men who passed through the fire of captivity and emerged unbroken. The tears remain for those who never returned and gave their lives in the service of others.

NOTES TO CHAPTERS

M OST DIRECT QUOTATIONS are taken from diaries, letters and other contemporary sources supplied by ex-POWs or their relatives to the author. In addition, some accounts have been taken from the archives of the Public Record Office (PRO) and Imperial War Museum (IWM).

CHAPTER ONE

Details of how Churchill and Alanbrooke received the news of the fall of Tobruk are recorded in W. S. Churchill, *The Second World War*, IV, *The Hinge of Fate* and Arthur Bryant, *The Turn of the Tide 1939–1943: A Study based on the Diaries and Autobiographical Notes of Field-Marshal the Viscount Alanbrooke, K.G., O.M.* According to the *Statistical Digest of the War* the total of men serving in the U.K. armed Forces who were taken into captivity in the war against Germany, including men serving in the Forces from overseas, was 135,009. This figure is made up as follows: RN – 5,518; Army – 119,764; RAF – 9,727 (Table 14, p. 13). The accuracy of these numbers seems open to question; they are suspiciously precise and camp nominal rolls, compiled at the end of the war, upon which they were presumably based, were notoriously inaccurate. The total of men in captivity was almost certainly well in excess of this figure.

CHAPTER TWO

Details of the Geneva Convention can be found in *Oppenheim's International Law*, ed. H. Lauterpacht. Second Lieutenant Heasman's remarks are quoted by 'H.S.' in *My Brother John: British Prisoner of War*, copy loaned by the authoress. Adrian Vincent's comment is taken from his *The Long Road Home*. The account of French POWs at Hemer is from Robert Guerlain, *A Prisoner of Germany*.

The order to stay put in Italian POW camps in 1943 is dealt with by M.R.D. Foot and J. M. Langley, *MI9: Escape and Evasion 1939–1945*. Ivelaw-Chapman's comment about *Oberarzt* Ittershagen is quoted by Eric Cuddon, ed., *The Dulag Luft Trial*. Other information can be found in 'Memoirs of Air Chief Marshal Sir Ronald Ivelaw-Chapman', in IWM.

The organization of Dulag Luft and interrogation techniques there are dealt with by David Kahn, *Hitler's Spies* and from a short unpublished history (in typescript) prepared for the later occupants of Camp King (as Dulag Luft became known) – the United States Army, Europe. The comment about Scharff is quoted by Ronald H. Bailey, *Prisoners of War*. Saunders' suspicions about the traitor at Dulag Luft is from his account in Daniel A. Dancocks, *In Enemy Hands*. Sydney Smith in '*Wings' Day* tells the full story of the inspirational RAF leader at Dulag Luft and later.

CHAPTER THREE

The Hon. T. C. F. Prittie's remark on POW camps comes from his *South to Freedom* written in conjunction with Captain W. Earle Edwards.

Information about the German command structure is fragmentary but can be compiled from material in the Bundesarchiv-Militärarchiv [B-M], series RH 53-17/45 and in IWM (Papers on Stalag Luft III Murders). Incidental details come from B-M, Series RH 49/20; 24; 25 and 41.

Michael Duncan in *Underground from Posen* reproduces his diary entry in June, 1940, concerning the German reply to Major-General Fortune's complaint about violations of the Geneva Convention. Hitler's after-dinner monologue is reported in *Hitler's Table Talk 1941–1944*, translated by Norman Cameron and R. H. Stevens.

Information about the new German questionnaire, produced in 1942, and narrow focus of material comes from Kahn, *Hitler's Spies*. There is no definitive map or list of camps where British POWs were held but a useful, though incomplete, checklist is in B-M, Series RH 49/20.

Details of Oflag IX at Spangenberg are taken from Prittie, *South to Freedom* and W. Wynne Mason, *Prisoners of War*. Despite the fact that it deals specifically with New Zealanders taken POW during World War II this volume is virtually indispensable for an understanding of all aspects of Allied prisoners in captivity; it is at once both scholarly and informative and I have made extensive use of it in my own work.

The history of Stalag VIIIB at Lamsdorf and numbers of British POWs there are taken from the handbook published for visitors to the site, Stefan Popiolek, *Museum of Martyrology of Prisoners of War in Lambinowice* and from an article, 'Lamsdorf – the Death-Place of about 100 Thousand', in *Contemporary Poland*, No. 7 (April, 1978). Göring's efforts to control Stalag Lufts come from the 1945 interrogation reports of *Generalmajor* Westhoff and *Generalleutnant* Grosch, now in IWM.

Oliver Philpot's account of Stalag Luft III is taken from his *Stolen Journey*; for the recollection of Arnhem prisoners, see John Dominey's *The Sergeant Escapers*. Moran's account of the fake medical examination is confirmed by the practical joker himself, Howard Gee, in *Detour: The Story of Oflag IVC*, ed. Lieutenant J. E. R. Wood. Captain Monckton's account is in IWM while Guy Morgan's arrival at Marlag Nord is recorded in his *Only Ghosts Can Live*.

CHAPTER FOUR

Marcel Junod's own account of his work for the ICRC is in his *Warrior Without Weapons* and this can be supplemented by details from *Report of the International Committee of the Red Cross on its activities during the Second World War*.

I have found the ideas put forward by Stanley Cohen and Laurie Taylor, *Psychological Survival: the Experience of Long-Term Imprisonment*, useful when analysing the ways in which POWs marked off the passage of time while in camps; see esp. Ch. 4.

Lord Percy of Newcastle, *Some Memories*, was the President of the Board of Education who commented on the background of men who fought in World War II. The Canadian who became a religious fanatic is mentioned by John A. Vietor, *Time Out: American Airmen at Stalag Luft I*. Information about *Bau und Arbeitskommandos* is to be found in J. M. Green, *From Colditz in Code*.

For an interesting examination of the utilization of POW labour see Gerald H. Davis, 'Prisoners of War in Twentieth-Century War Economies', *Journal of Contemporary History*, 12 (1977). The Liverpool and Glasgow razor gangs are mentioned by Ewart C. Jones, *Germans under my Bed*.

CHAPTER FIVE

A comparison of official British arrangements for dealing with POW problems during the First and Second World Wars can be made by consulting John A. Fairlie, *British War Administration*; N. B. Dearle, *Dictionary of Official War-Time Organisations*. A history of the War Office's POW Directorate in World War II has been written but remains unpublished: Col. H. J. Phillimore, 'Historical Monograph: Prisoners of War' (typescript, War Office, 1949). A note appended to this MS, now in the Ministry of Defence, explains perhaps why it was not published: '[This monograph] is really an apologia for the Prisoners of War Directorate and not a full story of the War Office dealing with prisoners of war.'

Sir Arthur Harris's *Bomber Offensive* provided his comment on bomber crews. Information about the use of codes between POW camps and London can be found in Foot and Langley, *MI9*, some of which, in turn, derives from Green's *From Colditz in Code* where detailed examples are given. Among Camp Histories in the PRO there are also a few details of coded letters; PRO WO 208/3270; 3274; 3276, etc. In his excellent account of POW life, Calton Younger explained how the term 'mespot' came to be used. It had 'enjoyed pre-war currency in the R.A.F., men isolated in Mesopotamia having been jilted in such numbers that a 'Mesopotamian letter' came to have a special connotation. The inevitable construction stuck'; taken from his *No Flight from the Cage*, as are his other comments.

Some details of the camp newspaper for Americans and *Pow Wow* are given by David A. Foy *For You the War is Over*. The Radio Padre's talks are noted in Foot and Langley, *MI9*, while Francis Ambrière mentions the trouble caused by escapers in *The Exiled*. Roger Coward comments on escapes from Stalag VIIIB in his *Sailors in Cages*. The punishment meted out by the Kommandant of Stalag Luft I in 1945 is from papers in B-M, Series RL 23/91.

Information about medical conditions is from John Borrie, *Despite Captivity*. The appalling state of Russian POWs is from Douglas Thompson, *Captives to Freedom*.

Sam Kydd has written amusingly of his POW life in *For You the War is Over*. The 'Barbed Wire University' is dealt with by Robert W. Holland, *Adversis Major*. The Canadian who hated Germans is mentioned by Geoff Taylor, *Piece of Cake*.

The names of Munkert and Sommers come from Aidan Crawley's *Escape from Germany* which is the first full published version although an edited edition was put out by Collins in 1956; see also Dominey, *The Sergeant Escapers*. In Younger's book, Munkert appears as Monckhart but I believe this to be mistaken. Squadron Leader Calnan's comment comes from his *Free as a Running Fox*.

CHAPTER SIX

The British Red Cross War Organization is dealt with comprehensively in *The Official Record of the Humanitarian Services of the War Organization of the British Red Cross Society and Order of St John of Jerusalem 1939–1947*, compiled by P. G. Cambray and G. G. B. Briggs. Hilary St George Saunders, *The Red Cross and the White* and the *Prisoner of War* add further details.

The account of dogs hunting down the German guard is from Derek Thrower, *The Lonely Path to Freedom*. Lieutenant James's escape from Marlag Nord is re-told in his own way in *A Prisoner's Progress*. A

plan of Marlag 'O' compound is shown in the frontispiece of Lieutenant James's volume which matches exactly a plan drawn on 6 April
1945 by Lieutenant-Commander Muir – copy in author's possession
supplied by Captain Norwood. A plan of Marlag 'M', showing little
difference from the basic layout of Marlag 'O' was supplied to me by
Leading Stoker Reading.

The scatological comments by *Leutnant* Güssefeld come from
Green, *From Colditz in Code*. I have relied heavily for information
about the British Free Corps on Rebecca West, *The Meaning of Treason*
and Ronald Seth, *Jackals of the Reich*. Copy of the BFC leaflet was
supplied by C. Upton, J. Laurie (and others); on Laurie's is written,
'German Wit'. Material about the Irish Brigade is taken from Carolle
J. Carter, *The Shamrock and the Swastika* and for the final effort in late
1944 from Seth, *Jackals of the Reich*. A copy of the letter from McGrath
is among Payne-Best's papers in IWM. The Reverend David Read's
ideas on reading in captivity may be found in his 'Books in Prison:
Reflections of a P.O.W. Chaplain', Parts I and II, *Chambers's Journal*,
9th Series, I (Oct–Nov, 1947).

Material on educational facilities in camps and the Educational
Books Section of the Red Cross is taken from Holland, *Adversis Major*
and from Red Cross and St John War Organization, POW Department, Educational Books Section, 'Results of Examinations, POW
Camps, Jan 1st to June 30th 1945'; provided by Laurie. My account of
the way in which cigarettes were used as currency in POW camps is
based on R. A. Radford, 'The Economic Organisation of a P.O.W.
Camp', *Economica*, XII (1945), reprinted in Paul A. Samuelson, *et al*,
Readings in Economics. I am grateful to a colleague, Dr. Richard Szreter,
for bringing this to my attention. Donald Edgar has written of his time
as a POW in *The Stalag Men*.

CHAPTER SEVEN
There are a few details of exchanges of British and German POWs by
Count Folke Bernadotte, *Instead of Arms* (Hodder & Stoughton, 1949).
Cambray and Briggs, *Red Cross and St John* is also useful.

CHAPTER EIGHT
Goebbels's newspaper articles are mentioned by Marlis G. Steinert,
Hitler's War and the Germans. The incidents with Hayer and Amberger
are fully documented in *The Trial of German Major War Criminals:
Proceedings of the International Military Tribunal sitting at Nuremburg,
Germany* and in *Law Reports of Trials of War Criminals* (U.N. War
Crimes Commission), see Vol. 1, 'The Dreierwalde Case' and 'The
Essen Lynching Case'.

Trooper Moreton's account of the battle between Canadians and Glaswegians is in Dancocks, *In Enemy Hands*. Bad blood between the Americans, French and British is noted by Ian Sabey, *Stalag Scrapbook*. Air Marshall Harris's comment on leaflet raids is taken from his *Bomber Offensive*.

Details of the *Prominente* at Oflag IVC come from Giles Romilly and Michael Alexander, *The Privileged Nightmare*. Some material relating to this can also be found in P. R. Reid, *The Latter Days at Colditz*. The tough march from Stalag Luft III is commented on by George Harsh, *Lonesome Road*, while my general account of the forced transfer of POWs in 1945 is based closely on Mason, *Prisoners of War*.

CHAPTER NINE

A. J. Evans has given a personal account of the liberation of Milag und Marlag Nord in *Escape and Liberation 1940–1945*. A part of Wing Commander Beaumont's POW diary is reproduced by Edward Lanchbery, *Against the Sun: the story of Wing Commander Roland Beaumont*.

For the inhumane Allied treatment of Russian POWs Nikolai Tolstoy's *Victims of Yalta* is useful, as is Nicholas Bethell, *The Last Secret: Forcible Repatriation to Russia 1944–7*. Churchill's comment about Poland is from his *Second World War*, VI, *Triumph and Tragedy*, p. 377. Details of the liberation of Oflag IVC come from Reid, *Latter Days at Colditz*; Reinhold Eggers, *Colditz: the German Story*; Lieutenant Wood (ed), *Detour: Oflag IVC*. The arrival of the *Prominente* at Innsbruck is related in Romilly and Alexander, *The Privileged Nightmare*.

Details of Gottlob Berger's considerable SS career can be found in Heinz Höhne, *The Order of the Death's Head*. The broadcasts by Chester Wilmot and Robert Barr are in *War Report: A Record of Dispatches broadcast by the BBC's War Correspondents with the Allied Expeditionary Force 6 June 1944 – 5 May 1945*, Ch. XIX.

CHAPTER TEN

Guy Morgan's comments come from his *Only Ghosts Can Live*. Much information on CRUs can be found in 'Transitional Communities and Social Re-Connection: A Follow-up Study of the Civil Resettlement of British Prisoners of War', Part 1 by Adam Curle in *Human Relations*, I, 1 (1947) and Part 2 by Adam Curle and E. L. Trist in *op. cit.*, I, 2 (1947). See also Lieutenant-Colonel Wilson, 'The Serviceman Comes Home', *Pilot Papers*, 1, No. 2 (April, 1946) quoted by Robert H. Ahrenfeld, *Psychiatry in the British Army in the Second World War*; esp. Ch. IX 'Rehabilitation and Civil Resettlement of Repatriated

Prisoners of War' which gives in detail the background planning of CRUs.

Details of war-service entitlements can be found in two booklets issued to servicemen shortly before the war ended: *To All British Commonwealth Prisoners of War* and *Release and Resettlement*. Comments on his prison experiences by Tom Burns come from his article, 'Men and Barbed Wire', *The Fortnightly*, CLVII, N.S. (April 1945). Research on POW captivity and ill-health in later life has been examined by Donald L. Patrick and Peter J. D. Heaf, *Long Term Effects of War-Related Deprivation on Health*. I am indebted to Dr Heaf for a copy of this pamphlet and for his comments on this matter.

The problem of officers' pay has been publicized in various articles in *The Guardian* and *Daily Telegraph* in October, 1980. I am also grateful to C. P. Lynam Esq., (Head of F2 [Air]) at the Ministry of Defence, who wrote to me summarizing the Ministry's position in this matter.

SOURCES AND BIBLIOGRAPHY

Manuscript Sources

I am most grateful to the ex-POWs, whose names are listed below, who filled in questionnaires and sent me tapes, diaries, letters and other items of information. Most of the questionnaires and related material are now lodged permanently in the archives of the Imperial War Museum. Prisoners who died in captivity and former prisoners who have not survived to see this book in print are marked with an asterisk and I am indebted to their relatives and friends who kindly allowed me to use their reminiscences, set down before they died, and memorabilia which they left behind.

ARMY

Guardsman H. A. Adams; Corporal G. E. Adkins; Private S. G. Aldous; Sergeant C. Allwood; Private L. Andrews; Private F. Annal; Sergeant G. Askew; Private E. Ayres; Private E. Ayling; Guardsman D. S. Bailey; Lance-Corporal A. J. Barlow; Signalman E. Bardsley; Private G. G. Barker; Private A. Barraclough; Private E. Bartlett; Sapper L. Beard; Corporal A. E. Bell; Corporal J. D. Berry; Lance-Corporal T. W. Berry; Private M. Blaza; Private A. Blake; Sapper D. Bletsoe; Private J. G. Booth; Private H. S. Bowers; Sapper A. J. Bradford; Gunner B. J. Bridgeman; Private H. H. Broomhead; Private A. C. Bryant; Sergeant S. M Casson; Lance-Bombadier E. Chadwick; Corporal E. A. Chainey; Captain F. Christopher-son; Private R. C. Clark; Private Z. J. Clarke; Private J. Cocker; Private J. F. Collett; *Private J. Copland; Fusilier F. B. Cook; Private J. L. Corderoy; *Staff Quarter-Master Sergeant H. C. Crisford; Gunner A. Crossley; Lieutenant F. Cundy; Private F. L. Cusworth; Sergeant O. S. D'Alcorn; Private F. W. Daniels; Private W. Darbyshire; Private H. V. Davies; Private E. B. Davis; Private V. C. Davis; Gunner G. Davison; Gunner G. T. Delamore; Sergeant R. R. Dexter; *Private G. Dickie; Sapper J. Dickinson; Private F. T. Dobbins; Private E. H. Drysdale; Private L. F. Dunn; Private D. T. Dunne; Private K. Dyson; Private G. Dickie; Rifleman C. Edwards; Gunner F. Edmunds; Private W. S. Eldred; Lance-Corporal J. P. Fahey; *Signaller J. Fall; Lance-Corporal N. Farrer; Sapper S. A. Fennell; Trooper A. Fesel; Lance-Corporal J. Finneran; Private R. H. Firmage; Gunner A. E. Fry; Gunner R. Folkard; Sergeant R. Folley; Private F. Freeman; Sergeant E. J. Geary; Lieutenant-Colonel G. German; Fusilier G. Gerner; Corporal

H. W. Goodrich; Corporal L. L. Gordon; Driver C. J. Green; Lance-Corporal A. E. Groom; Staff Sergeant A. E. Grover; Driver A. A. Hall; Private J. A. Hames; Lance-Corporal P. R. W. Hancy; Private G. W. Handley; Staff Sergeant E. A. Harling; Fusilier W. E. Harrison; Sergeant J. Hawkes; Private H. R. Hawkins; Private S. Hayden; Rifleman A. J. Haynes; *Driver J. A. Haynes; Lance-Corporal F. Harrison; Gunner W. Harrison; Private F. Hennebry; Fusilier J. Hester; Private F. J. Hill; Rifleman H. L. Hill; Signalman W. Hoare; Lance-Bombardier G. A. Hogan; Major J. R. Holden; Corporal V. J. Hope; Sergeant C. Houliman; Private W. Howarth; Private E. Howe; Private P. E. Howell; Sergeant Major F. C. Hudson; Fusilier T. Hughes; Staff Sergeant A. G. Hunter; *Trooper W. L. Hutchings; Captain C. L. Irwin; Sergeant M. R. B. Jacklin; Rifleman F. E. Jackson; Trooper J. Jameson; Sergeant F. C. Jeanes; *Signalman E. Jevons; Private A. R. Jones; Private H. Jones; Gunner V. E. Jones; Gunner J. J. Joyce; Driver R. S. Kerridge; *Lance-Corporal H. S. Key; Lieutenant P. B. Kingsford; Sapper E. W. Kirk; Lance-Bombardier S. P. Larke; *Sergeant F.W.P. Lawrence; Private C. W. Lawson; Private J. E. Leighton; Private F. G. Lenthall; Corporal I. J. L. Lewis; *Private G. C. Lillyman; Private J. Lindsay; Private P. H. C. Lister; *Private J. A. Little; Lance-Corporal C. Longmore; Captain R. E. Loder; Private W. H. Lodge; Private R. Low; Sergeant A. Longstaff; Lance-Corporal D. W. Luckett; *Private J. J. Lusted; Captain A. G. Lyon; Private R. L. Maggs; Gunner E. T. Magill; Gunner L. Mallett; Private J. H. Marriott; Second Lieutenant R. G. Marshall; Lance-Corporal W. Massam; Signalman L. Matthews; Private K. J. Maxwell; Staff Sergeant J. E. McGee; Private J. McIntosh; Lance-Corporal A. McKechnie; Trooper A. J. Medler; Lance-Corporal H. H. Merryweather; Private J. L. Miles; Private E. Monaghan; Trooper A. H. Moore; Bombardier W. Mordue; Lance-Corporal S. Morley; Signalman A. B. Moses; Major J. H. Munro Fraser; Lance-Corporal W. Mussom; The Reverend J. S. Naylor; Sergeant D. Nell; Sergeant R. S. Newton; Captain A. L. Nicholls; Corporal H. J. Noy; Corporal W. O'Loughlin; Staff Quarter-Master Sergeant G. Ovens; Private A. Page; Gunner D. B. Palmer; Driver W. L. B. Parslow; Gunner F. Peacock; Private C. Pearson; Private G. H. Perry; Private W. G. Phillips; Private A. D. Pickering; Sapper E. A. Pickering; Private R. Poll; Rifleman W. J. Porter; Driver A. E. Potterton; *Sergeant J. H. Prosser; Lance-Corporal P. Pugh; Private C. F. Quartermaine; *Corporal B. Quinn; Private C. Randall; Fusilier M. P. Reavey; Private W. Reay; Lance-Corporal C. R. Rich; *Lieutenant J. J. T. Roberts; *Private P. Roberts; Corporal F. A. Robertson; Gunner T. Robinson; Bombardier W. R. Robinson; Regimental Sergeant Major W. Rogan; Second Lieutenant C. P. Rossiter; *Private W. E. Rowe; Private R. R. Rowley; Corporal T. W. Rowley; Sergeant H. Royle; Private A. J. Rudd; Sergeant C. Ruddock; Trooper S. Sabin; Driver W. H. Sadler; *Sapper T. Scott; Sergeant T. Sedgwick; Sergeant J. S. Sharpe; *Lieutenant G. R. Shaw; Private W. Shaw; Sergeant Major J. Sherriff; Gunner R. Shilham; Private V. Simmons; Lance-Corporal R. Simpson; Sapper A. F. Smith; Private M. A. F. Smith; Company Sergeant-Major G. E. Soane; Lance-Corporal J. C. Sollars; Private W. Southern; Trooper E. L. Spencer; *Warrant Officer F. O. Squirrell; Bombardier E. W.

Stonard; Trooper R. R. Stopford; Driver J. Stoppard; Private A. Strudwick; Sergeant F. A. Suckling; Private W. J. Sudworth; Corporal W. Swift; Private H. Taylor; Private J. Taylor; Sergeant W. Taylor; Driver W. H. Taylor; Gunner W. H. Taylor; Lance-Corporal E. J. Tibbitts; Driver B. A. Tomkins; Signalman C. H. Trewin; Sergeant H. W. Tuck; Sergeant G. Upton; Second Lieutenant J. P. Varley; Private F. A. Wale; Private H. J. Walker; Corporal S. R. Walker; Private S. C. Ward; Sergeant R. Watson; Private J. J. Webster; Corporal J. R. Welland; Gunner D. A. H. West; Private P. C. J. Whelan; Private E. Whitaker; Corporal J. G. White; Guardsman S. Whitehouse; Corporal J. Williams; Corporal R. W. S. Williams; *Company Quarter-Master Sergeant E. R. Willis; Trooper A. H. Wilson; Private C. T. Wilson; Private P. A. Wilson; *Private H. F. Wiseman; Gunner A. M. Woodley; Gunner A. W. Woolley; Sergeant A. W. Wren; *Private H. H. Yapp.

RAF

Sergeant R. W. Anderson; Sergeant C. Aynsley; Sergeant J. K. Banfield; Flying Officer A. Bolton; Flying Officer I. D. Bolton; *Flight-Sergeant W. K. H. Bowden; Sergeant D. Bruce; *Flight-Sergeant J. H. Bulmer; Sergeant J. S. Caton; Sergeant D. C. Dunphy; Flying Officer C. Dilly; Flying Officer K. F. East; Sergeant R. H. Eeles; Sergeant R. Esling; Sergeant B. B. Fereday; Sergeant R. S. Fermor; Corporal R. E. Fletcher; Flying Officer L. L. Ford; Warrant Officer E. Frais; Sergeant M. A. Green; Flying Officer G. A. Griffiths; Pilot Officer W. A. Hancock; Pilot Officer K. J. S. Harvey; Sergeant L. H. Harcus; Sergeant L. H. Humes; Squadron Leader F. W. M. Jensen; Sergeant M. Kelly; Pilot Officer W. H. Layne; Sergeant H. R. C. Lowman; Sergeant W. W. M. Margerison; Sergeant H. G. McLean; *Wing Commander C. C. McCarthy Jones; Sergeant H. W. Owen; Sergeant D. Peachey; Flying Officer N. G. Price; Sergeant O. Roberts; Pilot Officer L. R. Sidwell; Sergeant G. J. W. Simister; Sergeant J. B. Smith; Sergeant A. K. Snell; Sergeant E. Spencer; *Flight-Sergeant F. J. W. Steele; Sergeant M. Stretton; Sergeant D. Taylor; Sergeant D. S. Veale; Sergeant H. Wagner; Sergeant W. P. Wood; *Sergeant F. Webster; Pilot Officer T. W. S. Wilson.

NAVY

Able Seaman A. Bailey; Marine W. E. Blockley; Lieutenant N. K. Cambell; Able Seaman I. A. Clark; Ordinary Seaman R. N. Flowers; Ordinary Seaman A. T. M. Gant; Able Seaman F. O. Garbutt; Marine E. J. Hill; Technical Officer L. Haddow; Leading Telegraphist J. H. Laurie; *Petty Officer H. M. Macey; Marine E. F. Mine; Lieutenant Commander R. Mercer; Captain (RM) L. Norwood; Able Seaman (MN) U. Peters; Able Seaman J. P. Read; Leading Stoker R. G. Reading; Petty Officer H. F. Ship; *Stoker (MN) E. Tipple.

Material sent to the author:

Guardsman H. Adams – Log Book

Private L. G. Aldous – Letters

Private E. Ayling – Account, '"Eleven More Months", the Journal of a Private Soldier', Unpub. TS, Letters, etc.

Marine W. E. Blockley – Letters, etc.

Flying Officer A. Bolton – Log Book

Flying Officer I. D. Bolton – Log Book

Gunner B. J. Bridgeman – Log Book

*Flight-Sergeant J. H. Bulmer – Letters, etc.

Lance-Bombardier E. Chadwick – Diary

Private R. C. Clark – Letters

Private J. L. Corderoy – Account

Private F. W. Daniels – Account

Gunner G. T. Delamore – Diary (fragmentary)

Sapper J. Dickinson – Letters, etc.

Sergeant R. H. Eeles – Log Books

Gunner R. Folkard – Letters, etc.

Able Seaman A. T. M. Gant – Diary, Letters

Sergeant M. A. Green – Log Book, etc.

Lance-Corporal A. E. Groom – Diaries

Technical Officer L. Haddow – Log Book

Corporal V. J. Hope – Diary (fragmentary), etc.

*Trooper W. L. Hutchings – Letters

*Signalman E. Jevons – Notebook, Letters, etc.

Gunner J. J. Joyce – Account

Pilot Officer W. H. Layne – Log Book

Leading Telegraphist J. H. Laurie – Log Book, Papers, etc.

Private F. G. Lenthall – Diary, Papers, etc.

*Private G. C. Lillyman – Diary (2)

*Private J. A. Little – Letters

Private W. H. Lodge – Account

*Private J. J. Lusted – Diary (fragmentary)

Gunner L. Mallett – Papers

Flight-Sergeant W.W.M. Margerison – Diary (fragmentary)

*Wing Commander C. C. McCarthy Jones – Log Book

Marine E. F. Mine – Papers

Bombardier W. Mordue – Notebook

Lieutenant H. C. M—— Log, Papers, etc.

Major J. H. Munro Fraser – Log Book, Papers, etc.

Reverend J. S. Naylor – Diaries

Sergeant D. Nell – Notebooks (5) Diary

Captain A. L. Nicholls – Log Book, etc.

Sergeant H. W. Owen – Log Book

Private G. H. Perry – Letters, Papers

Private R. Poll – Diary (fragmentary)

Flying Officer N. G. Price – Log Book

*Sergeant J. H. Prosser – Notebook Diary

Leading Stoker R. G. Reading – Log Book, Papers, etc.

*Lieutenant J. J. T. Roberts – Letters, Photographic album

Gunner T. Robinson – Diary

Corporal T. W. Rowley – Notebook, Diary

Trooper S. Sabin – Account

*Sapper T. Scott – Papers

*Lieutenant G. R. Shaw – Diary

Petty Officer H. F. Ship – Log Book, Papers

Lance-Corporal R. Simpson – Diary

Company Sergeant-Major G. E. Soane – Diary

Trooper E. L. Spencer – Diaries, Papers
*Flight-Sergeant F. J. W Steele – Letters, Papers
*Stoker E. Tipple – Log Book
Sergeant H. W. Wagner – Diaries, Papers
*Sergeant F. Webster – Papers, etc.

Private P. C. J. Whelan – Log Book, Papers
*Company Quarter-Master Sergeant E. R. Willis – Notebook, Papers
Trooper A. H. Wilson – Account
Gunner A. M. Woodley – Diary (fragmentary)
*Private H. H. Yapp – Letters

Imperial War Museum Archives
Second Lieutenant E. H. Baxter – 'Oflag Occasions', Unpub. TS
Major E. Booth – 'The Diary of a Prisoner of War', Unpub.
Major A. T. Casdagli – Diary, TS transcript, Letters, etc.
Lieutenant M. Freer Roger – Diary, Oct 1942–Dec 1943
Sergeant L. H. Harcus – Diaries, TS transcript
Sergeant A. G. Hickmott – Scrapbook
Sir Ronald Ivelaw-Chapman – 'Memoirs', Unpub. TS
Gunner W. W. Jamieson – Account
Colonel L. E. Le Souef – 'To War Without a Gun', later pub. under same title by Artlook (Western Australia, 1980)
Gunner B. H. Martin – Account
Private D. C. Mason – Diary, Account
Second Lieutenant F. Robson – 'Human Worms: One Who Turned', Unpub. TS
Captain J. H. Sewell – Log Books, Papers, etc.
Private L. B. Shorrock – Account
Bombardier J. Tonkin – 'No Tunnels – No Wooden Horses', Unpub. TS
Sergeant H. J. Walden – 'A Scar On My Mind', Unpub. TS
Signalman G. F. Warsop – 'In God's Pocket', Unpub.
Major A. C. Whitcombe – 'Some notes on experiences and reactions of a POW', Unpub. TS, Papers
Captain G. F. Wilson – Diaries, Papers

Public Record Office
The PRO has produced a useful guide to its records on this subject – Leaflet 39, *'Prisoners of War: Documents in the Public Record Office.'*
Material relating to POWs in German captivity is to be found scattered throughout various sets of files. The most useful are:
WO 32 (War Office Registered Files. These cover all aspects and are the main source for British POWs in German captivity)
WO 163 (Minutes of the Imperial POW Committee, 1941–45)
WO 165 (Official War Diaries of POW Directorate in War Office including meetings of the Imperial POW Committee)
WO 193 (Directorate of Military Operations)
WO 208 (Includes Camp Histories compiled in 1945)

WO 222 (Medical Historian's Papers)
WO 224 (International Red Cross Reports on German and Italian camps)
Air 2 (Air Ministry Correspondence)
Air 20 (Air Ministry Unregistered Papers)
Air 40 (Directorate of Intelligence, includes escapes from camps)
DEFE 2 (Ministry of Defence, includes papers on German treatment of
    British POWs)
FO 371 (Material on Foreign Office exchanges with the Vatican)
FO 916 (Foreign Office Consular (War) Department, includes welfare of
    POWs in Germany)
CAB 66 (War Cabinet Memoranda, Acts of Violence towards British POWs)
CAB 122 (Policy concerning Allied POWs)
PREM 3 (Prime Minister's Office, includes details of Imperial POWs in
    PREM 4 German captivity and inter-governmental discussions on Allied
    POWs)

Bundesarchiv-Militärarchiv

Only fragmentary material has survived. There is no trace of the central
archive of the German organization for POW matters – the *Kriegs-
gefangenenwesen*. The main files used were:
RH 19/41
RH 49/3–41
RH 53/4–58
RL 23/91

Bibliography

Allen Andrews, *Exemplary Justice* (Harrap, 1976).
Francis Ambrière, *The Exiled* (Staples Press, 1951).
Robert H. Ahrenfeldt, *Psychiatry in the British Army in the Second World War*
    (R & KP, 1958).
R. Anderson and D. Westmacott, *Handle with Care: A Book of Prison Camp
    Sketches, Drawn and Written in Prison Camps in Germany* (privately printed,
    Cookham, 1946).
Ronald H. Bailey, *Prisoners of War* (Time-Life Books, Chicago, 1981).
A. J. Barker, *Behind Barbed Wire* (Batsford, 1974).
Capt E. G. C. Beckwith (ed), *Selections from The Quill: a Collection of
    Prose, Verse and Sketches by Officers Prisoner-of-War in Germany, 1940–1945*
    (Country Life, 1947).
George Beeson, *Five Roads to Dresden* (Corgi edn., 1958).
Lowell Bennett, *Parachute to Berlin* (Vanguard Press, N. Y., 1945).
Count Folke Bernadotte, *Instead of Arms* (Hodder & Stoughton, 1949).
Nicholas Bethell, *The Last Secret: Forcible Repatriation to Russia 1944–47*
    (André Deutsch, 1974).
Gregory Blaxland, *Destination Dunkirk; the Story of Gort's Army* (William
    Kimber, 1973).
John Borrie, *Despite Captivity: A Doctor's Life as Prisoner of War* (William
    Kimber, 1975).

Paul Brickhill, *Escape – or Die: Authentic Stories of the R.A.F. Escaping Society* (Evan Bros., 1952).

John Brown, *In Durance Vile* (Hale, 1981).

Arthur Bryant, *The Turn of the Tide 1939–1943: A Study based on the Diaries and Autobiographical Notes of Field-Marshal the Viscount Alanbrooke, K.G., O.M.* (Collins, 1957).

Tom Burns, 'Men and Barbed Wire', *The Fortnightly*, CLVII, N.S. (April 1945).

Kendal Burt and James Leasor, *The One that Got Away* (Michael Joseph and Wm. Collins, 1956).

T. D. Calnan, *Free as a Running Fox* (Macdonald, 1970).

P. G. Cambray and G. G. B. Briggs, *Official Record of the Humanitarian Services of the War Organisation of the British Red Cross Society and Order of St John of Jerusalem 1939–1947* (Red Cross & St John War Organization, 1949).

Paul Carell and Günter Böddeker, *Die Gefangenen: Leben and Uberleben deutscher Soldaten hinter Stacheldraht* (Verlag Ullstein, Frankfurt, 1980).

Carolle J. Carter, *The Shamrock and the Swastika* (Pacific Books, Paolo Alto, California, 1977).

W. S. Churchill, *The Second World War*, IV, *The Hinge of Fate* (Cassell, 1951).

——, *The Second World War*, VI, *Triumph and Tragedy* (Cassell, 1954).

James B. Chutter, *Captivity Captive* (Cape, 1954).

Stanley Cohen and Laurie Taylor, *Psychological Survival: the Experience of Long-Term Imprisonment* (Penguin, 2nd edn., 1981).

Roger V. Coward, *Sailors in Cages* (Macdonald, 1967).

Edward Crankshaw, *Gestapo: Instrument of Tyranny* (N.E.L. edn., 1973).

Aidan Crawley, *Escape from Germany* (H.M.S.O., 1985).

Eric Cuddon, *The Dulag Luft Trial*, War Crimes Trials Series, IX (Willm. Hodge & Co., 1952).

Adam Curle, 'Transitional Communities and Social Re-Connection: A Follow-up Study of the Civil Resettlement of British Prisoners of War', Part 1, *Human Relations*, I,1 (1947); Part 2 with E. L. Trist in *Human Relations*, I, 2 (1947).

Leo Daldrup, *The Other Side* (Hodder & Stoughton, 1954).

Daniel A. Dancocks, *In Enemy Hands: Canadian Prisoners of War 1939–45* (Hurtig, Edmonton, Canada, 1983).

Gerald H. Davis, 'Prisoners of War in Twentieth-Century War Economies', *Journal of Contemporary History*, 12 (1977).

N. B. Dearle, *Dictionary of Official War-Time Organisations* (O.U.P., 1928).

John Dominey, *The Sergeant Escapers* (Ian Allen, 1974).

Michael Duncan, *Underground from Posen* (William Kimber, 1954).

Donald Edgar, *The Stalag Men* (John Clare, 1982).

Reinhold Eggers, *Colditz: the German Viewpoint* (Robert Hale, 1961).

Major L. F. Ellis, *The War in France and Flanders 1939–1940*, U.K. Military Series (H.M.S.O., 1953).

A. J. Evans, *Escape and Liberation 1940–1945* (Hodder & Stoughton, 1945).

John A. Fairlie, *British War Administration* (O.U.P., New York, 1919).

M. R. D. Foot and J. M. Langley, *MI9: Escape and Evasion 1939–1945* (The Bodley Head, 1979).

David A. Foy, *For You the War is Over: American Prisoners of War in Nazi Germany* (Stein and Day, N.Y., 1984).

Richard Garrett, *P.O.W.* (David & Charles, 1981).

Jimmy Graham and Jack Thomas, *Joe in Germany* (Privately published, Bognor Regis, 1946).

Roland Gant, *How Like a Wilderness* (Gollancz, 1946).

J. M. Green, *From Colditz in Code* (Robert Hale, 1971).

Robert Guerlain, *A Prisoner of Germany* (Macmillan, 1944).

Sir Arthur Harris, *Bomber Offensive* (Collins, 1947).

George Harsh, *Lonesome Road* (Longmans, 1981).

Hitler's Table Talk 1941–1944, translated by Norman Cameron and R. H. Stevens (Weidenfeld & Nicolson, 2nd edn., 1973).

Heinz Hohne, *The Order of the Death's Head* (Secker and Warburg, 1969).

Robert W. Holland, *Adversis Major: a short history of the Educational Books Scheme of the Prisoners of War Department of the British Red Cross Society and Order of St John of Jerusalem* (Staples Press, 1949).

H.S., *My Brother John: British Prisoner of War* (King Bros. & Potts, St. Leonard's-on-Sea, privately printed, 1942).

Leslie C. Hunt, *The Prisoner's Progress: An Illustrated Diary of the March into Captivity of the last of the British Army in France – June 1940* (Limited edn., Hutchinson, n.d. [c 1946?]).

David James, *A Prisoner's Progress* (William Blackwood, Edinburgh & London, 1947).

Ewart C. Jones, *Germans under my Bed* (Arthur Barker, 1957).

Francis S. Jones, *Escape to Nowhere* (Bodley Head, 1952).

Marcel Junod, *Warrior Without Weapons* (Cape, 1951).

David Kahn, *Hitler's Spies: German Military Intelligence in World War II* (Hodder and Stoughton, 1978).

Sam Kydd, *For You the War is Over* (Bachman & Turner, 1973).

Edward Lanchbery, *Against the Sun: the story of Wing Commander Roland Beaumont* (Cassell, 1955).

Terry Lovell, *Camera in Colditz* (Hodder & Stoughton, 1982).

Law Reports of Trials of War Criminals (U.N. War Crimes Commission, H.M.S.O., 1947).

John Mansel, *The Mansel Diaries: the diaries of Captain John Mansel, P.O.W., and camp forger in Germany, 1940–45* (Wildwood House, 1977).

W. Wynne Mason, *Prisoners of War*, War History Branch, Dept. of Internal Affairs, Wellington, N.Z. (O.U.P., 1954).

M. N. McKibbin and A. G. Dallimore, *Barbed Wire: Memories of Stalag 383* (Staples Press, 1947).

Guy Morgan, *Only Ghosts Can Live* (Crosby Lockwood, 1945).

George Moreton, *Doctor in Chains* (Howard Baker, 1970).

Airey Neave, *They Have their Exits* (Hodder & Stoughton, 1953).

Richard Pape, *Boldness be my Friend* (Paul Elek, 1953).

Lord Percy of Newcastle, *Some Memories* (Eyre & Spottiswood, 1958).

Oppenheim's International Law, ed. H. Lauterpacht (Longman, 7th edn., 1952).

Donald L. Patrick and Peter J. D. Heaf, *Long Term Effects of War-Related*

Deprivation on Health (British Members' Council of the World Veterans Federation, July 1981).

Oliver Philpot, *Stolen Journey* (Hodder & Stoughton, 1950).

J. Ellison Platt, *Padre in Colditz* (Hodder & Stoughton, 1980).

Prisoner of War (Horace Marshall & Sons, 1942).

The Prisoner of War, May 1942 – July 1945 (monthly).

Stefan Popiolek, 'Lamsdorf – the Death-Place of about 100 Thousand', in *Contemporary Poland*, No. 7 (April, 1978).

——, *Museum of Martyrology of Prisoners of War in Lambinowice* (Lambinowice, Poland, n.d.).

Hon. T. C. F. Prittie, *South to Freedom: A Record of Escape*, written in conjunction with Captain W. Earle Edwards (Hutchinson, 1946).

J. E. Pryce, *Heels in Line* (Barker, 1958).

R. A. Radford, 'The Economic Organisation of a P.O.W. Camp', *Economica*, XII (1945), reprinted in Paul A. Samuelson, *et al.*, *Readings in Economics*, 5th edn., (McGraw Hill, N.Y., 1967).

David Read, 'Books in Prison: Reflections of a P.O.W. Chaplain', Parts I and II, *Chambers's Journal*, 9th Series, I (Oct–Nov, 1947).

Miles Reid, *Last on the List* (Leo Cooper, 1974).

P. R. Reid, *The Colditz Story* (Hodder & Stoughton, 1952).

——, *The Latter Days at Colditz* (Hodder & Stoughton, 1953).

Release and Resettlement (W.O., 1945).

Report of the International Committee of the Red Cross on its activities during the Second World War (Geneva, May 1948).

Anthony Richardson, *Wingless Victory* (Odhams, 1950).

Cyril Rofe, *Against the Wind* (Hodder & Stoughton, 1956).

Giles Romilly and Michael Alexander, *The Privileged Nightmare* (Weidenfeld & Nicolson, 1954).

Ian Sabey, *Stalag Scrapbook* (F. W. Cheshire, Melbourne & London, 1947).

Hilary St George Saunders, *The Red Cross and the White* (Hollis & Carter, 1949).

Ronald Seth, *Jackals of the Reich: the Story of the British Free Corps* (N.E.L., 1972).

Sidney Smith, *'Wings' Day: The Man Who Led the RAF's Epic Battle in German Captivity* (Collins, 1958).

Marlis G. Steinert, *Hitler's War and the Germans* (Ohio U. Press, 1977).

Statistical Digest of the War (H.M.S.O., 1951).

Geoff Taylor, *Piece of Cake* (Peter Davies, 1956).

——, *Return Ticket* (Davies, 1972).

Douglas Thompson, *Captives to Freedom* (Epsworth Press, 1955).

Derek Thrower, *The Lonely Path to Freedom* (Robert Hale, 1980).

To All British Commonwealth Ex-Prisoners of War (W.O. [D.P.W.], Feb 1945).

Nicolai Tolstoy, *Victims of Yalta* (Corgi revised edn., 1979).

Trial of the German Major War Criminals: Proceedings of the International Tribunal sitting at Nuremburg, Germany (H.M.S.O., 1946).

John A. Vietor, *Time Out: American Airmen at Stalag Luft I* (Smith, West Ridge, N.H., 1951).

Adrian Vincent, *The Long Road Home* (Allen & Unwin, 1956).

War Report: A Record of Dispatches broadcast by the BBC's War Correspondents with the Allied Expeditionary Force 6 June 1944 – 5 May 1945 (O.U.P., 1946).

Eric Williams, *The Wooden Horse* (Collins, 1949).

Lieutenant-Colonel Wilson, 'The Serviceman Comes Home', *Pilot Papers*, I, No. 2 (April 1946) quoted by Robert H. Ahrenfeld, *Psychiatry in the British Army in the Second World War* (Routledge & Kegan Paul, 1958).

Rebecca West, *The Meaning of Treason* (Macmillan, 1949).

Lieutenant J. E. R. Wood, ed., *Detour: The Story of Oflag IVC* (Falcon Press, 1946).

Calton Younger, *No Flight from the Cage* (Star Pbk edn., 1981).

INDEX